PAT BROWN, MBA

Financial Literacy For NIL for Parents of Student Athletes

A Parent's Guide to Protecting, Supporting, and Empowering Your Student-Athlete in the NIL Era

ABRAM 47 BROWN

First published by AbramBrown47 2025

First edition

ISBN: 978-1-967737-02-4

This book was professionally typeset on Reedsy.
Find out more at reedsy.com

Contents

Preface

When I first heard the phrase "Name, Image, and Likeness," I didn't immediately think of business deals, contracts, or logos. I thought of kids—teenagers and young adults—many of them from neighborhoods like mine, schools like mine, and families like mine, now suddenly navigating money, exposure, and pressure that none of us were prepared for.

I wrote this book because I've lived both sides of the game.

As a former Division I college football player and team captain at the University of Kansas, I know firsthand the demands, dreams, and distractions that come with being a student-athlete. And now, as a financial advisor, NIL educator, and most importantly, a parent, I see how the world around these athletes has changed—and how fast it's changing.

Opportunities have exploded. NIL allows student-athletes to build businesses, support their families, and get paid for what they bring to the table. But with those opportunities come real responsibilities: taxes, contracts, budgeting, branding, and long-term financial planning.

Most athletes aren't taught these things in the classroom. And most parents—especially in Black, brown, immigrant, working-class, and first-generation families—never had the chance to learn this either. We're all learning in real time. That's what this book is for.

This isn't just a financial manual. It's a cultural conversation. It's a guide for families who want to protect their kids from scams, overspending, and stress—and instead, equip them to turn NIL into a stepping stone toward long-term wealth, freedom, and purpose.

Whether you're the parent of a rising high school freshman or a college senior fielding NIL offers, you belong here. Whether you grew up with money or without, whether you're well-versed in finance or figuring it out as you go—this book is for you.

You won't find fluff in these pages. You'll find real talk, practical steps, questions to ask, and red flags to watch for. You'll find the conversations I've had with student-athletes, parents, coaches, compliance officers, and financial professionals across the country. You'll find lessons from my own journey—from being the kid who didn't understand credit, to the man who now teaches student-athletes how to use it wisely.

This book is your playbook. Not just for NIL—but for life.

Because when your child succeeds off the field as much as they do on it, that's the real win.

Let's get to work.

— Pat Brown, MBA

Author | Former Athlete | Financial Advocate for Families

Creator of *Financial Literacy for NIL* and *Financial Literacy for Student-Athletes*

How to Use This Book

Welcome to *Financial Literacy for Parents of Student-Athletes*

This book was written with one goal in mind: **to help you, as a parent, confidently guide your student-athlete through the complex world of money, NIL (Name, Image & Likeness), and life decisions that come with opportunity—and responsibility.**

Whether your child is just entering high school or already navigating college athletics and NIL deals, this book is your companion. It equips you with the tools, questions, and conversations needed to **protect and empower them every step of the way.**

And here's something even more important:

This book is also your *gateway* to better understanding the financial literacy journey your student-athlete is on.

It serves as a **parental companion to my other books written specifically for student-athletes**, including:

- **Financial Literacy For NIL**
- **Financial Literacy For NIL – High School Student-Athletes Edition**
- **Financial Literacy For NIL – International Student-Athletes Edition**

These books are written *for them*. This one is written *for you*, so you can engage in their journey, speak their language, and be the guiding presence they need when the stakes are high and the opportunities are even higher.

How to Use This Book

This isn't a book to read once and put away. It's a **reference, a workbook, a guide, and in some ways, a mirror**. You'll find yourself going back to different chapters as your child reaches new stages in their athletic and financial journey.

Here's how to get the most out of this resource:

1. Read by Section, Not Necessarily in Order

This book is broken into key parts—each focused on a specific phase of the student-athlete's development:

- **Part I:** Lays the foundation for why financial literacy and parental involvement matter in the NIL era.
- **Part II:** Walks you through each year of high school—what to watch for, what to teach, and what conversations to have.
- **Part III:** Focuses on year-round and summer athletics, especially travel sports like AAU and 7-on-7, where exposure and risk collide.
- **Part IV:** Dives into the realities of college NIL—taxes, agents, deals, and compliance.
- **Part V:** Breaks down the business side: LLCs, contracts, working with professionals, and protecting your child's brand.
- **Part VI:** Covers life skills—budgeting, mental health, lifestyle pressure, credit, and identity safety.
- **Part VII:** Offers tools, checklists, and conversation starters to help you take action.

2. Use It as a Conversation Starter

This book isn't just for you—it's for your family. Pick a chapter, read it with your student-athlete, and ask:

- "What part of this feels relevant to you right now?"
- "Does any of this confuse or worry you?"
- "Have you seen anything like this happen to a teammate or friend?"

Your goal is to **create a safe space** where money and opportunity aren't taboo—they're topics your child can approach with confidence.

3. Highlight, Annotate, Revisit

Make this book yours.

Highlight passages that resonate. Write your own questions in the margins. Revisit key chapters before every sports season, major NIL conversation, or financial milestone.

You might not need the LLC section now—but in six months? You will.

You may not need the tax guidance yet—but when that first 1099 form arrives? You'll know exactly where to turn.

4. Use the Checklists and Templates

Throughout the book, you'll find **checklists, sample questions, planning tools, and budgeting frameworks**. Don't skip them.

They're here to make the information *actionable*—tools you can use now and customize over time.

5. Don't Try to Master Everything at Once

You're not expected to become a financial expert overnight.

This book is designed to **walk alongside you**, not overwhelm you.

Start where you are. Build from there. Use what's helpful now. Come back to the rest later.

6. Be Honest About What You Don't Know

If you weren't taught these things growing up, that's okay. Many of us weren't.

Use this book to **break generational patterns**, ask better questions, and get support where needed.

If something doesn't make sense, underline it. Look it up. Ask a trusted advisor. Your *willingness to learn* is the best gift you can give your student-athlete.

7. Return to It Year After Year

This book grows with your child.

What you teach a freshman is different from what a senior needs to know. What a college sophomore faces is different from a high school sophomore.

Use this book as a **long-term playbook**. Each chapter is designed to meet you at a different mile marker in the journey.

Final Note

You are your child's most important financial influence—**whether you feel like it or not**.

The world they're stepping into is bigger, faster, and more public than the one we grew up in. NIL, branding, business formation, taxes—these aren't things they'll automatically know.

But they *can* learn. And you *can* lead.

This book gives you the road map—and with the student-athlete versions by their side and this guide in your hands, you'll both be ready for the road ahead.

How This Book Connects to the Full NIL Financial Literacy Series

This book, *Financial Literacy for NIL for Parents of Student-Athletes,* is not a stand-alone manual. It's part of a comprehensive educational series built to support families and student-athletes at every stage of their journey—from high school to college, from the first NIL deal to long-term financial independence.

If you've picked up this book, it likely means you care about your child's future—not just their athletic performance, but their ability to manage money, protect their brand, and build something that lasts far beyond game day. But to support them fully, you need context. You need a system. And that's exactly what this book provides—while tying into a larger blueprint for NIL success.

Here's how this book correlates with the rest of the series:

1. Financial Literacy for NIL

Audience: College student-athletes (and aspiring high school athletes preparing for that leap)

Focus: Direct financial education for student-athletes managing NIL income

This foundational book dives deep into the core topics every student-athlete must understand:

- How to handle self-employment income
- Budgeting NIL money

- Avoiding scams and bad contracts
- Understanding taxes, credit, LLCs, and agents
- Building a personal brand and protecting it legally
- Investing early and planning for the future

It's written in plain language, packed with real-life examples, and structured to be accessible for athletes who've never had a financial education course.

How This Parent Book Connects:

As a parent, you are your child's first financial mentor. While *Financial Literacy for NIL* speaks directly to your athlete, *this* book speaks directly to you—giving you the tools to understand what your child is being taught, what challenges they're facing, and how to reinforce those lessons at home.

Together, both books form a partnership—you learning how to guide, your child learning how to execute.

2. Financial Literacy for NIL for High School Student-Athletes

Audience: High school freshmen through seniors who are beginning to hear the buzz about NIL

Focus: Early preparation for NIL—before the money, deals, or spotlight arrive

This version is designed to introduce young athletes to:

- The basics of money and mindset
- Budgeting, saving, and understanding credit
- Building a personal brand online
- Managing peer pressure, hype, and ego
- Knowing when to say yes—and when to wait
- Preparing academically and socially for the college recruiting process

It's meant to spark early conversations, set a strong foundation, and help high school athletes think like pros long before they sign a deal.

How This Parent Book Connects:

If your child is still in high school, this parent guide helps you understand:

- What you should be teaching year by year (freshman through senior)
- What red flags to watch for in travel ball, AAU, and showcase events
- What to ask summer coaches, recruiting advisors, and brands
- How to help your child develop a healthy relationship with money, social media, and exposure

It aligns directly with the student version, but gives you the *parent perspective*—so you can support without smothering, guide without controlling.

3. Financial Literacy for NIL for International Student-Athletes

Audience: International student-athletes studying or competing in the U.S.

Focus: Navigating the intersection of NIL, U.S. tax law, immigration status, and cross-border banking

This book helps international athletes understand:

- Visa restrictions (F-1, CPT, OPT) and NIL eligibility
- Whether and how they can legally earn NIL income
- Currency conversion, banking access, and reporting requirements
- Tax obligations in both the U.S. and their home country
- Cultural and language barriers in financial education
- Personal branding with international appeal

It's written to demystify a complex system and protect athletes from losing visa status, violating school rules, or accidentally committing tax fraud.

How This Parent Book Connects:

For parents of international athletes, this parent edition helps bridge the cultural gap. Even if you live outside the U.S., or if English isn't your first language, you can use this book to:

- Understand the U.S. financial system as it applies to your child
- Know what professionals your student-athlete needs to hire or consult
- Monitor international money transfers and banking rules
- Ask better questions of agents, advisors, and school compliance staff

If your child is an international athlete in the U.S., this book helps *you* stay in the loop—even from afar.

Why the Series Works Together

Think of this series like a coaching staff:

- *Financial Literacy for NIL* is the **playbook** for the athlete
- *Financial Literacy for NIL for High School Athletes* is the **developmental guide** for early training
- *Financial Literacy for NIL for International Athletes* is the **rulebook** for the unique road they walk
- *Financial Literacy for NIL for Parents of Student-Athletes*—this book—is the **sideline headset**, helping you guide your child through it all

Every athlete needs a team. These books are built to work together, giving every member of the family or support network the tools they need to succeed.

A Shared Language

When families read these books together, they're not just absorbing information—they're building a shared language. The athlete learns how to protect their NIL opportunity. The parent learns how to support them in that pursuit. And together, they make more informed, confident, and values-driven decisions.

This book shows you how to lead at home. The others show your student-athlete how to lead in life.

Final Thought: NIL is a Family Journey

You might be here because your child has potential. Maybe they've already signed a deal. Maybe they're headed to college. Or maybe you're just trying to prepare for what's coming.

Wherever you are, just know this: *NIL is not just about the athlete. It's about the family.*

This book gives you a seat at the table. The others make sure your child is ready to eat at it.

Read them together. Discuss the lessons. Build the habits. Protect the opportunity.

Because when NIL is handled right—it doesn't just change one athlete's life. It can change a whole generation.

The Foundation – Why Parents Matter in the NIL Era

When the NIL (Name, Image, and Likeness) era officially arrived in July 2021, a floodgate of opportunity was opened for student-athletes across the country. From local businesses to national brands, the playing field shifted virtually overnight. Suddenly, student-athletes—many still teenagers—had access to an entirely new economy that hadn't existed for generations before them. From endorsement deals and paid appearances to social media sponsorships and merchandise sales, young athletes were being handed opportunities—and money—without ever going pro.

It was a long-overdue development, correcting decades of imbalance where athletes helped generate billions in revenue for their schools but couldn't earn a dime themselves. But with that new opportunity came a wave of complexity that no one—least of all the student-athletes—was truly prepared for.

That's where parents come in. And that's why this book starts here—with you.

A New Era Requires a New Role for Parents

In the past, a parent's role in the athletic journey was centered around support: getting kids to practice, cheering at games, managing schoolwork, and helping them through the recruitment process. Those responsibilities are still vital. But in the NIL era, the job description for parents has expanded. Dramatically.

Today's parents must become:

- Financial mentors
- Legal watchdogs
- Brand protectors
- Contract reviewers
- Tax preparers
- Emotional anchors
- Risk managers
- Digital advisors

That's a tall order, especially considering many of today's parents never received financial literacy themselves. Yet the stakes have never been higher. Because while NIL represents progress and possibility, it also presents real dangers if mishandled.

Why NIL Is Different From Anything We've Seen Before

There's never been a generation of high school and college athletes with this level of financial opportunity and exposure. In the past, a scholarship was the dream. Today, a scholarship might come second to signing with a national clothing brand, launching a YouTube channel, or getting paid for a TikTok dance. The NIL era isn't just about business—it's about identity, influence, and image.

That means families are navigating new terrain. NIL isn't just about whether your child gets paid—it's about how they get paid, who pays them, whether that income is reported properly, how it impacts eligibility, and how it affects their mental health. There are contracts, taxes, agents, managers, endorsements, social media sponsorships, team collectives, legal agreements, and public scrutiny—all layered on top of the already intense demands of being a student-athlete.

It's not just a job—it's a small business. And your kid is the CEO, often without the tools or maturity to run it alone.

Why Parents Must Take the Lead

Let's be honest. Most 16-to-22-year-olds aren't equipped to manage sudden money, complex negotiations, and long-term planning. They've spent their lives being coached on performance—not finances. Most student-athletes:

- Don't know how to read a contract
- Don't understand tax brackets
- Don't track their expenses
- Don't save or invest
- Don't know how to distinguish a good deal from a bad one
- Don't fully grasp how social media can both build and destroy their image

And why should they? No one ever taught them. In most cases, schools and sports programs still don't.

That's why your role as a parent is more critical now than ever before. You are their first line of defense—and their most trusted guide. You don't need to be a financial expert, but you do need to be financially engaged.

This book will help you do that.

When NIL Starts (Hint: Sooner Than You Think)

Many parents mistakenly believe they don't need to worry about NIL until their child is in college. But that's no longer the case.

More than 30 states now allow high school athletes to profit from NIL. In some states, there are no restrictions at all. That means your 15-year-old daughter playing club volleyball might be eligible to sign a deal tomorrow. Your 17-year-old son playing travel baseball may already have DMs from companies or agents.

If you're not paying attention, someone else will. And not all of those people will have your child's best interests at heart.

NIL isn't something that starts in college anymore—it's something parents need to prepare for starting in middle school and early high school, particularly for athletes involved in nationally competitive programs, summer leagues, 7-on-7 tournaments, AAU, track meets, or private training academies.

The Silent Struggle: Families Navigating Sudden Wealth

Imagine this: Your son signs a $25,000 NIL deal at 17. He's still living in your house. You don't know whether that income affects your household taxes, your FAFSA application, or his financial aid. You don't know if he's supposed to set aside money for taxes or whether he's being paid as a contractor or employee. You don't know what's in the contract—or even who reviewed it.

Now imagine he wants to spend it all on clothes, jewelry, or a new car. You say no. He says it's his money. Now what?

These aren't theoretical situations. They're happening every day to real families, in real time, across the country.

Sudden money is powerful. But it's also dangerous—especially for young people without structure. And for families who may have struggled financially, that money can spark hope, resentment, entitlement, or confusion. The psychological side of NIL is as real as the financial side. And parents must be ready to manage both.

The Values Conversation

NIL is not just about money—it's about values. Parents must have intentional conversations with their student-athletes about:

- What kind of deals align with your family's values?

- What brands or causes do you want your child representing?
- What are they willing—and not willing—to promote?
- How will they manage attention, praise, and criticism?
- How does this impact their academic and athletic focus?

Money without a value system will eventually create problems. NIL is an opportunity to teach your child about integrity, leadership, and the long-term impact of their choices.

What NIL Is... and Isn't

Let's clarify some things. NIL is:

- The right for student-athletes to profit from their **Name, Image, and Likeness**
- Legal in most states and under NCAA rules
- Still subject to federal and state tax law
- Not a guaranteed income stream
- Often based on social media presence, marketability, and brand alignment
- Subject to eligibility restrictions in high school and college

But NIL is **not**:

- Free money with no consequences
- A get-rich-quick system
- A replacement for scholarships or academics
- A sign that your child is destined for the pros
- A reason to stop planning for life after sports

Understanding what NIL is—and what it isn't—will help you set realistic expectations for your child and your family.

The New Financial Playbook for Parents

In this new NIL era, parents must adopt a new financial playbook. It includes:

1. **Education:** Learn the basics of personal finance, business formation, and tax law. You don't need to be an expert—you just need to be literate.
2. **Communication:** Have regular, open conversations with your child about money, priorities, goals, and expectations.
3. **Protection:** Ensure contracts are reviewed by professionals. Avoid handshake deals or pressure tactics.
4. **Monitoring:** Keep an eye on spending, savings, social media activity, and mental health.
5. **Planning:** Help your child create short- and long-term plans. Where is the money going? What will it be used for? What happens if the deals dry up?
6. **Partnership:** Build a team. That might include a CPA, financial advisor, NIL attorney, or trusted coach. You are your child's manager—make sure you have a support system, too.

The Emotional Toll on Parents

Let's not sugarcoat it. This new responsibility can feel overwhelming.

You're balancing your own job, bills, family needs—and now you're being asked to manage contracts and build a brand strategy for your child. It's a lot.

Many parents feel:

- Out of their depth
- Worried they'll give the wrong advice
- Pressured to say yes to things they don't understand
- Unsure how to set boundaries or say no

- Concerned about their child's mental health and maturity

All of those feelings are valid. This is uncharted territory for everyone. But you are not alone. This book—and the community behind it—exists to support you as you support your child.

The Parent Power Principle

Here's the truth: NIL success starts at home.

You have more influence than you think. Your child is watching how you talk about money, how you handle stress, how you ask questions, and how you respond to opportunities. You are their model for how to navigate this world.

Even if you've made financial mistakes in the past—even if you've never had money yourself—you can still teach your child the lessons you've learned.

And if you're willing to grow, ask questions, and engage, you'll find yourself not just managing NIL, but mastering it—for the benefit of your child, your family, and generations to come.

What's Coming Next in This Book

In the chapters to follow, we'll walk through every step of the student-athlete journey, from freshman year of high school to college graduation. You'll learn:

- What to teach your child at each stage of development
- What questions to ask at every turn—college visits, contract signings, financial meetings, and more
- How to navigate taxes, legal issues, insurance, agents, scams, and business formation
- How to support your child emotionally as they navigate pressure, public scrutiny, and expectations

- How to build a lasting foundation of financial literacy that goes far beyond NIL

This book isn't just about NIL. It's about parenting in a new world. It's about helping your child build a life—not just a highlight reel.

You're the most important person in your child's NIL journey. And your time is now.

Chapter 1: Introduction Why This Book Matters Now

Your Role as a Parent in Your Child's Financial and Athletic Future

How NIL Changed the Game for Families

In households across America, parents have long been the backbone of their children's athletic journeys. From driving hours to games, paying for trainers, cutting oranges for halftime snacks, and cheering from the sidelines, the commitment has always been real. But in today's world—where your child's name, image, and likeness (NIL) now have real market value—that commitment requires a new type of preparation: **financial leadership**.

As a parent, you are no longer just a fan in the stands or a chauffeur to tournaments. You are now a guide, an advisor, a protector, and in many ways, a gatekeeper of your child's financial potential. This isn't a role most parents ever expected to play—but it's one they must rise to. Because in the new NIL economy, families that aren't prepared risk watching opportunity turn into overwhelm, income turn into liability, and freedom turn into financial chaos.

This book exists to make sure that doesn't happen to your family.

From Sports Parents to Strategic Advisors

In the past, parents of student-athletes focused on the basics: effort, eligibility, and exposure. You worried about grades, playing time, recruiting letters, and scholarships. And those things are still important. But now, there's a new dimension to consider: **money**.

Your child might get paid for a tweet, an appearance at a camp, wearing a local brand, or doing a shoutout on Instagram. Some students might make a few hundred dollars. Others could pull in thousands—some even millions. While that kind of income used to only come after "making it," today it could show up in high school.

Parents must now make a mindset shift: you're not just raising an athlete—you're potentially guiding a **young entrepreneur**, a **public figure**, and in many cases, the **financial leader of the household.**

And that comes with enormous opportunity and responsibility.

You're now being asked to help your child:

- Understand the difference between gross and net income
- File taxes for the first time
- Protect their brand and digital reputation
- Evaluate contracts from businesses and sponsors
- Set boundaries with agents and managers
- Decide whether or not to start an LLC
- Determine what's a fair endorsement deal
- Avoid scams, fraud, and financial predators
- Learn what it means to be a business owner at 17 or 19 years old

Most parents have never been taught these things themselves. That's okay. This book is here to teach you, so you can teach—and protect—your child.

Why NIL Changed Everything

The term "NIL"—short for Name, Image, and Likeness—refers to an athlete's right to monetize their identity. In 2021, the NCAA changed its rules to allow college athletes to profit from their NIL. This change didn't come out of nowhere—it was the result of years of pressure and legal battles demanding that student-athletes be allowed to share in the value they help create.

It was a historic win.

For the first time, athletes could earn income from sponsorships, social media, merchandise, appearances, and more—all without jeopardizing their eligibility.

But what started as a college movement has quickly made its way into high schools. Today, **more than 30 states allow high school athletes** to sign NIL deals. This means that NIL isn't just a college issue anymore—it's a family issue.

And it's here to stay.

NIL Is About More Than Money—It's About Access

To be clear, not every student-athlete will make six figures—or even four figures—from NIL. But it's not just about how much they earn—it's about **what NIL makes possible**:

- NIL gives students a chance to **build a personal brand**.
- NIL introduces them to **financial systems early**.
- NIL helps some families **bridge financial gaps** through legitimate income.
- NIL teaches **entrepreneurship** in real time.
- NIL opens the door for student-athletes to **fund their own education**, **start businesses**, or **help their families**.

These are powerful outcomes—but only if approached with the right mindset and support.

That's where you come in.

The Opportunity and the Risk

Let's be honest: money changes things.

Whether it's $500 or $50,000, a teenager receiving income for the first time—especially in the public eye—is stepping into uncharted territory. And the stakes are high.

The Opportunity:

- **Financial Literacy:** NIL can teach kids how to budget, save, invest, and give.
- **Business Skills:** Athletes learn about contracts, branding, taxes, and marketing.
- **Independence:** Earning money builds confidence and can reduce student loan dependence.
- **Family Relief:** For some, NIL can help offset family expenses or support younger siblings.
- **Legacy Building:** Done right, NIL income can be the seed for generational wealth.

The Risk:

- **Misinformation:** Many young athletes get advice from TikTok instead of trusted professionals.
- **Predators:** Agents, managers, or even friends may try to take advantage.
- **Financial Illiteracy:** Without guidance, young people spend recklessly or ignore taxes.
- **Eligibility Risks:** Violating school or state rules can cost scholarships or team standing.

- **Mental Health:** Fame, pressure, and financial stress can be overwhelming without a support system.

So how do we make sure your child experiences the **opportunity** and not the **fallout**?

It starts with education. And the first educator is **you**.

What Parents Need to Understand About NIL

This book will go into detail later, but for now, here are the basics you need to know:

1. **Income Is Taxable:** NIL money is not free money. It counts as self-employment income. Many student-athletes will receive 1099 forms from brands and businesses. If taxes aren't paid on time, there could be fines or worse.
2. **Contracts Are Legally Binding:** If your child signs an agreement—even digitally—they're bound to it. Parents must read the fine print, ask questions, and sometimes say no.
3. **State Laws Vary:** NIL rules are different depending on the state and sometimes even the school district. What's legal in California may be restricted in Texas.
4. **Social Media Matters:** Your child's online persona is now a financial asset—or liability. Posts, comments, and DMs can make or break deals.
5. **College Coaches Are Watching:** Even if your child is offered NIL deals in high school, they must stay focused on their grades, development, and recruitment.
6. **Not All Money Is Good Money:** Just because a company offers a check doesn't mean it aligns with your child's values or long-term goals.

You don't have to be an expert. But you do have to be engaged.

The Role Parents Now Play

Your new role in the NIL era can be summed up in five areas:

1. Educator

Teach your child what you're learning in this book: budgeting, saving, taxes, contracts, and brand awareness. If you don't know it yet, that's okay—we'll walk you through it.

2. Protector

Scams are everywhere. Be the person who reads the contract, checks credentials, verifies advice, and asks the questions your child might be too excited or intimidated to ask.

3. Accountability Partner

Create financial routines. Sit down once a month with your child to go over earnings, spending, goals, and issues. Help them understand what it means to build a sustainable financial life.

4. Advocate

You may need to speak up with coaches, schools, or companies. You might need to push back on deals that aren't in your child's best interest. Your voice matters.

5. Student

Don't be afraid to admit what you don't know. Learn with your child. Build a family culture of curiosity and growth. That's how legacies are built.

How This Book Will Help You

In the chapters that follow, this book will give you:

- **Year-by-year advice** on what to teach and watch for from freshman year of high school to college graduation
- **Questions to ask** coaches, agents, managers, accountants, and financial advisors
- **Checklists and templates** for organizing NIL offers, building budgets, and tracking income
- **Case studies and stories** of real families navigating NIL successfully—and others who learned the hard way
- **Tools for mental health, brand safety, and decision-making**

We'll take you from confusion to confidence. From reaction to preparation.

Closing Thought: Why You Matter More Than Ever

Your child may have a great coach. They may have a scholarship offer. They may even have a team or collective supporting them. But at the end of the day, **no one knows them like you do**. No one loves them like you do. And no one has more power to shape their mindset and their future than you do.

You don't need a degree in finance to make a difference. You just need to care enough to show up, learn, ask questions, and stay involved.

In the NIL era, families who prepare will thrive. Those who don't may regret it for years to come.

This is your chance to help your child not only succeed in sports, but also win in life.

That's why this book matters.

That's why **you** matter.

And that's why we're just getting started.

Chapter 2: What is NIL? A Parent's Guide to Name, Image & Likeness

In every generation, parents have had to adjust to the evolving challenges that come with raising children in a changing world. For some, it was the rise of the internet. For others, it was social media, school safety, or the ever-increasing cost of college. Today, for parents of student-athletes, that new reality is **NIL**—Name, Image, and Likeness.

If you've heard the term "NIL" tossed around but still aren't quite sure what it really means, you're not alone. Most parents—even those who have had kids recruited by major programs—are still wrapping their heads around this new landscape. This chapter is here to clear up the confusion and give you a solid foundation of what NIL actually is, how it impacts your child, and what you need to be aware of as their number one advocate.

Understanding NIL: The Basics

NIL refers to a student-athlete's right to profit from their **Name**, **Image**, and **Likeness**—in other words, their personal brand. This includes:

- Their **name** (e.g., signing autographs or having their name appear on merchandise)
- Their **image** (e.g., photos, videos, likeness used in promotional materi-

als)

- Their **likeness** (e.g., video game avatars, NFTs, digital representations)

Under NIL, student-athletes can legally earn income by allowing companies or organizations to use their identity in various commercial ventures.

Examples of NIL activities include:

- Signing endorsement deals with sportswear or nutrition brands
- Participating in paid autograph sessions or fan meetups
- Promoting products or services on social media (TikTok, Instagram, YouTube)
- Launching personal merchandise lines (clothing, gear, collectibles)
- Giving private lessons or hosting camps and clinics
- Appearing in commercials or online ads
- Creating monetized YouTube channels or podcasts

The key is this: **the student-athlete is getting paid for who they are**, not just how they perform. That includes their reputation, their following, their influence, and their story.

Before July 1, 2021, NCAA rules prohibited student-athletes from earning any money related to their athletic status. That meant no brand deals, no autograph payments, and no compensated appearances—even if the athlete was a household name. College athletes were often used to promote the school, sell tickets, and appear in national broadcasts without ever seeing a dime.

When the NCAA suspended those restrictions, and states began passing NIL legislation, a new era was born—one where athletes at both the college and high school level could participate in the free market and benefit from their personal brands.

What NIL Means for Your Child

Whether your child is a nationally ranked five-star recruit or a solid role player on their varsity squad, NIL is something that you, as a parent, need to be paying attention to. Why? Because NIL isn't only about big names or national headlines. It's about **access and awareness**.

Your child may not sign a six-figure deal with Nike—but they might be offered a free meal from a local restaurant in exchange for a social media post. They might be invited to appear at a youth camp or partner with a small brand that aligns with their sport. Even these "smaller" deals still have legal and financial implications, which we'll get into in later chapters.

Here's what NIL can mean for your child:

1. **Early Financial Opportunity**
2. NIL allows your child to earn money during high school and college—sometimes even enough to help with family expenses or save for the future.
3. **Brand Development**
4. NIL gives student-athletes a chance to build a personal brand, including logos, merchandise, websites, and followers—skills that translate into post-athletic careers.
5. **Business Experience**
6. Signing contracts, managing partnerships, and paying taxes teaches valuable business skills that most people don't learn until adulthood—if ever.
7. **Pressure and Responsibility**
8. NIL also brings new demands. Balancing school, sports, training, and now business can be overwhelming. Parents play a crucial role in providing structure and emotional support.
9. **Social and Ethical Choices**
10. Your child will need to learn how to evaluate brands, determine their values, and decide what kind of image they want to put into the world.

Common Myths About NIL

Because NIL is still so new, there's a lot of misinformation out there. Let's clear up some of the biggest myths.

Myth #1: "Only Division I college athletes can benefit from NIL."

Truth: NIL is not limited to D1 schools. Athletes in D2, D3, NAIA, JUCO, and even high school can earn NIL income depending on state and school regulations. Talent, following, and opportunity matter more than division status.

Myth #2: "You have to be a social media influencer to get NIL deals."

Truth: While social media can boost NIL appeal, it's not required. Many athletes earn NIL income from camps, speaking engagements, or working with local businesses—regardless of follower count.

Myth #3: "If my child earns NIL money, they'll lose their scholarship or eligibility."

Truth: As long as your child follows their school, state, and NCAA rules, they will not lose their eligibility. The key is staying compliant—something we'll cover in depth later in this book.

Myth #4: "It's free money with no strings attached."

Truth: All NIL income is considered taxable. In addition, many NIL deals include deliverables (posts, appearances, obligations). Failing to fulfill the contract can result in penalties or legal trouble.

Myth #5: "If my child is getting NIL deals, they don't need to focus on school."

Truth: Academic eligibility is still required to play and to maintain scholarship status. NIL does not replace the need for strong grades, character, and commitment.

NIL Deal Sizes: From Micro to Mega

NIL deals are not just for household names like college quarterbacks or viral stars. Athletes of all levels are earning income from creative, localized, and personal opportunities. Here's a basic breakdown of deal types:

- **Micro deals** ($50–$500): Sponsored posts, small business appearances, merchandise discounts
- **Local deals** ($500–$5,000): Community-based businesses offering endorsements or appearances
- **Mid-range deals** ($5,000–$50,000): Regional campaigns, clothing collaborations, recurring brand partnerships
- **Major deals** ($50,000+): Endorsements with national brands, NIL collectives, exclusive merchandise lines

Every athlete's NIL journey is unique. What matters most is that families approach every opportunity—big or small—with clarity, strategy, and structure.

High School NIL: State-by-State Overview

One of the most confusing aspects of NIL is that high school rules vary widely depending on your state—and sometimes your school district. As of 2025, here's a general snapshot:

States That Allow High School NIL Participation

These states have officially passed rules allowing high school athletes to engage in NIL activities(As of 2025):

- California
- New York
- Illinois
- Nebraska
- Alaska
- Colorado
- Louisiana
- Kansas
- Minnesota
- Utah
- Iowa
- New Jersey
- Connecticut
- Idaho
- Arkansas
- New Mexico
- North Dakota
- Oregon
- Rhode Island
- Washington
- Maine
- Oklahoma
- Massachusetts
- Pennsylvania
- Missouri

Note: Rules still vary. Some states allow NIL deals only with prior approval. Others restrict promotional materials or require parental oversight. Always check with your school's athletic association.

States That Prohibit High School NIL

Some states still prohibit high school athletes from earning money from NIL deals, meaning doing so could cost your child eligibility. These include (As of 2025):

- Texas
- Florida
- Georgia
- South Carolina
- Kentucky
- Alabama
- Mississippi
- North Carolina
- Tennessee
- Nevada

Important: These rules are evolving quickly. New states are proposing legislation every month, and athletic associations are regularly revising their stances. Check with your **state high school athletic association** and **your school's athletic director** for the latest information.

What Parents Should Do Now

Now that you understand what NIL is, what it isn't, and how it varies by state, here's what you can do next:

1. **Know Your State Rules:** Visit your state's high school athletic association website. Know what's allowed, what's prohibited, and what paperwork might be required.
2. **Talk With Your School:** Speak with your athletic director or coach

to clarify school policies. Some schools are more proactive than others about NIL education.

3. **Start the Money Conversation:** Don't wait for a brand to approach your child. Begin talking about taxes, saving, budgeting, and social media responsibility now.
4. **Build a Trusted Network:** Start identifying professionals—financial advisors, CPAs, lawyers—who you can turn to when needed.
5. **Encourage Value-Based Branding:** Help your child think about what they stand for, what they want to promote, and how to stay authentic.

Conclusion: NIL is an Opportunity—With Structure

NIL has given student-athletes more freedom than ever before. But that freedom comes with responsibility. The families who thrive in this new environment are not the ones with the most followers or the flashiest deals—they're the ones with the most **structure**.

As a parent, you don't need to be an expert in endorsements, contracts, or tax law. But you do need to understand the foundation—and this chapter gives you that.

Now that you have a clear picture of what NIL is, how it works, and what it means for your family, the next step is learning **how to prepare your child for each stage of the journey**—starting with high school.

In the next section, we'll break down exactly what parents should be doing in **freshman, sophomore, junior, and senior year**, including what to teach, what to watch out for, and what conversations to have along the way.

Are you ready? Let's keep building.

Chapter 3: Financial Literacy Starts at Home

How to Teach Budgeting, Saving, Credit, and Smart Spending Early

Why This Matters Before a Kid Ever Signs an NIL Deal

Before your child ever signs a contract, cashes a check, or makes a sponsored Instagram post, they will face a series of financial decisions. Some of these decisions will be small: Do I spend this money or save it? Others will be much larger: Should I buy a car with my NIL earnings? Should I sign with this company? Should I pay my own phone bill?

Each decision will shape how your student-athlete handles money when it really matters. That's why financial literacy must start long before NIL income shows up.

Whether your child is 13 or 18, now is the time to build a solid financial foundation at home. And that foundation starts with four key concepts:

- Budgeting
- Saving
- Credit
- Smart spending

In this chapter, we'll walk through how to teach these principles, why they matter, and how they will directly affect your child's NIL journey—even if they never go pro.

The Power of Early Financial Education

Imagine this: Your 16-year-old daughter just landed a small NIL deal with a local brand. She gets $300 to post a video promoting a sports drink. The money hits her Venmo account, and she's thrilled. Now what?

If she's never been taught how to manage money, that $300 might be gone by the end of the weekend. She might spend it on shoes, fast food, or a shopping spree. She might think she's being smart by giving some to her friends or using it for gas.

But here's the problem: she never saved any of it. She never put money aside for taxes. She didn't realize that accepting that payment meant she just became self-employed in the eyes of the IRS. And no one ever taught her how to make a simple budget.

That small mistake may seem harmless. But repeated over time, it sets the tone for financial habits that can follow her into adulthood.

Early financial education doesn't just teach kids how to handle money. It teaches them how to think about money. And that mindset will impact everything they do—from NIL earnings to career choices to retirement savings.

Step 1: Teach Budgeting – Give Every Dollar a Job

Budgeting is not about restriction—it's about intention. It's simply giving every dollar a purpose.

Too many young athletes (and adults, for that matter) operate with a "spend first, think later" mindset. Budgeting flips that. It teaches your child to plan ahead.

How to Teach Budgeting

1. Use Real Money

Start with their allowance, chore money, or any small earnings. Help them divide that money into categories:

- Spending
- Saving
- Giving
- Taxes (if they're earning NIL income)

2. Introduce the 50/30/20 Rule

Once they have regular income (even small NIL earnings), introduce this basic formula:

- 50% needs (or savings if they live at home)
- 30% wants
- 20% savings or investments

3. Use Budgeting Apps

Apps like Greenlight, GoHenry, and Step are designed for teens and let parents monitor spending. Older teens can graduate to Mint, YNAB (You Need A Budget), or EveryDollar.

4. Have a Monthly Budget Meeting

Make this a family habit. Sit down once a month to review where money went. Celebrate wins. Talk about what can improve.

Why Budgeting Matters for NIL

NIL income often arrives sporadically—$250 one month, $2,000 the next. Without a budget, it's easy for athletes to burn through their earnings, especially when the next check seems just around the corner.

Budgeting teaches them how to manage irregular income, plan for taxes, and think long-term.

Step 2: Teach Saving – Pay Yourself First

Most young people treat saving like leftovers: if there's anything left after spending, then they'll save. That doesn't work.

The golden rule of saving is: **pay yourself first.**

How to Teach Saving

1. Open a Savings Account Together

Choose a bank or credit union with a teen program. Look for no monthly fees, mobile access, and parental oversight.

2. Set Simple Saving Goals

Encourage your child to save for:

- A new phone
- College spending
- A future car
- Emergency fund (yes, even for teens!)

3. Use Percentages

Teach your child to save 20% of every dollar earned—even NIL money. Make it automatic. The habit is more important than the amount.

4. Introduce Interest and Compound Growth

Use online calculators to show how money grows. Let them see that saving $50 a month for 5 years adds up.

5. Match Contributions

If you're able, consider matching their savings. For every $10 they save, you add $5. It reinforces the habit and builds motivation.

Why Saving Matters for NIL

NIL deals may not last forever. Injuries happen. Trends change. Companies pivot. A saving habit ensures your student-athlete can:

- Handle taxes and emergencies
- Avoid taking on credit card debt
- Fund big goals (like starting a business or going pro)
- Maintain peace of mind

Step 3: Teach Credit – Build It Before They Need It

Credit is one of the most misunderstood—and under-taught—areas of personal finance.

If your child is 17 and getting NIL income, they are likely being offered pre-paid debit cards, credit card promotions, and "buy now, pay later" options. And unless they understand how credit works, they may destroy their score before they even have one.

How to Teach Credit

1. Start with Education

Explain what credit is: a measure of trustworthiness in borrowing money. Walk them through:

- What a credit score is
- What affects it (payment history, credit usage, length of credit history)
- Why it matters (loans, apartments, even job applications)

2. Consider a Secured Credit Card

Once your child turns 18, they can open a secured credit card with a cash deposit. Use it for small purchases and pay in full monthly.

3. Cosign With Caution

If you cosign for a card, make sure they understand it's a shared responsibility. One missed payment affects both scores.

4. Monitor Together

Use apps like Credit Karma or your bank's credit tracking tools to show them how scores move over time.

5. Teach the Dangers

Explain interest rates, minimum payments, and late fees. Show how $1,000 in spending can turn into $1,500 in debt.

Why Credit Matters for NIL

Your child may want to buy a car, rent an apartment, or invest in a business. A strong credit history opens doors. A weak one closes them.

Teach credit early—before they "learn the hard way."

Step 4: Teach Smart Spending – Needs vs. Wants

Student-athletes under NIL are now being flooded with marketing. Brands are in their inboxes. Social media is filled with influencers showing off clothes, cars, and jewelry. It's easy to fall into the trap of "I need to look successful to be successful."

That mindset can lead to lifestyle inflation—spending more just because they're making more.

How to Teach Smart Spending

1. Needs vs. Wants

Work with your child to list needs (food, transportation, equipment) vs. wants (designer gear, fast food, luxury items). Help them practice mindful spending.

2. Set Spending Limits

Use prepaid debit cards or app-based spending rules to help younger teens manage money in safe amounts.

3. Talk About Marketing

Teach them how ads target emotions. Discuss how companies use athletes for influence—and how that doesn't mean they care about the athlete's well-being.

4. Delay Purchases

Create a 24-hour or 48-hour rule for large purchases. If they still want it after waiting, it's probably worth considering.

5. Share Family Stories

Be transparent about past money mistakes or successes. Share what you've learned about spending wisely.

Why Smart Spending Matters for NIL

NIL income can disappear fast. Many student-athletes go broke before the season ends—not because they're bad people, but because they've never been taught how to spend wisely.

Smart spending is a discipline. And like any discipline, it takes practice.

Real Life NIL Cautionary Tales

Let's look at two true-to-life composite examples:

Example 1: The Over-Spender

Derek, a high school senior in California, lands a $2,000 NIL deal. He spends the entire amount in one weekend—new clothes, AirPods, a hotel party with friends. Two months later, the brand asks for a follow-up post, but Derek has deleted the video. The company pulls out. Derek is left with no money, no deal, and an upset coach who had vouched for him.

What Went Wrong?

- No budget
- No savings
- No understanding of contract obligations

Example 2: The Financially Literate Athlete

Sophia, a junior volleyball player in Florida, gets $1,200 from NIL across two deals. She saves $400, uses $200 for business cards and a website, and gives $50 to her church. The rest goes into her college savings. She also sets aside 20% for taxes. She sends a thank-you note to both brands—and is offered renewal deals the next season.

What Went Right?

- Budgeting
- Strategic spending
- Savings habit
- Professionalism and gratitude

These two students had the same opportunity. Their outcomes were shaped by their financial literacy.

Building a Financial Culture at Home

You don't have to have money to teach about money. You just need to create a culture in your home that talks openly, honestly, and consistently about:

- Income
- Responsibility
- Gratitude
- Delayed gratification

- Financial goals

Include your child in family budget meetings. Talk about bills and how decisions get made. Model what it looks like to manage money with intention.

Remember: NIL is not just about money—it's about maturity.

Conclusion: Habits Before Headlines

Every dollar your child earns under NIL is an opportunity to teach a lesson that will benefit them for a lifetime. And those lessons start at home, before the lights, before the cameras, and long before the contracts.

You are your child's first financial coach. And the earlier you start, the more confident and capable they'll be when the money starts rolling in.

Teach them how to budget.

Show them how to save.

Explain how credit works.

Model smart spending.

Because NIL doesn't create character—it reveals it. The habits you build now will determine how your child handles success later.

Part II: High School Years – Year-by-Year Parent Playbook

The high school years are a critical runway—not just for college athletics, but for building the mindset and habits student-athletes need to navigate NIL successfully. Each year presents new opportunities for growth, and new risks if parents aren't paying attention. This section helps parents take a strategic, year-by-year approach to supporting their student-athlete, so when the NIL spotlight comes, their child is ready in every way.

Freshman Year is about **foundation**. Parents should focus on building healthy academic habits, reinforcing discipline, and establishing character as the most important currency. Financial conversations begin early—even if the athlete isn't earning money yet. Now is the time to introduce simple concepts like budgeting, saving, and smart spending using allowance, gift money, or small earnings. It's also the right time to clean up and shape social media presence, which will eventually become part of your child's public brand. Parents should start forming relationships with coaches, school counselors, and mentors, while also teaching their child about reputation, responsibility, and online safety.

Sophomore Year is when **exposure increases**, and so does pressure. At this stage, athletes may begin receiving early attention from recruiters, media outlets, and even small NIL interest from local brands. Parents should double down on teaching financial literacy—this includes opening bank accounts, setting up a monthly budget review process, and using digital tools to track spending and saving. It's important to help your child understand taxes, even at a basic level, and to introduce the idea that any NIL money is real income with responsibilities. This is also the time to encourage smart decisions around personal branding, including how they show up online and who they allow into their circle. Parents need to pay close attention to potential distractions: early ego, overuse of social media, and unsolicited NIL or recruiting pitches from unverified sources.

Junior Year is often when things start to get real. Recruiting picks up, official visits begin, rankings carry weight, and NIL inquiries may start coming in more frequently—especially in states that allow high school NIL. Families must be financially and emotionally prepared. Parents should guide their student-athlete through real-world simulations: what to do if a brand offers a deal, how to read a simple contract, and how to decide what aligns with their values. It's time to involve professionals—such as NIL consultants, accountants, or attorneys—if meaningful money is on the table. Parents must also ensure their child understands the impact NIL income could have on eligibility, taxes, or future scholarship needs. On the personal side, this is when character gets tested—can the student stay focused amid rising attention? Can they say "no" to distractions? That's where parental leadership really shines.

Senior Year is the culmination of everything built over the previous three years. By now, your child may be committed to a school, actively receiving NIL offers, or stepping into media spotlights. Parents must serve as protectors and partners: reviewing contracts, setting up legal entities if needed (like an LLC), preparing for tax season, and ensuring your child is not signing away long-term rights for short-term gain. Financial discipline must be second nature by this point—your child should know how to budget, save for taxes, invest, and plan for irregular income. Beyond the business side, parents should also focus on emotional wellness. The pressure to perform, represent a brand, and transition to college life is intense. Parents play a key role in ensuring their child's identity remains rooted in more than just money or athletics.

Across all four years, the consistent theme is this: **parents are not just**

spectators—they are financial and emotional coaches. This playbook is your sideline guide for helping your child stay grounded, make smart decisions, and build a foundation for success far beyond high school.

Chapter 4: Freshman Year – Fresh Start: Setting the Tone in 9th Grade

Freshman year sets the tone for everything that follows. It's not about NIL deals or brand partnerships just yet—it's about **establishing habits, priorities, and values** that will become the foundation of your child's success both on and off the field. Ninth grade is where student-athletes begin to take their goals seriously, and where parents have a unique window of influence to shape the way their child approaches school, sports, money, and life.

Key Conversations to Have Now

This is the year to begin having open, honest, and regular conversations with your child that go beyond athletics. The goal is to create a relationship where your student-athlete feels supported, guided, and held accountable.

Important topics include:

- **Vision for the future**: Ask your child what they want their next four years to look like—not just in sports, but in school and life. Help them begin connecting their daily actions to long-term goals.
- **Grades and eligibility**: Explain that high school grades will directly impact college opportunities. Establish a GPA goal and monitor it together.
- **Balancing priorities**: Talk about how sports, school, family, friends, and rest all compete for time—and how to build a routine that honors each one.

- **Values and behavior**: Reinforce the importance of integrity, accountability, and how small decisions (like skipping homework or posting something inappropriate) can have long-term consequences.
- **Social media**: Review their online presence together. Talk about how what they post today could be seen by college coaches and brands years from now.

These conversations don't have to be formal lectures—they can happen in the car on the way to practice or over dinner. The key is consistency and creating a safe space where your child can learn and grow with your support.

Discipline, Time Management, and Focus

Freshman year is a transition year—your child is now in a bigger academic environment, playing with older teammates, and possibly feeling pressure to perform. This is when time management and discipline must become daily habits.

As a parent, help your child:

- **Create a weekly schedule**: Include time for homework, training, rest, meals, and screen time. Review it together and adjust as needed.
- **Set short-term goals**: These could include reading one book a month, improving a vertical leap, or raising a math grade. Make goals specific and trackable.
- **Limit distractions**: Set healthy boundaries around video games, phones, and social media use—especially during the school week.
- **Stick to commitments**: If they've joined a team, club, or tutoring program, encourage them to follow through and honor their word.
- **Build routines**: Morning checklists, bedtime wind-downs, and Sunday planning sessions help create a rhythm that reduces stress and increases focus.

Helping your student-athlete understand that time is a valuable resource—and teaching them how to manage it—is one of the most powerful NIL-preparation tools you can give them. Why? Because when the time comes for money, contracts, and media attention, the habits formed in freshman year will determine how they respond.

Why This Matters for NIL (Even Before NIL is a Factor)

Some parents assume that NIL is only relevant when the offers come in junior or senior year. But NIL readiness begins in ninth grade—with mindset, maturity, and responsibility.

Brands, college recruiters, and advisors all look for student-athletes who:

- Handle pressure well
- Stay on top of schoolwork
- Show leadership on and off the field
- Make wise decisions
- Respect coaches, teammates, and deadlines

These are the exact same qualities you can begin nurturing in your child right now. You're not just preparing them for a sport—you're preparing them for life. And whether they ever sign an NIL deal or not, those skills will pay off in every area of their future.

Freshman year is the clean slate. This is the time to build systems, structure, and support before the spotlight shines. Because when it does, your child will rise or fall on the strength of the foundation you've helped them lay.

Chapter 5: Car Chase

This Is So Random, But…

I always wanted to write a book with a car chase.

No joke. Any time someone tells me about a book—whether it's a mystery, romance, financial guide, or even a cookbook—I always ask with a grin:

> ***"But does it have a car chase?"***

It's my thing. My signature move.

And now, it's a tradition.

When I wrote *Financial Literacy For NIL,* I made sure to include a car chase in there.

This book—*Financial Literacy For NIL for Parents of Student Athletes*? Yep. It's got one too.

And trust me—every future book in the *Financial Literacy* series will have a car chase somewhere in its pages. Why? Because it's not just about action—it's about movement. It's about momentum. It's about **making the topic exciting**.

So yes, this book absolutely has a car chase.

But not in the *Fast & Furious* way (although if Vin Diesel wants to narrate the audiobook, let's talk).

This chase is the one you're already in.

Right now.

It's the unpredictable, high-speed, high-stakes pursuit called **Name, Image, and Likeness (NIL)**.

And you?

You're the driver.

Welcome to the NIL Car Chase

You've got the keys.

The engine's running.

The road ahead is wide open.

And the decisions you make today could affect the next 10–20 years of your child's life.

But before you press the pedal, let's take a second to check your dashboard:

- **Are you watching your fuel?** That's your *budget*. A lot of student-athletes run hot and blow through their NIL money before the first season wraps.
- **Is your check engine light on?** That might be that NIL contract you didn't fully read. Or the taxes you haven't planned for. Or that cousin who keeps texting, "Let me hold something real quick."
- **Are you checking your rearview mirror?** Behind you are the IRS, school compliance, sketchy dealmakers, and even old spending habits. Don't let them sneak up on you.
- **Do you even have a GPS?** Are you heading toward long-term wealth? Entrepreneurship? Financial freedom? Or just taking flashy exits that look good online but lead nowhere?

This isn't about speed.

It's about **control**.

Your Role in the Driver's Seat

As a parent, you're not just along for the ride.

You're part coach, part navigator, part pit crew.

You're helping your student-athlete:

- Shift gears with purpose
- Hit the brakes when needed
- Refuel when they're low
- And pull over when it's time to ask for help

Sure, other kids are zooming past on social media—posting checks, flashing new cars, rocking endorsements. But what you *won't* see are the breakdowns, the burnout, and the financial dead ends that come from driving blind.

That's why this book exists.

That's why *every* book I write will have a car chase—because the financial journey is real, it's fast, and it matters.

This is your moment.

This is your map.

This is your manual for navigating NIL with clarity, confidence, and a clean dashboard.

So yeah—this book has a car chase.

You're the one steering.

Let's make sure you know where you're going.

Chapter 6: What Parents Should Be Teaching This Year

Introduction to budgeting, credit awareness, and the value of money

The importance of grades and character off the field

Freshman year is the perfect time to start laying the groundwork for smart financial habits and strong personal values. While most student-athletes won't sign NIL deals at this stage, they're likely beginning to handle their own spending decisions—whether it's allowance, cash from chores, small part-time jobs, or gift money from birthdays and holidays. These small moments create the perfect learning environment to introduce foundational concepts about money and personal responsibility.

Introduction to Budgeting

Teaching your child how to budget is one of the most impactful things you can do this year. A budget doesn't need to be complicated—it simply shows your child how to plan where their money goes instead of wondering where it went.

Start with these simple steps:

- **Use what they have now**: Whether it's $20 from chores or $50 from a birthday, help them split it into spending, saving, and giving categories.
- **Set goals together**: Want a new pair of shoes or sports gear? Create a savings plan to reach that target gradually.

- **Track spending**: Use a notebook, a budgeting app for teens, or a digital debit card that allows parental monitoring.
- **Introduce delayed gratification**: Talk about the benefits of waiting and saving instead of buying immediately—an essential skill if they earn NIL money later.

The goal isn't just to make them financially literate; it's to help them understand that money is a tool, not a toy.

Credit Awareness

While your child can't open a credit card yet, this is the ideal time to explain what **credit** is, how it works, and why it matters.

Key concepts to introduce:

- **What a credit score is** and why it's important for renting apartments, buying a car, or getting approved for a loan later in life.
- **The dangers of debt**: Explain how interest works and what happens when people don't pay their credit card bills on time.
- **Responsibility over reputation**: Talk about how credit is built slowly through trust and consistency—just like their reputation with coaches and teachers.

Think of this year as planting seeds. The earlier your child begins to understand credit, the better choices they'll make when they're old enough to build it.

Teaching the Value of Money

Whether your family is well off, living paycheck to paycheck, or somewhere in between, it's vital your child understands that **money is earned, not just given**. Too many young athletes with NIL income struggle because they've never learned how to respect money—they just spend it because it's there.

What to emphasize:

- **Effort = earnings**: Connect household chores, academic success, or athletic performance with rewards—teaching the link between hard work and income.
- **Show real-life examples**: Take your child grocery shopping and talk about budgeting. Involve them in small decisions like comparing prices or calculating discounts.
- **Talk about opportunity cost**: If they buy that $50 hoodie, what are they giving up? Teach them to think in trade-offs, not just purchases.

These early conversations will prepare them to handle larger sums of money responsibly when NIL offers come their way.

The Importance of Grades + Character Off the Field

It's easy for a young athlete to believe that talent alone will open doors. But you, as the parent, must remind them that **character and academics** are just as important—if not more.

Here's why:

- **Grades are eligibility**: Poor academics can ruin recruitment potential and shut down NIL opportunities entirely. Many schools require a minimum GPA to even participate in NIL deals.
- **Character is currency**: Brands and coaches are watching. A student-athlete with a strong work ethic, good attitude, and leadership off the field is more likely to attract both scholarships and endorsements.
- **Discipline matters**: Teach your child that how they treat teachers, teammates, and even opponents reflects on their family, school, and future.

What to do:

- **Set academic expectations now**: Consider a minimum GPA goal. Check grades weekly or biweekly and praise progress.
- **Talk about integrity**: Ask your child, "What do you want to be known for?" and help them align their daily actions with that identity.
- **Celebrate character**: When they show maturity, leadership, or selflessness, point it out. Reinforce that success isn't just about stats—it's about who they are becoming.

Why It All Matters Before NIL Ever Starts

Too many student-athletes get thrown into the NIL spotlight with no preparation. Money without maturity leads to mistakes. But parents who start early—like in freshman year—give their child a head start that's more valuable than any deal they'll sign.

By teaching budgeting, credit awareness, and the value of money now, you're not just preparing them to manage NIL money—you're preparing them for adulthood.

And by reinforcing grades and character off the field, you're helping them build a brand that sponsors, coaches, and future employers will trust.

NIL success isn't built during the deal. It's built years before, in the way a young athlete carries themselves when no one's watching.

Freshman year is when it all begins.

Chapter 7: Sophomore Year – The Sophomore Spark: Talent Meets Exposure

Sophomore year is when potential starts to look like performance. Your child is no longer just trying to make the team—they're competing, producing stats, and maybe even standing out. This is the year when the spotlight begins to flicker. Camps, rankings, showcase events, and social media clips can start drawing attention from recruiters, fans, and even businesses looking to align early with rising stars.

For many families, this is the first time the idea of "NIL" starts to feel real—even if the checks haven't come yet.

The key challenge for parents during this time? **Balancing excitement with discipline, growth with humility, and confidence with character.**

The Sophomore Surge: Why Exposure Increases

By 10th grade, many student-athletes begin participating in larger-scale events outside their school environment:

- **Position-specific camps** run by colleges or scouting services
- **Showcases and combines** where performance is timed, measured, and ranked
- **Travel teams or club teams** that play in front of college scouts

- **National or state rankings** on sports websites, social media, or recruiting platforms

These events often bring visibility—and visibility brings pressure. Some athletes thrive in that pressure, while others become distracted by it. That's where parents play a vital role.

Camps, Rankings, and Buzz: What Parents Should Know

Exposure is a double-edged sword. A strong showing at a summer camp can boost a child's confidence and recruiting interest. A poor performance—or negative attitude—can stick with them longer than the game itself.

What parents should focus on:

- **Encourage effort over outcome**: Help your child see these events as opportunities to learn and grow, not just prove themselves.
- **Vet the events**: Not all camps or combines are created equal. Some are cash grabs with no real exposure. Research who's attending, who's coaching, and who benefits.
- **Understand the politics**: Rankings are subjective. Don't get caught up in internet hype. What matters is consistent performance and coachable behavior.
- **Prepare your child mentally**: Discuss how to handle disappointment, how to interact with scouts, and how to stay focused on their team responsibilities during the school year.

Managing Hype and Ego

Sophomore year can bring the first real "buzz" around your student-athlete. Maybe a coach retweets a highlight video. Maybe a recruiting site ranks them among the best in the region. Maybe they're the talk of their school—or even their town.

This is where you, the parent, become **the emotional thermostat** in your home.

How to manage ego and entitlement:

- **Keep praise balanced**: Acknowledge accomplishments but stay focused on the bigger picture.
- **Model humility**: Share stories of hard work, failure, and perseverance—especially if you've walked a similar path.
- **Keep them grounded in reality**: Remind your child that for every highlight clip, there's another athlete grinding in silence.
- **Focus on team culture**: Make sure your child continues to be a good teammate, not just an individual standout.
- **Watch for changes** in behavior, attitude, or motivation. Sophomore success can quickly lead to sophomore slumps if humility is lost.

This is also when parents must **set the tone on social media and branding**. With more eyes comes more scrutiny. If your child is being followed by college pages, brands, or agents, every tweet, comment, and story matters.

Why This Matters for NIL

Brands aren't just watching stats—they're watching **how your child carries themselves.** Sophomore year is often when NIL circles start quietly paying attention. They're looking for:

- Clean social media
- Positive interactions with coaches and teammates
- Leadership skills
- Community involvement
- Personal stories that align with brand values

If your child gets noticed for the wrong reasons—showboating, negativity, disrespect—those early NIL opportunities may never materialize. Sophomore year is the time to **start acting like a professional**, even if no one's writing checks yet.

Parental Priorities in Year Two

Your role this year is to:

- Be a sounding board, not just a cheerleader
- Monitor mental and emotional shifts as exposure grows
- Celebrate effort, character, and consistency—not just rankings and offers
- Help your child understand what true "value" means—not just athletic worth, but leadership, humility, and work ethic

This is also a great year to **bring in educational resources**: a financial literacy podcast, a YouTube channel on athlete branding, or a trusted mentor who has experience with the recruiting or NIL process.

The Bottom Line

Sophomore year is often when student-athletes go from "playing for fun" to realizing, *"This could really take me somewhere."* That realization is both exciting and risky.

Exposure is only helpful if your child is ready for it. And readiness starts with structure at home—mentally, emotionally, and financially. Sophomore year is not about chasing deals or followers. It's about becoming the kind of person brands, teams, and universities want to invest in.

Help your child focus on becoming that person.

Chapter 8: What Parents Should Be Teaching This Year

Social Media Literacy and Digital Brand Building

Starting a Savings Account and Creating a Simple Budget

By sophomore year, your child likely has access to a phone, social media accounts, and is making more independent financial decisions. Whether or not NIL money is on the table yet, this is the ideal time to deepen their financial education and elevate their digital presence. These are two areas that often go overlooked—until it's too late.

Social Media Literacy and Digital Brand Building

Sophomore year is when many student-athletes begin attracting attention—sometimes from local media, sometimes from recruiters, and increasingly, from brands scouting early NIL potential. Every tweet, post, and comment becomes part of your child's digital résumé.

What parents should be teaching now:

1. Every post is permanent

Even if they delete it, screenshots last forever. Teach your child to pause and ask: *"Would I want a coach, brand, or college administrator to see this?"*

2. What you like and share matters

It's not just about what your child posts—it's also what they engage with. Liking or resharing offensive content can be just as damaging as posting it.

3. Their online voice is part of their brand

Help your child identify what they want to be known for. Is it leadership? Positivity? Work ethic? Encourage them to post with intention and authenticity.

4. Clean up existing profiles

Now is the time to review and delete anything that could be misinterpreted or cast them in a negative light. That includes old jokes, lyrics, rants, or party photos.

5. Create a consistent look and feel

If your child is serious about their athletic identity, help them create consistent usernames across platforms, use a professional-looking profile photo, and update bios to reflect goals, sports, and accomplishments.

6. Understand NIL visibility

Brands aren't just looking at performance—they're looking at *who your child is online.* A student-athlete with 1,000 followers and a positive, consistent voice may attract more NIL opportunities than someone with 20,000 followers and chaotic content.

7. Control their narrative

Encourage your child to highlight achievements, training progress, academic successes, community involvement, and other moments that reflect their values and personality.

Starting a Savings Account and Creating a Simple Budget

This is also the year to build **real-world financial systems** your student-athlete can use—before any NIL money ever arrives.

1. Open a student checking and savings account

If you haven't already, visit your local credit union or bank to open joint accounts. This allows your child to:

- Get used to managing digital money
- Make mobile deposits or transfers
- See how interest works (even if minimal)
- Begin separating spending money from savings

Make sure you discuss:

- ATM fees
- Overdraft risks
- Online safety
- How to track balances and transactions

2. Introduce them to digital money tools

Apps like Greenlight, GoHenry, or Step allow parents to oversee teen accounts while teaching independence. For older or more mature students, platforms like Chime or Capital One offer simple student-friendly accounts.

3. Create a basic monthly budget

Even if their income is low or irregular, it's the *habit* that matters. Use these categories:

- **Earnings**: Allowance, part-time job, holiday money
- **Giving**: Donating to a cause or church
- **Saving**: At least 10–20% of income
- **Spending**: Meals out, small purchases, entertainment
- **Sports-related expenses**: Training gear, travel snacks, etc.

Review it together monthly. Help them ask:

- Where did my money go?
- What could I have done differently?
- What am I saving for?

4. Set a short-term savings goal

Whether it's a new pair of cleats, tickets to a concert, or a gift for a sibling, teach your child to plan and wait—two skills that will serve them greatly when larger NIL checks start coming in.

5. Teach the importance of building financial muscle now

Let your child know that:

- NIL income is not guaranteed
- The habits they build now will be the habits they carry when the stakes are higher
- Managing $50 well prepares them to manage $5,000 wisely

Why These Lessons Matter in Sophomore Year

This is the transition year—when raw talent becomes visible and attention begins to build. Your student-athlete may not have major NIL opportunities yet, but their digital footprint and financial habits are already speaking for them.

- A clean, confident online presence builds trust with future partners
- A basic budget creates the discipline needed for managing larger income
- A savings habit builds independence and resilience
- A clear brand identity sets your child apart from the crowd

As a parent, you don't need to micromanage every post or dollar. You just need to create systems, have regular conversations, and model the behavior you want your child to adopt.

Because the truth is: NIL doesn't create new habits—it reveals existing ones. And sophomore year is when those habits really start taking shape.

Chapter 9: Junior Year – The Recruitment Year: What's Really at Stake

Offers, visits, verbal commitments

Summer travel teams, rankings, and sponsorship attention

Junior year is the inflection point—the moment when dreams start becoming decisions. For many student-athletes, it's the year when their performance, exposure, and reputation start converging to create tangible opportunities. And for parents, it's the year when **your involvement matters more than ever—not just emotionally, but strategically and financially.**

This is where recruiting becomes real. It's also when NIL begins to shift from a distant idea to an immediate consideration.

Offers, Campus Visits, and Verbal Commitments

This year is when college coaches begin making formal offers, scheduling official and unofficial visits, and asking for verbal commitments. Your child might start receiving regular contact from programs, attending prospect days, or getting handwritten notes and calls. These experiences are exciting—but also overwhelming.

What's at stake:

- A verbal commitment could shape your child's next 4–5 years.
- Some offers come with time pressure ("commit now or we'll move on").

- NIL opportunities may be used as a recruiting tool—both subtly and directly.

What parents should do:

- Be a calm, informed presence during the process.
- Help your child understand what each school really offers: coaching stability, academic support, location, alumni network, NIL infrastructure.
- Don't get caught up in hype—rankings and gear don't build futures.
- Prepare questions for coaches: Does your program have an NIL coordinator? What financial literacy resources are provided to athletes? Do you support athletes starting LLCs or using campus media studios for brand content?

Remind your child that the goal is not to *just* get recruited—it's to find the right fit where they can thrive athletically, academically, and financially.

Summer Travel Teams, Rankings, and Exposure

Between junior year and the summer before senior year, exposure events hit their peak. Your child may be invited to:

- National camps
- Elite showcases
- AAU or 7-on-7 tournaments
- Travel baseball or softball leagues
- Junior Olympics or national combines

These are the events where college recruiters, media scouts, and now—brand representatives—are watching.

Why it matters:

- Performance at these events can influence scholarship offers.
- Attitude and coachability during these weekends matter as much as stats.
- NIL-minded companies may scout these events looking for marketable athletes to approach early.

What parents should monitor:

- Are these events worth the time, money, and travel? (Some are cash grabs.)
- Is your child staying grounded, or becoming consumed by rankings?
- How is your family handling rising expectations—financially and emotionally?

Encourage your student-athlete to focus on growth, not just performance. Rankings shift. Exposure can fade. But character, humility, and work ethic create long-term opportunity.

Increased Sponsorship Interest: The NIL Window Cracks Open

For some athletes, junior year brings the first real **NIL flirtations**—a DM from a local brand, a parent on the team asking about partnerships, a coach mentioning a potential NIL-friendly program.

While some states still restrict NIL at the high school level, others fully allow it. This creates a patchwork of legality, risk, and opportunity.

What parents should understand:

- Brands may approach your child subtly—offering "free gear" or a "collaboration."
- These interactions could jeopardize eligibility depending on your state and school rules.
- Accepting the wrong deal too early could impact recruitment.
- Many families fail to consult legal or financial professionals before

saying yes.

What you should be doing now:

- Educate your child on **what NIL is** and how to recognize a legitimate opportunity.
- Help them build a **simple system for reviewing offers** (always sleep on it, always discuss it with you, and never post about it until signed).
- Start thinking about how to **vet a brand, contract, or agent**.
- Begin documenting any income or partnerships, even small ones.

This is also the time to involve professionals: a financial advisor who understands NIL, a CPA who can explain tax obligations, and possibly a lawyer with contract experience. Don't wait until senior year when things are moving too fast.

What's Really at Stake in Junior Year

Junior year is about **setting up the launch pad**. Every visit, every impression, every online post can influence the next chapter of your child's life. Your family must now operate with a mix of discipline, discernment, and long-term thinking.

What's truly at stake isn't just a scholarship or a sponsorship—it's your child's **future financial foundation, reputation, and emotional readiness**.

This year, teach your child to:

- Protect their image
- Ask for help
- Think long-term
- Say no to distractions
- Prioritize fit over flash

As a parent, your job isn't to chase the dream—it's to **build the structure that supports it**.

Junior year is the proving ground. The spotlight is brighter, the stakes are higher, and the rewards are real. But only families who stay focused, informed, and intentional will navigate it successfully.

Chapter 10: What Parents Should Be Teaching This Year

Taxes 101: Understanding Income and Consequences

Explaining Endorsement Deals and Their Impact

By junior year, financial education moves from hypothetical to practical. As recruiting interest intensifies and NIL opportunities become more than just a buzzword, parents must prepare their student-athlete for two important financial realities: **income has consequences** and **endorsement deals are legal contracts, not casual handshakes.**

These conversations may feel early, but if you wait until the money shows up, you'll be playing catch-up in a high-stakes environment. Now is the time to teach your child the foundational truths behind taxes and sponsorships—concepts that will affect every NIL dollar they may earn.

Taxes 101: Understanding Income and Consequences

Too many student-athletes—and their parents—are shocked to learn that NIL income is not tax-free. In fact, most NIL money is treated as **self-employment income**, meaning your child may be responsible for paying **federal, state, and possibly local taxes** on their earnings.

If your child earns even a few hundred dollars through NIL, they may owe taxes—and if they don't plan accordingly, they'll face penalties, interest, or worse.

Key Tax Concepts to Teach Now:

1. All NIL income is reportable

If your child receives money through Venmo, PayPal, CashApp, Zelle, or even a check from a local business, it likely counts as income. Ignoring it doesn't make it disappear.

2. W-9s and 1099s

Brands and companies may ask your child to fill out a W-9 form, which provides their Social Security Number and declares them a contractor. At the end of the year, they'll receive a **1099-NEC** summarizing what they were paid. That income will be reported to the IRS—and must be included when filing taxes.

3. Self-employment taxes

Unlike W-2 employees, self-employed individuals (which your child becomes when they accept NIL money) must pay **both income tax and self-employment tax**, which includes Social Security and Medicare contributions—currently 15.3%.

4. The importance of setting money aside

Teach your child to save **20%–30%** of every NIL dollar they earn for taxes. This avoids scrambling at tax time or borrowing money to pay the IRS.

5. State tax rules vary

Depending on where you live—and where the income was earned—state taxes may apply. If your child participates in a national NIL deal that crosses state lines, things can get even more complicated.

6. Filing quarterly taxes may be required

If your child earns a significant amount through NIL (typically $1,000+ per quarter), they may be required to file and pay **estimated quarterly taxes** to avoid IRS penalties.

7. Professional help is worth it

This is the year to consider building your NIL team—especially a **CPA** or tax preparer with experience working with young entrepreneurs or athletes. Don't wait until the filing deadline.

Why Tax Education Matters Now

Even if your child hasn't received a dime yet, these conversations prepare them for:

- What questions to ask when offered a deal
- How to spot red flags in payments and paperwork
- How to avoid owing money or violating tax laws down the road
- Understanding that NIL is **not free money—it's income with legal strings attached**

The earlier they grasp this, the more confident and responsible they'll be when the opportunity comes.

Explaining Endorsement Deals and Their Impact

An endorsement deal sounds simple on the surface: a brand pays your child to promote its product. But in reality, **endorsement deals are business agreements**—sometimes complex, often legally binding, and always tied to your child's public image and credibility.

Now is the time to help your student-athlete understand:

- What an endorsement deal really is
- What they're agreeing to when they sign
- How one deal could impact future opportunities

What Parents Should Teach About NIL Deals:

1. Deliverables matter

A brand may offer your child $500 to post two videos and attend a photoshoot. If they don't complete those deliverables—or post late—they may forfeit payment or damage their reputation.

2. Read the fine print

Many NIL agreements include clauses around:

- **Exclusivity** (e.g., can't promote a competing brand)
- **Usage rights** (e.g., the company can use your child's image for a year)
- **Non-disparagement** (e.g., your child can't criticize the company publicly)
- **Termination clauses** (e.g., the brand can cancel the deal for misconduct or poor performance)

3. Your child is the product

Unlike employees, NIL athletes are monetizing their identity. This means:

- Their image may be used in marketing they didn't control
- A mistake or scandal could cause sponsors to pull out
- A bad deal could hurt future partnerships

4. There's no such thing as "just a free hoodie"

If a brand gives your child gear in exchange for a post, that's still a transaction. The moment there's an exchange of value, it may be a taxable event—and it often constitutes a contract, even informally.

5. Bigger isn't always better

Help your child evaluate opportunities based on:

- Brand alignment with their values
- Long-term potential vs. quick cash
- How the partnership may affect their public image or recruiting

6. Don't sign anything without review

This is the year to normalize the idea that **every contract gets reviewed by a parent or professional**. Teach your child that it's not about trust—it's about business.

Practical Teaching Tips for Parents

- **Role-play**: Practice what your child would do if a brand reached out on Instagram. Who would they tell? What questions would they ask?
- **Create a "decision checklist"** for evaluating deals, including questions like:
- What do they want me to do?
- How long is the deal for?
- What happens if I change my mind?
- Is this the type of brand I want representing me?
- **Track everything**: Encourage your child to create a folder (digital or physical) to store deal documents, receipts, and brand contacts.
- **Use real-world examples**: Share stories of pro athletes who lost endorsements due to poor choices—and those who built empires from smart partnerships.

Why These Lessons Matter Now

Junior year isn't just about being recruited—it's about preparing to operate like a business. NIL offers aren't theoretical anymore. And even if your child doesn't sign one this year, they're likely to be in conversations that could shape their reputation, eligibility, and financial life.

By teaching them about taxes and endorsement basics now, you're setting them up to:

- Be cautious instead of careless
- Ask smart questions
- Build a reputation as a responsible, professional athlete
- Protect themselves legally and financially

Most importantly, you're reinforcing that NIL is not just about the money—it's about maturity, responsibility, and long-term thinking.

And junior year is the perfect time to instill all three.

Chapter 11: Senior Year – Senior Year Game Plan: Preparing for the Leap

Signing Day, College Decisions, Agent Conversations Begin

Staying Eligible and Focused

Senior year is the final lap of a long and often emotional race. It's the year where everything your family has worked for starts to crystallize—college commitments, potential NIL contracts, and the looming transition into adulthood. It's a year of celebration, pressure, and decision-making, all at once.

For student-athletes with NIL potential, senior year often feels like the starting line of a business career that's layered on top of their sports and academic responsibilities. That's why your guidance, structure, and steadiness are more important than ever.

Signing Day and College Decisions

By senior year, your child may already be verbally committed or entering the final stages of recruitment. Signing Day becomes a major milestone, and with it comes new realities:

- **Scholarship terms and fine print**
- **Fit beyond athletics** (academic support, location, NIL readiness)
- **School-specific NIL policies** and support systems
- **Social media attention and public pressure**

What parents should do:

- **Review scholarship offers carefully.** Understand whether they're renewable annually or guaranteed for four years. Not all "full rides" are equal.
- **Talk about life off the field.** What major will your child pursue? What's the backup plan if sports ends early?
- **Evaluate the school's NIL infrastructure.** Does the university have an NIL collective? On-campus resources for branding and content? Financial literacy programming?
- **Ask about compliance.** Every school must monitor its student-athletes' NIL activities. Make sure your child understands the rules before they get there.

Agent and Advisor Conversations Begin

For top-tier athletes—especially those in football, basketball, and Olympic sports—**agents, managers, and brand consultants may begin reaching out before graduation.** These professionals may offer to help with:

- NIL brand deals
- Social media strategy
- Contract negotiations
- Financial or tax planning
- Business formation (LLCs, trademarks)

What parents need to know:

- **Anyone can call themselves an "NIL agent."** There is no nationwide licensing requirement yet, so due diligence is essential.
- **Protect your child from early exploitation.** Many so-called agents offer "exclusive" contracts with hidden fees, long terms, or revenue splits that heavily favor the agent.

- **You are still legally responsible.** If your child is under 18, any contract may require parental consent. Even after they turn 18, they'll likely still lean on you for guidance.

What to do now:

- Create a **list of questions** to ask every agent or advisor. Examples:
- Who else have you worked with?
- How are you paid—flat fee or percentage?
- Can we terminate this contract at any time?
- What happens if my child gets injured?
- **Consult a lawyer** to review any contracts.
- Consider working with a **registered financial advisor** who understands NIL—not just investment professionals, but someone who can explain taxes, budgeting, and income planning.

This is also a great time to start building a **personal advisory team**—trusted professionals who can help your child manage the business side of being an athlete.

Staying Eligible and Focused

With all the attention, excitement, and decisions happening senior year, it's easy for a student-athlete to lose focus. But **eligibility can be lost in a moment**, and a bad semester or misstep can derail even the most promising career.

Parents should help their student-athlete stay locked in on:

- **Academics:** GPA and core course completion still matter for final NCAA eligibility.
- **Training:** Injuries from overtraining, distractions, or burnout can derail momentum.
- **Time management:** College visits, social media activity, content

creation, and NIL meetings can eat into schoolwork, workouts, and recovery if not well-balanced.

- **Mental health:** The pressure to "succeed" with NIL and college choices can take a toll. Check in regularly. Make space for open conversations that don't revolve around sports or business.

This is also the year to talk about **life skills** like:

- Living on a budget
- Managing dorm life
- Speaking professionally in meetings or interviews
- Handling public criticism or backlash
- Protecting personal information online

Your child may be stepping into more public visibility than ever before. Help them understand what's expected of them—and how to advocate for themselves as both athletes and young professionals.

Why Senior Year Matters More Than Ever

Everything leading up to this year has been preparation. But now the spotlight is real. Colleges are making decisions. Brands are watching. Agents are circling. And your child may be just months away from earning more money than many adults—before they even get a diploma.

That's why your role in senior year is not just supportive—it's strategic.

- Be the calm voice when hype gets loud.
- Be the eyes that read every contract and ask every hard question.
- Be the anchor that keeps your child focused on their values, goals, and long-term vision.
- Be the teammate who celebrates wins, manages setbacks, and keeps the mission in view.

This year isn't just the end of high school. It's the beginning of an entirely new chapter in your student-athlete's life—one that could include college, competition, NIL income, a personal brand, and real-world financial responsibility.

Help them finish strong and step forward prepared.

Chapter 12: What Parents Should Be Teaching This Year

Contracts and Reading the Fine Print

Differences Between W-2, 1099, and LLCs

By senior year, your student-athlete may be offered NIL contracts—whether for social media promotions, merchandise sales, brand partnerships, or appearances. These deals are no longer hypothetical; they come with real legal, tax, and business implications. That's why one of the most important things you can teach your child this year is **how to understand what they're signing** and **how different types of income will affect them financially.**

This isn't about making them lawyers or accountants—it's about preparing them to ask the right questions, spot red flags, and make smart decisions.

Contracts: Reading the Fine Print

Every NIL opportunity—whether it's a $100 gift card or a $10,000 endorsement—is a **business transaction**, and that means there will (or should) be a contract. Too many young athletes (and their families) treat NIL agreements as informal, casual exchanges. That's how people get taken advantage of.

Key Contract Concepts to Teach Your Child:

1. Deliverables and Deadlines

- What exactly is the athlete expected to do?
- How many posts, appearances, or promotions are required?
- When are they due, and how should they be submitted?
- Failing to fulfill the deliverables—even unintentionally—can void the deal or lead to legal action.

2. Payment Terms

- How much are they being paid?
- Is payment a flat fee, performance-based, or commission-based?
- When and how will they get paid—upfront, after delivery, or in installments?
- What happens if payment is late or missed?

3. Length and Scope

- How long does the agreement last—30 days, six months, a year?
- Can your child work with other brands during this time, or is the deal **exclusive**?
- Does the brand retain rights to your child's image even after the deal ends?

4. Intellectual Property and Usage Rights

- Can the company use your child's image, video, or voice beyond the contract term?
- Will your child's name or content be used in ads, websites, or packaging?

5. Termination Clause

- Can either side cancel the agreement? Under what conditions?
- What happens if your child is injured, transfers schools, or loses

eligibility?

6. Dispute Resolution

- What happens if there's a disagreement? Is arbitration required?
- Is the agreement governed by your state's laws or another state's?

7. Morals Clauses

Many NIL contracts include a morals clause. This allows the company to cancel the deal if the athlete behaves in a way that reflects poorly on the brand (e.g., legal issues, offensive posts, poor sportsmanship).

What You Can Do as a Parent:

- Help your child adopt a simple rule: *"I don't sign anything without letting my parent or advisor review it first."*
- Teach them not to be rushed—"If they pressure you to sign today, that's a red flag."
- Involve a lawyer or NIL-savvy advisor to review any agreements over a few hundred dollars.
- Keep a digital folder with signed contracts, correspondence, deliverables, and payment records.

Understanding Income: W-2, 1099, and LLCs

Your child's NIL income is not like a part-time job at the mall. It doesn't come with automatic tax withholding, a manager overseeing everything, or a simple paycheck every two weeks. Most NIL income is **independent contractor income**, and it comes with responsibilities.

Now is the time to teach your child the **differences between common income types**:

W-2 Income (Traditional Employment)

- Used when your child is considered an **employee**

- Taxes are automatically withheld (federal, state, Social Security, Medicare)
- Employer may offer benefits like health insurance or retirement
- At year-end, the employer sends a **W-2 tax form**

NIL Relevance:

W-2 income is rare in NIL deals. Your child is unlikely to be classified as an employee of a brand or collective unless they're hired for a job unrelated to their athletic role.

1099 Income (Independent Contractor)

- Your child is **not an employee**, but is paid for services (e.g., promoting a product)
- **No taxes are withheld**—they must pay them later on their own
- Your child receives a **1099-NEC** form at the end of the year if they earned $600 or more from any single company
- Responsible for **self-employment taxes (15.3%)** in addition to income tax

NIL Relevance:

Most NIL income—endorsements, appearances, social media promos—is paid as **1099 income**. This means your child needs to:

- Save for taxes (20–30% of income)
- Track all income and expenses
- Possibly file **quarterly estimated taxes** if income is high

Forming an LLC (Limited Liability Company)

Some families begin exploring whether their student-athlete should form an **LLC** to manage their NIL activities. This adds a layer of professionalism and can help with:

- Separating personal and business finances

- Establishing a brand name or merchandise line
- Deducting legitimate business expenses (travel, gear, equipment)
- Working with brands that prefer dealing with a business rather than an individual

Important Points for Parents:

- An LLC must be registered with your state and usually requires an annual fee
- You may also need to apply for an EIN (Employer Identification Number)
- Your child will need to open a **separate business bank account**
- An LLC doesn't eliminate taxes—but it can provide deductions and limit liability

When it may be appropriate:

- If your child earns over $5,000–$10,000 per year through NIL
- If they want to build a brand or sell merchandise
- If they're entering long-term or high-profile deals

Professional guidance is a must when creating an LLC—don't do it alone.

How to Teach These Lessons Without Overwhelming Your Child

You don't have to make your student-athlete a tax expert or business owner overnight. Instead:

- Introduce one concept at a time
- Use real-life examples—like showing them a sample 1099 or a mock contract
- Make it visual—draw out how taxes work or walk through a checklist before signing a deal

- Include them in the decision-making—whether it's choosing an advisor, opening an LLC, or organizing paperwork
- Normalize asking for help—emphasize that no professional signs anything without legal review, and your child shouldn't either

Why This Education Is Critical Before Graduation

When your child steps onto a college campus, they may immediately be presented with:

- NIL contracts from collectives or sponsors
- Requests for W-9s and bank details
- Opportunities to start their own business or monetize their brand
- Scams or shady agents offering "free help" with legal strings attached

If you've helped them build the right mental framework—one that prioritizes caution, structure, and clarity—they'll be prepared.

They'll know how to say:

- "Let me run this by my parents and advisor."
- "I'd like this reviewed before I sign."
- "What does this clause mean?"
- "How will this affect my taxes?"

That kind of wisdom? It's what separates student-athletes who succeed in the NIL era from those who struggle.

And it all starts with what you're teaching right now.

Part III: Year-Round Athletes – What Parents Need to Know About Summer Leagues

For many student-athletes, **summer isn't an off-season—it's a second season**. Travel teams, club circuits, national showcases, skills camps, and invitationals have become essential to player development, recruiting visibility, and, increasingly, NIL relevance. While summer leagues offer opportunity, they also present risks—financial, physical, emotional, and legal. For parents, this is no time to coast.

This section helps parents understand what's really at stake in the summer and how to protect, guide, and position their student-athlete through the busiest and most unstructured part of the sports calendar.

Why Summer Matters More Than Ever

Summer is when:

- College coaches hit the road
- National and regional scouts build rankings
- Highlight videos get made
- Exposure to brands and agents quietly begins
- Injuries, burnout, and ego inflation can also creep in

The **stakes are high**, but the structure is loose. Unlike school-year sports, summer leagues are often run by third-party organizations with different priorities, less oversight, and inconsistent levels of professionalism.

Key Topics Covered in This Section:

1. Choosing the Right Summer Program

Not all summer leagues are equal. Parents need to ask:

- Who's coaching this team?
- What's the track record for college placement?
- Are there academic expectations or tutoring available?
- Will my child be overexposed or underdeveloped?

Some programs exist to develop athletes. Others exist to exploit them. Know the difference.

2. Understanding Summer NIL Exposure

- Can your child receive NIL offers during summer events?
- Do summer organizers or third-party recruiters have relationships with brands?
- Are there photographers or videographers creating content that will be monetized?
- What state rules govern NIL activity during offseason competition?

Summer is when brands and influencers often take notice—especially if your child's clips go viral or they're playing in high-profile tournaments.

3. Travel Costs and Family Budgeting

Summer leagues often mean:

- Flights and hotels
- Tournament fees
- New gear and uniforms
- Meals, gas, and day-to-day costs

Parents should budget in advance and evaluate return on investment—not every $800 tournament brings college offers or NIL opportunity.

4. Injury Risk and Overtraining

Year-round play, limited rest, and lack of medical oversight can lead to:

- Sprains, tears, and long-term wear
- Physical and emotional burnout
- Poor performance in front of scouts due to fatigue

Encourage off-days, recovery, and cross-training. Teach your child to speak up when something doesn't feel right.

5. Social Media and Image Control

With so much content created during summer:

- Who owns the videos of your child?
- Can that footage be monetized without your consent?
- Is your child being tagged, quoted, or filmed by influencers or recruiters?
- Are summer league coaches encouraging healthy branding, or promoting "look at me" behavior?

Parents should guide their child through responsible social media use during these events and monitor for digital overexposure.

6. Early NIL Conversations and Brand Interactions

Some families may experience their first "NIL feelers" during the summer:

- Brand reps offering free gear for shoutouts
- Event sponsors asking for promo posts
- Parent-coaches hinting at brand partnerships

Even if these offers are informal, they may count as NIL activity—and could affect eligibility depending on state laws or school policies.

7. Maintaining Academic Standards

It's easy for school to become an afterthought in the summer. But:

- Summer grades (if enrolled in summer school) affect eligibility
- Poor habits in June and July can create a sluggish senior year start
- Some schools request transcripts mid-summer during recruiting

Keep academics on the radar with summer reading, tutoring, and study routines—even during heavy travel.

8. Family Boundaries and Balance

Summer ball can take over the household. As a parent, set boundaries:

- Plan family time or vacations outside the tournament calendar
- Manage your child's screen time, sleep, and stress
- Keep NIL and recruiting in perspective—your child is still a teen

The Big Idea

Summer leagues are a preview of what NIL life looks like: unstructured schedules, performance pressure, travel, brand exposure, and public visibility.

If your child can learn to:

- Manage their time
- Show up consistently
- Protect their body and mind
- Engage with people professionally
- Represent themselves with maturity
- ...they'll be ready when real NIL opportunities arrive.

For parents, this section reinforces that your job doesn't stop in May—it shifts. Summer is where the brand, the buzz, and the business mindset all begin to form. And with the right approach, it can be an incredibly valuable—and joyful—part of your family's NIL journey.

Chapter 13: The AAU / 7v7 / Travel Ball Circuit – Big Exposure, Bigger Risks

Summer circuits—like **AAU basketball**, 7-on-7 **football**, **club volleyball**, **travel baseball/softball**, and **track club tours**—have become central to the identity and development of student-athletes. These leagues promise elite competition, national exposure, and the attention of college recruiters and, increasingly, NIL-savvy brands.

But behind the matching backpacks, livestreamed games, and highlight reels lies a more complex reality: **Who's really funding these leagues? Who's mentoring these kids? Who's protecting their future?**

This chapter gives parents a behind-the-scenes look at the summer sports machine—and the **red flags** and **boundaries** they need to be aware of.

Who's Funding These Leagues?

The summer circuit is big business.

- Some programs are funded by **shoe companies** (Nike, Adidas, Under Armour) looking to funnel talent toward sponsored college programs.
- Others are funded by **local business sponsors**, **"handlers,"** or **private investors** with less transparent motives.
- Some are self-funded—parents footing the bill through fees, travel costs, and fundraising.

It's important to ask:

- **Where is the money coming from—and where is it going?**
- **Are coaches being paid to promote certain players?**
- **Are brand reps quietly influencing team decisions?**
- **Are players being promised exposure or benefits that never materialize?**

Understanding the financial structure behind the program helps parents spot whether it's truly athlete-centered—or agenda-driven.

Who's Watching Your Kid (And Why)?

Summer leagues often involve:

- Overnight travel with **minimal adult supervision**
- Exposure to **non-certified coaches**, "trainers," and brand reps
- Frequent interaction with strangers—scouts, influencers, "advisors," content creators
- Social media livestreams, camera crews, and marketing teams recording every move

As a parent, you have to ask:

- **Who is my child with when I'm not there?**
- **What background checks have been done on the adults involved?**
- **What content of my child is being created, posted, or sold—and who owns it?**
- **Is my child being watched as a *student-athlete*, or as a *commodity*?**

The summer circuit is a magnet for **legitimate recruiters and shady opportunists** alike. Your role is to **stay close**, ask questions, and maintain visibility.

Red Flags Parents Can't Ignore

Here are warning signs that something might not be in your child's best interest:

- **No transparency** around team finances, fees, or sponsorships
- Coaches discouraging parent involvement or attendance
- Pressure to **switch teams or trainers mid-season** with no clear reason
- Promises of NIL deals, rankings, or college offers that seem too good to be true
- Adults asking for **direct access to your child's phone, social media, or banking info**
- Unofficial "agents" or "recruiters" offering help without contracts or credentials
- Emotional manipulation—*"If you don't play here, you'll ruin your shot."*

Your job isn't to be paranoid—it's to be **informed and protective**. If something feels off, it probably is.

Setting Parental Boundaries in the Summer Circuit

To keep your child safe and focused during summer sports, you need **clear boundaries and expectations**:

1. **No solo travel without trusted adult supervision**

- Know where your child is staying, traveling, and eating—at all times.

1. **Non-negotiable academic check-ins**

- Summer grades, reading, and prep shouldn't fall off the radar during travel season.

1. **Digital oversight**

- Know who's messaging your child on social media, especially "scouts," "trainers," and NIL reps.

1. **No signing anything without review**

- Whether it's a media release or a "collaboration" agreement, all documents go through you or a trusted advisor.

1. **Family-first mindset**

- Protect your child from pressure to perform for coaches, cameras, or clicks. They are a teenager first—an athlete second.

1. **Regular emotional check-ins**

- Long travel weekends, losses, and performance anxiety can build silently. Make space for rest and honest conversation.

1. **Be visible—but not intrusive**

- Attend games when you can. Stay plugged into the team dynamic. Build relationships with coaches and parents—but don't micromanage your child's athletic growth.

The Bottom Line

The summer circuit offers incredible opportunity:

- College exposure
- Personal development
- Early NIL buzz

- Confidence and competitive growth

But it also opens the door to:

- Burnout
- Injury
- Exploitation
- Financial waste
- Emotional fatigue

Parents who stay informed, present, and proactive help their child extract the best from the experience—without sacrificing health, safety, or integrity.

Because **exposure without protection** is dangerous.

And **talent without structure** is vulnerable.

This chapter arms you with the awareness to make sure your child's summer season is a launchpad—not a liability.

Chapter 14: What to Ask Summer Coaches and Sponsors

Are they talking to agents or brands?

Are they tracking your child's personal data?

Summer coaches and team organizers often serve as the gatekeepers to college exposure, high-profile camps, and early NIL visibility. They may have good intentions, strong connections, and a genuine passion for the game—but they also might be operating in a loosely regulated space where **athletes are viewed more as products than people**.

As a parent, you can't afford to be hands-off. You need to be asking the right questions to **understand who's influencing your child**, **what information is being collected**, and **what business is being conducted behind the scenes.**

This chapter provides a **parental checklist of questions**—broken down by topic—to help you vet coaches, teams, sponsors, and other adults involved in your child's summer athletics.

Questions to Ask About Brand and Agent Activity

1. Are you talking to brands or sponsors about our kids?

If yes:

- What companies?

- What kind of deals or conversations are taking place?
- Is anyone being paid to promote specific players?

2. Are you in contact with any NIL agents, collectives, or reps?

- Have any approached you directly about our team or my child?
- Have you recommended any of our athletes to agents?
- Are you receiving any form of compensation or referral fee?

3. Are brands providing anything to the team—gear, funding, sponsorships?

- If so, what's expected in return?
- Do players have to wear branded gear, post on social media, or appear in marketing content?

4. Do you help athletes navigate NIL offers or contract conversations?

- What's your process if a brand reaches out?
- Do you involve the family, or handle it through the team?

These questions help you identify **whether a coach is acting as a mentor or a middleman**, and whether they're equipped—or overstepping—when NIL conversations arise.

Questions to Ask About Personal Data and Digital Tracking

1. Is my child's data being collected through any platforms, apps, or devices?

- Does the team use recruiting services, wearable tech, or evaluation software?
- Who has access to the data?

- Is it being sold or shared with third parties (scouts, colleges, companies)?

2. Are you posting highlight clips, photos, or personal stats online?

- Where are they being published?
- Are athletes tagged by name or handle?
- Who owns the footage—us, the coach, or a third-party media outlet?

3. Are players being asked to provide their phone number, email, or social media logins?

- Who sees that information?
- Is it being used to create athlete profiles without parent oversight?

4. Do you share team rosters, contact info, or bios with external organizations?

- If so, are parents notified?
- Is there an opt-out process?

In the age of NIL, **data is currency**—especially for teenage athletes. You have the right to know how your child's name, image, and personal details are being tracked and shared.

Questions to Ask About Oversight and Communication

1. Who else has access to the players during travel and tournaments?

- Are there other staff, trainers, or "unofficial mentors" involved?
- What's the coach's policy on outside influencers?

2. Are players ever meeting with brand reps, agents, or media alone?

- Are parents notified when these meetings happen?
- Are guidelines in place for protecting athlete privacy?

3. How do you keep parents involved in major decisions or communications?

- Do you have a system for sharing updates about exposure, recruiting, or NIL contact?

Questions to Ask About Priorities and Player Development

1. What's your goal for these athletes—scholarships, development, brand-building, or exposure?

- How do you balance those priorities?
- What's your track record for player advancement?

2. How do you prepare athletes for NIL opportunities?

- Do you educate them on contracts, taxes, or brand strategy?
- Do you refer them to professionals when needed?

3. How do you handle off-the-field behavior, social media, and character building?

- What are your expectations for athletes?
- Do you talk to players about how NIL can be affected by their digital footprint?

Red Flags If a Coach or Sponsor:

- Dismisses or deflects your questions
- Pushes for exclusivity or secrecy
- Suggests NIL offers are being arranged without parental involvement
- Collects player data without transparency
- Says, "Don't worry about it—this is how the game works now"
- Encourages your child to prioritize exposure over education or rest

The Bottom Line

Summer coaches and sponsors can be incredible allies—or unintentional liabilities. Some truly want what's best for your child. Others may be pursuing side deals, leveraging your child's talent for personal gain, or exposing them to hidden NIL risks.

Your job isn't to hover—it's to investigate.

By asking the right questions early and often, you:

- Protect your child's privacy
- Maintain your role in decision-making
- Spot bad actors before contracts are signed or opportunities are lost
- Ensure that summer sports are a launchpad—not a detour—from your child's bigger goals

When it comes to your child's future, silence is not protection. **Questions are.**

Chapter 15: Managing NIL Offers Before College

Is it legal in your state?

What to do if a brand approaches your child

As early as sophomore or junior year—and especially during the summer showcase circuit—your student-athlete may attract NIL attention from brands, local businesses, or individuals offering free products, paid promotions, or even long-term partnerships. While this can feel like a breakthrough, it also raises serious legal, financial, and eligibility questions that parents need to be equipped to answer.

This chapter guides families through the *first NIL approach*, with practical steps for making informed, compliant, and future-focused decisions.

Step 1: Is It Legal in Your State?

High school NIL laws vary dramatically across the country. Some states have fully embraced NIL opportunities for high school athletes, while others **strictly prohibit** any form of brand partnership prior to college.

What you need to know:

- State athletic associations—not the NCAA—govern high school NIL rules.
- Even within a state, private schools may have different NIL policies than public schools.

- Accepting NIL compensation in a **restricted state** can result in **loss of eligibility**, disqualification from competition, or revoked college offers.

How to check:

- Visit your state's high school athletic association website (e.g., GHSA, CIF, UIL, etc.).
- Call your school's **athletic director or principal** to ask about NIL policy enforcement.
- If your child plays in another state during summer (e.g., travel ball), check **that state's** rules too.

Step 2: If It's Legal—Evaluate Carefully

If your child is in a state that **does permit** high school NIL, it's still not time to celebrate and sign. Most parents and teens aren't prepared to manage the financial and legal implications of brand deals.

If a brand approaches your child:

Ask yourself:

- **What is the company asking in return?**
- Posts, appearances, livestreams, tagging, wearing gear?
- **What does your child receive?**
- Cash? Free gear? Discounts? Exposure?
- **What are the terms and timeline?**
- Is this a one-time offer or a 6-month agreement?
- **Does this affect your child's eligibility for high school sports, club teams, or camps?**
- **Does it limit future partnerships with other brands?**

Step 3: Get Everything in Writing

No matter how small the opportunity seems—**treat it like a business deal**.

If a brand says, "We'll send you gear in exchange for a few posts," that's still NIL activity. And it comes with tax obligations and brand expectations.

Require a written agreement that includes:

- Description of what your child is expected to do
- Payment or product details
- Timeline
- Rights the brand is requesting (e.g., use of your child's image or name)
- Termination clause (how either party can back out)

Even if the brand insists it's "just a handshake deal"—**don't move forward without a written agreement and parental review**.

Step 4: Involve the Right People

Your child should never be responding to NIL offers on their own. You need to **build a protective circle** before any deal is signed.

People to involve:

- **You** (the parent or guardian)
- A **school official or compliance officer**
- A trusted **attorney** with contract experience
- A **CPA or tax preparer** (to plan for income taxes)
- If possible: a vetted **NIL consultant or financial advisor**

Avoid:

- Agents or "managers" who reach out uninvited
- Coaches acting as unofficial agents
- Anyone offering to take a cut or commission without a formal contract

and transparency

Step 5: Protect Your Child's Eligibility and Reputation

Even if a deal is legal, that doesn't mean it's smart. Help your child weigh:

- **Brand alignment**: Does this company reflect your child's values?
- **Image control**: Will the brand use your child's name, face, or story long after the deal ends?
- **Recruiting impact**: Could this partnership hurt your child's standing with college coaches or programs?
- **Online exposure**: Is the content being requested appropriate, respectful, and consistent with how your child wants to be seen?

Red flag deals to avoid:

- Multi-year agreements that stretch into college
- Partnerships with alcohol, gambling, tobacco, or political companies
- Companies asking for exclusivity or controlling language
- Offers that seem "too good to be true" with no track record or transparency

Step 6: Build a System for NIL Evaluation

If your child begins receiving multiple NIL opportunities, it's time to create structure.

Simple NIL decision checklist:

- Is this legal in our state?
- Who made the offer? Are they verified?
- What are they offering—and what's expected in return?
- Is there a contract?
- Have we consulted a professional?

- How will this affect future opportunities or eligibility?
- Does this align with our family values and goals?

You might even consider creating a **family NIL policy**—a shared agreement outlining what types of offers you'll accept, when to say no, and who gets involved in the decision.

The Bottom Line

Getting an NIL offer before college can feel like a win—but **what you do next matters more than what's being offered**.

As a parent, your job is to:

- Slow down the process
- Ask the tough questions
- Get the facts straight
- Surround your child with ethical guidance
- Prioritize long-term growth over short-term money

Remember: **NIL is not just about income—it's about identity**. And before your child builds a brand, they need a solid foundation.

This chapter ensures you have the tools to protect your child's name, image, and future—starting with the very first offer.

Chapter 16: Summer Money – Tracking & Teaching

S*etting Up a Checking Account*

Conversations About Saving vs Spending

For many student-athletes, summer is the first time they start receiving **real money**: from NIL appearances, social media promotions, coaching youth clinics, or even a part-time job to support their athletic dreams. But earning money is only the beginning. The real lesson lies in **what they do with it**—and that starts at home.

This chapter walks parents through how to **set up basic financial systems** and, more importantly, **use each dollar as a chance to teach discipline, self-awareness, and future-mindedness**.

Step 1: Setting Up a Checking Account

If your child is earning income—even $50 at a time—it's time for them to have their own bank account.

Why a checking account matters:

- It teaches **responsibility** and ownership
- It provides a **safe place** for NIL or work income (instead of Venmo or cash apps alone)
- It enables **tracking** and building a financial history
- It introduces concepts like **debit cards, balances, overdraft fees, and**

direct deposit

What kind of account should you open?

- A **joint teen checking account** (linked with your account for oversight)
- Low or no fees
- Mobile app access with parental notifications or controls
- Option to **separate checking and savings** accounts under one login

Consider banks that offer teen-focused programs or apps like:

- **Chase High School Checking**
- **Capital One MONEY Teen**
- **Fidelity Youth Account**
- **Step**, **Greenlight**, or **GoHenry** for financial literacy features

Step 2: Tracking Income and Expenses

Once the account is open, show your child how to:

- Log income sources (e.g., NIL payments, job wages, appearance stipends)
- Categorize spending (meals, clothing, sports gear, entertainment)
- Review statements regularly
- Spot unnecessary or impulse purchases
- Ask themselves: *Was this worth it?*

Even if they're not earning thousands, it's the habit that matters. It teaches that **money isn't just something you spend—it's something you manage.**

Step 3: The Saving vs Spending Conversation

This is one of the most important financial conversations you can have with your child—especially as summer money starts flowing in.

Teach the 70/20/10 (or 60/30/10) Rule:

- **70% for spending** (within a monthly budget)
- **20% for saving** (toward short-term or long-term goals)
- **10% for giving** (charity, church, or community)

Adjust the percentages based on your family's values—but the key is helping them **see money in categories**, not just as a single lump to burn through.

Talk about "wants" vs "needs":

- Wants: brand-name clothes, fast food, gadgets, entertainment
- Needs: sports equipment, travel costs, car maintenance, savings

Have your child reflect before purchases:

- "Why do I want this?"
- "Will I still value it a month from now?"
- "What will I be giving up by buying this now?"

Goal-setting builds purpose:

- Saving for a new laptop, phone, or car? Create a visual tracker.
- Starting a business or YouTube channel? Save for gear and branding.
- Want to give back? Create a giving fund or volunteer program tied to their NIL platform.

Step 4: Start Talking About Taxes (Gently)

If your child is earning income from NIL—even if it's just a few hundred dollars—they may owe taxes. Summer is a good time to:

- Introduce the concept of **self-employment income**
- Set aside a percentage of every dollar (10%–20%) in a separate savings account labeled "TAXES"
- Let them see what **net income** vs **gross income** means

No need to overwhelm them with IRS codes—just help them **respect the money** and understand that not all income is free and clear.

Step 5: Connect Their Money to Their Mission

For student-athletes, tying money to identity is powerful. Ask:

- "What does your money say about your goals?"
- "How can you use your earnings to support your dreams?"
- "How does saving now help you have freedom later?"

When NIL or job income is connected to personal values—education, training, impact—it becomes more meaningful and less likely to be wasted.

Bonus: Create a Family Financial Check-In Routine

Use summer downtime to build new habits:

- Weekly money conversations at the dinner table
- Monthly goal reviews (what was earned, spent, saved)
- Discussing one financial principle together each week (e.g., compound interest, debit vs credit, investing basics)

Make money talk **normal, empowering, and judgment-free**.

The Bottom Line

Summer income is more than just pocket change—it's a training ground for adulthood.

By helping your child open a checking account, track income, save intentionally, and spend with purpose, you're giving them tools that will matter **long after the games are over**.

And in the NIL era, where a single post or partnership can lead to five-figure payments, those habits could be the difference between success and struggle.

Teach them now—and they'll thank you for life.

Part IV: College Years – Managing the NIL Reality

College is when NIL becomes real. The money starts coming in, the contracts get longer, and the spotlight gets brighter. For student-athletes, college is often their first true experience as independent adults—balancing academics, athletics, brand responsibilities, and financial decisions all at once. This section of the book focuses on how parents can serve as behind-the-scenes guides as their children enter a new, high-stakes environment.

The section begins by addressing how to help your child live like a student, not a celebrity, even if they're earning NIL income. It's about setting boundaries, building smart habits, and maintaining financial discipline in a college environment that often encourages impulsive spending.

It then explores the business side of NIL—how to handle contracts, taxes, agents, and LLCs. Student-athletes are now technically small business owners, and this section equips parents with the knowledge to help their children manage that role responsibly.

Maintaining eligibility and compliance is another critical focus. With NIL laws constantly evolving and varying by school and state, athletes can unintentionally violate rules. Parents will learn how to help their child navigate compliance departments and avoid missteps that could lead to suspension or loss of scholarship.

The emotional and mental health impact of NIL is also covered. With the pressure to perform, post, and profit, many college athletes feel overwhelmed. This section teaches parents how to recognize warning signs of burnout or identity loss and how to help their children create balance and boundaries.

Building a purposeful personal brand becomes a key theme. Parents will learn how to encourage their child to be intentional with their online presence, align with brands that reflect their values, and use their platform to support causes or career goals that last beyond college.

The section also warns about NIL scams and predatory influences, providing real-world examples and advice for protecting your child from bad actors and manipulative contracts.

Finally, this part defines the evolving role of the parent in the college years—not as a manager, but as a mentor. It helps parents understand when to offer advice, when to step back, and how to maintain open communication without overstepping.

Part IV is about helping your student-athlete grow into a responsible adult who can earn, lead, and live with clarity and character in the NIL era. It equips parents with the tools to stay connected, informed, and impactful—without taking the wheel.

Chapter 17: From Signing Day to First Check – The Fast Shift

For student-athletes and their families, Signing Day represents the culmination of years of dedication, hard work, and sacrifice. It's a celebration, a relief, and a rite of passage. But for athletes entering college in the Name, Image, and Likeness (NIL) era, that moment also marks the beginning of a very different journey—one that involves contracts, money, expectations, and identity.

This chapter explores the transition from Signing Day to receiving a first NIL check and why that shift can be both thrilling and disorienting. We'll cover the emotional, financial, and logistical changes that occur, and how families can navigate them with clarity and care.

The Emotional Shift: When Celebration Becomes Pressure

The moment your child signs a National Letter of Intent (NLI), their life changes. They become a college athlete, a future representative of their school, and in many cases, a visible figure in their sport's online and recruiting communities. There's pride, of course, but there's also pressure.

Expectation and Exposure

Social media lights up. Friends, family, coaches, and strangers all have opinions. Expectations skyrocket. If your child was a top recruit, they might already be dealing with attention from NIL collectives, brand scouts, and fan bases. Even mid-level athletes may receive early NIL opportunities based on regional notoriety or niche marketability.

This added exposure comes with new responsibilities. Your child may now feel the need to "live up to" their Signing Day moment. That can lead to anxiety, self-comparison, and performance pressure. It's essential to provide a calm, stable home perspective: remind them they were recruited for who they are, not who they need to become overnight.

First NIL Offer, First Check: What Actually Happens

For some student-athletes, an NIL check may come before they even start classes. Deals can range from a few hundred dollars to thousands, depending on the sport, the athlete's following, their school, and their value to local or national sponsors. These deals often include:

- Social media posts
- Appearances at local events
- Merchandising or apparel partnerships
- Content creation or podcast features
- Joining a collective tied to their university

Even the smallest NIL transaction can be transformative for a young adult. It's likely the largest amount of money they've ever earned. But unlike a part-time job with structured pay and taxes withheld, NIL money comes with strings—and consequences.

Understanding Taxes, Contracts, and Income Types

It's easy for an 18-year-old to see $2,000 in a CashApp transfer and think it's free money. Parents must help shift that perspective.

Taxable Income

Most NIL payments are classified as self-employment income. That means:

- No taxes are withheld
- Your child is responsible for paying quarterly estimated taxes
- They must file a tax return and may owe federal, state, and self-employment taxes

Help your child set aside 20% to 30% of all NIL income for taxes immediately. Open a separate "tax savings" account if necessary.

Contracts and Deliverables

NIL agreements may come with a formal contract. It's critical that no one in your family signs anything without reviewing it thoroughly. Contracts outline:

- What your child must do (the "deliverables")
- Payment schedule and method
- Exclusivity clauses (can they work with competitors?)
- Termination clauses (how can either party back out?)
- Image usage rights (can the brand use their name or photo indefinitely?)

Even small deals can have lasting implications if poorly structured. It's worth hiring a lawyer or NIL-savvy advisor to review terms before signing.

Financial Aid Impact: The Overlooked Complication

One of the most commonly misunderstood consequences of NIL earnings is their impact on **need-based financial aid**. Many families celebrate new NIL income without realizing it could reduce or eliminate federal and institutional aid.

FAFSA Considerations

NIL income must be reported on the Free Application for Federal Student Aid (FAFSA) as untaxed income. This can:

- Lower your Expected Family Contribution (EFC)
- Reduce eligibility for Pell Grants or need-based scholarships

Institutional Aid

Some colleges include NIL earnings when calculating need. That means NIL money can offset financial aid packages or lead to a reevaluation of award amounts.

Families should consult with:

- The school's financial aid office
- A CPA familiar with student income
- An NIL consultant if large earnings are expected

Sometimes, it may be wiser to structure deals through an LLC or delay certain income to a future tax year to protect aid eligibility.

Building a Plan Before the Money Arrives

Preparation is everything. Help your child develop a simple NIL management plan before they accept their first deal.

Step 1: Set Up the Right Accounts

- **Checking Account:** For receiving payments
- **Savings Account:** For taxes and long-term savings
- **Business Account (Optional):** If your child is earning over $10,000/year or building a personal brand

Step 2: Create a Budget

Have your child categorize income:

- 50% for needs (rent, food, phone)
- 20% for taxes
- 20% for savings
- 10% for wants (entertainment, clothes, etc.)

Track spending with a budgeting app or spreadsheet. Teach them to review it monthly.

Step 3: Create a Deal Evaluation Checklist

Help your child answer:

- Does this brand align with my values?
- What is the total time commitment?
- Are there long-term implications (exclusivity, image rights)?
- Who can help me review this?

The Social Media and Identity Piece

NIL isn't just about money—it's about identity. Your child is now building a public brand, often for the first time. That brand lives online.

Remind them:

- Every post is part of their digital resume
- Brands, fans, and reporters are watching
- They must set boundaries around what they share

Help them develop a simple content plan:

- Weekly sports updates
- Shout-outs to teammates and brands
- Community involvement
- Behind-the-scenes insights (without oversharing)

Encourage authenticity and consistency—but also remind them to protect their privacy and mental health.

Managing New Pressures

With income comes responsibility—and sometimes guilt or confusion. Some student-athletes feel pressured to send money home, help friends, or keep up with others' spending.

Normalize saying "no."

- No to deals that don't make sense
- No to friends asking for favors
- No to comparing themselves to athletes in different NIL tiers

Help them stay grounded:

- Keep their long-term goals in focus
- Revisit their budget monthly
- Celebrate small wins, not just flashy deals

Conversations to Have as a Family

1. What are our values around money?
2. Who will help review deals and contracts?
3. How do we define success in college—on and off the field?
4. What happens if NIL slows down or never takes off?
5. How can we make this money last—and grow?

These conversations empower your student-athlete to make informed, intentional decisions in a fast-moving environment.

Conclusion: The Fast Shift, Slowed Down

Signing Day to first check might only take weeks, but the consequences of early decisions can last a lifetime. Help your child slow down that shift. Teach them to pause, plan, and protect their future.

They may be a student-athlete, but they're also a business owner, a brand, and a young adult with a lot to manage. With the right systems and support, they don't just survive the NIL era—they thrive in it.

Chapter 18: Questions Parents Must Ask the School & Coaches

As your student-athlete transitions to college, parents must recognize that the school and coaching staff are not only overseeing athletic and academic performance—they're also gatekeepers and influencers of how NIL is handled on campus. Knowing what resources, education, policies, and guardrails exist can help you support your child while holding the institution accountable for their development and well-being.

This chapter gives you a framework of essential questions every parent should ask athletic departments, coaches, and school administrators as their child enters the NIL era.

Start With the Basics: What Does the School Actually Offer?

Many schools promote themselves as "NIL-friendly," but that can mean anything from full-service NIL support to a single workshop. Begin by asking:

1. What NIL education do you provide to student-athletes?

- Is there a formal NIL training curriculum?
- How often are workshops or seminars held?
- Are financial literacy, taxes, branding, and contracts covered?
- Are these sessions mandatory, and how are they tracked?

2. Do you offer 1-on-1 NIL advising or mentorship?

- Is there an in-house NIL coordinator?
- Can athletes get help reviewing contracts or structuring deals?
- Are professionals (lawyers, agents, CPAs) ever brought in to speak or consult?

3. How do you help athletes balance NIL with academics and athletics?

- Are there time management tools or staff to support scheduling?
- Do athletes have access to mental health counseling specific to NIL-related stress?

Compliance and Protection Questions

4. What are your NIL policies and support structures?

- Are there written NIL guidelines specific to this school?
- What is the reporting process for NIL deals?
- Is prior approval required before signing a deal?
- Who ensures NCAA/state rules are being followed?

5. What happens if an athlete breaks a rule or signs a bad contract?

- Are there consequences to eligibility or scholarship status?
- Does the school intervene in disputes?
- Will the athlete be supported if they need to exit a deal?

6. How do you protect athlete data and privacy in NIL deals?

- Is the athlete's information shared with brands or collectives?
- Are athletes required to work with certain platforms?

- Is there any tracking of social media or earnings?

Questions for Coaches

7. What is your role in your athletes' NIL journey?

- Do you encourage or discourage NIL involvement?
- Are you involved in the review or approval process?
- How do you help players stay focused amid NIL opportunities?

8. Do you have relationships with collectives or local sponsors?

- Are players introduced to these groups through the program?
- How are those introductions managed and monitored?

9. How do you ensure fairness and team cohesion with NIL?

- Do you address NIL-related jealousy or competition among teammates?
- How do you support walk-ons or non-starters in NIL conversations?

Evaluating the Culture

10. What are the school's values around NIL?

- Do you emphasize education, entrepreneurship, or quick income?
- Are athletes taught to align deals with their long-term goals?
- What happens when an athlete turns down a deal that doesn't fit their brand?

11. What does success in NIL look like at your school?

- Is it based on earnings alone, or on personal and professional growth?

- Are there success stories you can share?
- Are alumni involved in mentoring current athletes?

Final Thoughts for Parents

This isn't about overstepping—it's about due diligence. When your child chooses a school, they're not just choosing a coach or campus. They're choosing a system that will influence their development as an athlete, student, and now, as a business.

Asking these questions won't just inform your understanding—it will demonstrate to the school that your family takes NIL seriously and expects professionalism, protection, and partnership. And that's exactly what your student-athlete deserves.

Chapter 19: What to Know About NIL Collectives & Team Deals

As NIL continues to evolve, one of the most powerful forces shaping the landscape is the rise of **NIL collectives** and **team-based deals**. These entities play an increasingly important role in how athletes earn, engage, and interact with sponsors and their universities. But with increased opportunity comes complexity—especially when it comes to taxes, eligibility, contracts, and fair treatment.

This chapter breaks down what NIL collectives are, how team deals work, and what parents must know to ensure their student-athlete is both informed and protected.

What Are NIL Collectives?

NIL collectives are organizations—usually separate from the university—that raise money from donors, boosters, and businesses to fund NIL opportunities for athletes at a particular school. These collectives often:

- Broker endorsement or promotional deals for athletes
- Organize group licensing deals (e.g., video games, merchandise)
- Facilitate appearances, social media campaigns, or brand work
- Sometimes provide educational, financial, or legal support

Some collectives are sport-specific (e.g., football-only), while others serve all varsity athletes. They may offer guaranteed monthly payments or tie compensation to appearances and performance metrics.

Key Questions for Parents to Ask About Collectives

- Is the collective affiliated with or endorsed by the university?
- How are deals structured—is it a flat stipend, or based on work completed?
- Are athletes signing contracts? For how long? What are the terms?
- What rights are athletes giving up—name, image, likeness, content, merchandise?
- Is the money taxed, and are 1099s issued?
- Can the athlete opt out of participating without penalty?
- What happens if the athlete is injured, transferred, or no longer eligible?

Group Licensing & Team Deals

Group licensing allows a company to use the name, image, or likeness of a group of athletes—such as the entire football or basketball team—without needing separate agreements with each individual. Examples include:

- Jerseys with player names sold at the campus bookstore
- Athlete appearances in video games
- Co-branded merchandise and trading cards

While group deals can provide widespread benefit and fairness, they also raise questions:

- Does your athlete have the right to opt in or out?
- Is everyone paid equally, or based on performance or visibility?
- Are there exclusivity clauses that prevent your athlete from doing individual deals?
- What companies are licensing the group, and how are they using the

athletes' likenesses?

Tax Concerns with Collective & Group Deal Income

Whether from a collective or a group licensing deal, any NIL money received is likely taxable. In most cases, athletes are considered **independent contractors**, meaning:

- No taxes are withheld up front
- A 1099 form is issued if more than $600 is earned from one source
- Athletes must track income and pay self-employment taxes
- Quarterly estimated tax payments may be required

If a collective pays athletes on a recurring basis (e.g., $2,000/month), your child may need to:

- Set aside 25% to 30% of that income for taxes
- Track business expenses (travel, gear, training) that may be deductible
- Consider forming an LLC to manage NIL income more efficiently

Parents should help their athlete:

- Open a separate account to hold taxes
- Work with a tax advisor who understands NIL
- Keep records of every deposit, contract, and receipt

Power Dynamics & Pressure

While collectives can empower athletes, they also introduce subtle power dynamics. Athletes may feel:

- Pressured to accept deals that don't align with their brand
- Obligated to perform outside of school/team responsibilities

- Confused about what's required or allowed under school rules

Make sure your student-athlete knows:

- They are not required to say yes to every opportunity
- They should review every contract before signing
- They can walk away from deals that don't fit their goals

Final Takeaways for Parents

Collectives and group deals are quickly becoming a core part of college athletics. They offer access, equity, and structure—but also bring risk and responsibility. As a parent, your role is to:

- Understand how these systems work
- Help your child vet opportunities
- Reinforce that not all money is good money

The NIL era isn't just about getting paid—it's about making smart, informed choices that build toward a future. And that starts with knowing what questions to ask, what rights to protect, and what kind of legacy your student-athlete wants to create.

Chapter 20: Common NIL Pitfalls & Parent Warning Signs

As exciting and empowering as NIL opportunities can be, they also open the door to potential mistakes, manipulation, and stress. The sudden access to money, attention, and business offers can easily overwhelm student-athletes who are still maturing emotionally and financially. For parents, being able to spot the red flags early—before they turn into regrets—is essential.

This chapter identifies the most common NIL pitfalls and the key warning signs that parents should watch for. Whether your child is just getting started or already signing deals, your awareness can serve as a protective shield.

Pitfall #1: Isolation from Family and Support Systems

Success can be isolating—especially when money is involved. Some athletes start making NIL income and slowly pull away from trusted advisors, family, or school resources. They might think:

- "I can handle this myself."
- "They don't understand NIL."
- "I don't want to bother anyone."

Warning Signs:

- Reduced communication with parents or mentors
- Withholding details about new opportunities
- Avoiding conversations about contracts or finances
- Making major decisions without input

What to Do:

- Stay involved without being controlling
- Check in consistently, especially after big games or media exposure
- Offer to review contracts or budgets together
- Reinforce that asking for help is a strength, not a weakness

Pitfall #2: Spending Sprees and Lifestyle Inflation

NIL income often comes fast—and so does the urge to spend. New clothes, tech, jewelry, travel, and gifts for friends or family can quickly eat away at income meant to cover taxes or savings.

Warning Signs:

- Unexplained or excessive spending
- Social media posts showing lavish purchases
- Constant online shopping or late-night delivery
- Asking for more money despite earning more

What to Do:

- Talk openly about budgeting and taxes
- Encourage use of apps to track expenses and categorize spending
- Help them set up a 50/30/20 or 70/20/10 money rule
- Share stories of athletes who lost wealth due to lifestyle creep

Pitfall #3: Taking Bad Advice from the Wrong People

The NIL era has attracted a wave of self-proclaimed "experts," influencers, and agents—many without proper credentials. Some mean well. Others are exploitative.

Warning Signs:

- Your child starts quoting unfamiliar "advisors"
- They mention offers or deals without knowing the terms
- They're hesitant to let you or a trusted adult see agreements
- They commit to someone who isn't a registered agent or lawyer

What to Do:

- Teach your child to ask: "What are your qualifications?"
- Make it a family rule: no contracts without a review
- Help them build a team of vetted professionals
- Research advisors together before agreeing to anything

Pitfall #4: Falling for Scams or Fraudulent Offers

Scammers prey on young athletes by offering easy money, free gear, or promises of fame. These scams can involve identity theft, phishing, fake deals, or schemes designed to take a cut of future earnings.

Warning Signs:

- Messages from unknown accounts promising money or deals
- Requests for bank info, Social Security numbers, or login credentials
- High-pressure tactics to "sign today or lose the opportunity"
- Poor grammar or vague contracts

What to Do:

- Remind your child: if it sounds too good to be true, it probably is
- Help them verify every offer and sender
- Report suspicious contacts to school compliance or NIL support staff
- Keep a list of approved contacts for reference

Pitfall #5: Losing Focus on School and Sport

Chasing deals can sometimes replace chasing goals. Some athletes become consumed with building a brand, posting content, or managing their "business," and start to neglect their academic, athletic, or emotional growth.

Warning Signs:

- Drop in grades or missed assignments
- Late practices or skipped training
- Constant social media activity
- Mental fatigue or burnout

What to Do:

- Re-establish priorities: school and sport are still the foundation
- Encourage balance and time-blocking for NIL work
- Suggest unplugging from social media during exams or training blocks
- Celebrate effort and integrity over online engagement

Pitfall #6: Burnout, Anxiety, and Loss of Identity

The pressure to perform, maintain a public image, and monetize every opportunity can create emotional exhaustion. Your child might feel they can never turn off, never say no, and never show weakness.

Warning Signs:

- Mood swings or emotional withdrawal
- Avoidance of public or team events

- Doubting their abilities or self-worth
- Expressing a desire to quit or "disappear"

What to Do:

- Normalize talking about mental health
- Connect your child with therapy or counseling support
- Take NIL pressure off the pedestal; remind them who they are beyond the game
- Revisit their goals and values as a family

Final Thoughts for Parents

You don't need to control your child's NIL journey—but you do need to stay close to it. Every dollar, post, and contract is an opportunity to teach, support, and protect. These early experiences can shape not just their income, but their identity.

Stay curious. Stay connected. Stay grounded.

Your involvement is not about the money—it's about the mission: helping your child build a life, not just a brand.

Chapter 21: Parents & the Power of Financial Mentorship

In the NIL era, student-athletes aren't just navigating sports and school—they're stepping into a world of contracts, income, taxes, and long-term financial decisions. For many, it's their first real experience with money management. That's why parents have never been more important. As the most trusted adults in a young athlete's life, parents play a crucial role in shaping the mindset, habits, and values that determine whether NIL success becomes a stepping stone or a setback.

This chapter is about how parents can become financial mentors—not by being experts, but by being examples. It outlines how to lead by action, engage in real conversations, and build a financial roadmap with your student-athlete that sets them up for lasting success.

Leading by Example

Your child is watching you. They see how you talk about money, how you respond to stress, how you budget, save, give, or spend. Even if they don't say it out loud, they are learning from you.

To be a financial mentor, model the behavior you want your child to develop:

- Pay bills on time and explain why it matters
- Talk openly (not fearfully) about budgeting and saving

- Set and track personal financial goals
- Admit past mistakes and what you learned from them

You don't have to be perfect—you just have to be honest. Vulnerability creates teachable moments. Show them what financial responsibility looks like, not just what it sounds like.

Start with a Conversation, Not a Lecture

Sit down and ask your child:

- What do you want your money to do for you?
- How would you describe your relationship with money right now?
- What are you excited or nervous about with NIL?

Use those questions to open a dialogue. Keep the tone casual, not critical. This isn't about control—it's about collaboration.

Setting Financial Goals Together

Help your child think beyond the next check or the next purchase. Guide them to dream bigger and plan further. Start with simple categories:

Short-Term Goals (3–6 months)

- Save $500 for an emergency fund
- Pay off a credit card
- Build a budget and stick to it for 90 days

Mid-Term Goals (6–18 months)

- Save for a car or apartment deposit
- Launch a small NIL-related business
- Fund a travel experience or training opportunity

Long-Term Goals (2–5+ years)

- Build an investment account
- Graduate debt-free
- Create a brand or platform that outlives their playing career

Help them put these goals in writing. Revisit and revise them quarterly. Celebrate progress.

Teach the Basics Together

Make it a shared learning journey. Pick a topic each month to explore:

- January: Budgeting apps and tools
- February: Credit scores and reports
- March: Taxes and self-employment income
- April: Investing and compound interest
- May: Understanding insurance (health, disability, renter's)

Watch a video together. Read a short article. Talk about what you each learned. Let them see you growing, too.

Create a Safe Space for Mistakes

Your child will make financial mistakes. So will you. The goal isn't to avoid all failure—it's to create an environment where mistakes are addressed, not punished.

- If they overspend, help them rebuild.
- If they fall behind on taxes, connect them with a CPA.
- If they get scammed, walk through what happened and how to prevent it.

Normalize mistakes as part of financial growth.

Mentorship Beyond Money

Financial mentorship is about more than dollars—it's about values.

- Teach generosity: Set up a giving plan together.
- Teach patience: Show them how to save for something they really want.
- Teach boundaries: Help them say no to pressure from friends or fans.

These lessons translate into every part of life: relationships, career choices, leadership, and legacy.

Final Thoughts

You don't need to be a financial planner to be a financial mentor. You just need to be present, proactive, and purposeful.

Your child may have NIL money and a personal brand—but you have something they can't Google: experience, values, and perspective.

Use it. Share it. Build something together that lasts longer than a sponsorship. Because in the end, the most valuable deal your child can ever make is the one they make with their own future.

Part V: The Business Side – Money Management, LLCs, and More

Once your student-athlete begins earning regular NIL income, they've officially entered the business world—even if they don't realize it. Whether it's a few hundred dollars from social media or thousands from a recurring collective deal, they are now entrepreneurs managing taxes, contracts, personal branding, and financial systems. Part V is designed to help parents support this evolution and ensure their student is operating responsibly, legally, and with a long-term plan.

This section begins by breaking down the basics of money management for young earners. It covers budgeting with irregular income, managing multiple income streams, setting aside money for taxes, and building savings and emergency funds. Parents will learn how to help their children create financial systems that reduce stress and increase control.

Next, it introduces the idea of forming an LLC (Limited Liability Company)—what it is, why it matters, and when it's the right time. Readers will learn how LLCs can help protect a student-athlete's name and image, simplify tax reporting, and provide legitimacy when working with brands or starting their own ventures. The section outlines the process for creating an LLC, opening business bank accounts, and keeping personal and professional finances separate.

The section also explains essential business tools for NIL athletes, including bookkeeping apps, payment processors (like PayPal or Stripe), invoicing tools, and even simple content management systems for keeping track of brand deliverables and deadlines.

Tax education is another major theme. Parents will be guided through self-employment taxes, quarterly estimated payments, and common write-offs. The section encourages building a professional team—CPA, attorney, advisor—as income and brand complexity grows.

Finally, Part V emphasizes the mindset shift: helping student-athletes go from seeing themselves as just "athletes who post" to understanding that they are young professionals building a brand, managing revenue, and setting themselves up for financial independence long after college.

This section gives parents and athletes the tools, language, and systems to treat NIL income as more than a bonus—but as the foundation for a sustainable financial future.

Chapter 22: Should My Kid Start an LLC?

With more student-athletes earning income through NIL, many families are asking whether their child should create a formal business entity like an LLC (Limited Liability Company). For some, the answer is yes—but it depends on how much they're earning, how many deals they're managing, and whether they want to scale their brand into something long-term. This chapter breaks down when and why an LLC makes sense, what the risks and benefits are, and how to navigate state-specific rules and tax considerations.

What Is an LLC?

An LLC is a legal business structure that separates your personal assets from your business activities. It allows your child to conduct NIL business—like brand partnerships, social media deals, and merchandise sales—under a company name rather than their personal identity. It provides credibility, legal protection, and in some cases, tax advantages.

When Should a Student-Athlete Consider Starting One?

While not every athlete needs an LLC, here are signs it might be the right move:

- They're earning **$10,000 or more per year** from NIL deals
- They're working with **multiple brands or agencies**
- They want to **sell merchandise** or start a business around their name/image
- They need a more professional way to **send invoices** or manage payments
- They plan to **hire help**, such as an assistant, graphic designer, or video editor
- They want to **separate business finances** from their personal spending

If the NIL activity is consistent, public-facing, and growing, it might be time to take that next step.

Benefits of Creating an LLC

1. Legal Protection

An LLC can protect your child from personal liability. If there's ever a legal issue—such as a contract dispute, copyright claim, or business debt—their personal assets (like a car or bank account) are generally protected.

2. Business Credibility

Brands may take your student more seriously if they conduct business through an LLC. It adds professionalism and creates an official channel for communication and payments.

3. Simplified Finances

An LLC allows your child to separate business income and expenses. That makes budgeting, tax filing, and tracking much easier.

4. Tax Flexibility

An LLC is usually taxed as a sole proprietorship by default, but it can elect to be taxed as an S-corp or partnership later. This flexibility may offer advantages as income increases.

5. Branding Opportunities

An LLC can have its own name, bank account, website, and social media handles. This makes it easier to market products, sell digital content, or build a brand beyond athletics.

Risks and Responsibilities

1. Cost

Forming an LLC usually costs between $50 and $500 depending on the state. Annual fees or reports may also apply.

2. Complexity

LLCs require paperwork, recordkeeping, and often a business license or registered agent. It's not overly complicated, but it does add responsibility.

3. No Automatic Tax Savings

An LLC doesn't reduce taxes automatically. Your child still needs to set aside money for self-employment taxes and may need to file quarterly estimates.

4. Must Stay Separate

Mixing personal and business funds can compromise the legal protections of the LLC. That means keeping business and personal bank accounts, cards, and expenses separate.

State Rules and Requirements

Each state has its own rules for forming and maintaining an LLC. Things to check:

- **Filing fees and annual fees**
- **Business license requirements**
- **Name availability and naming rules**
- **Registered agent requirements**
- **Deadlines for renewal or reporting**

Some states also tax LLCs at the entity level. Before filing, review the state's small business portal or speak with a CPA.

You can usually file online through your state's Secretary of State website. Services like LegalZoom, ZenBusiness, or IncFile can also help, but they charge extra fees.

Tax Considerations

Once your student-athlete forms an LLC, they need to:

- Apply for an **EIN (Employer Identification Number)** from the IRS
- Open a **separate business bank account**
- Track income and expenses using software or spreadsheets
- File an annual federal return and possibly a state return

An LLC doesn't pay taxes directly unless elected. Instead, the income "passes through" to the individual's tax return (Schedule C for a sole proprietor).

If NIL income is substantial, a CPA may recommend electing S-Corp status for potential tax savings—but this is only worth considering at higher income levels (generally $50,000+ per year).

Final Thoughts for Parents

An LLC can be a powerful tool for structuring and growing a student-athlete's NIL business. It adds professionalism, improves financial organization, and provides a foundation for long-term brand development.

However, it also adds responsibility. Parents can help by:

- Helping their child research state rules and fees
- Connecting them with a trusted CPA or advisor
- Setting up a system to track income, expenses, and tax obligations

The goal isn't just to form a business—it's to build a mindset of structure, discipline, and long-term vision. If your child is ready for that step, an LLC might be the right move.

Chapter 23: NIL Taxes: What Parents Need to Know

When student-athletes begin earning money from NIL opportunities, they also begin a new chapter of financial responsibility: taxes. Unlike traditional part-time jobs, most NIL income isn't taxed up front, and it comes with specific filing requirements, deadlines, and complexities. This chapter is designed to help parents understand how NIL taxes work, what forms to expect, and when to bring in a professional to avoid costly mistakes.

Understanding NIL taxes is about much more than numbers. It's about making sure your child stays eligible, keeps their earnings, avoids penalties, and learns how to build a responsible financial future. Every payment your student-athlete receives can affect their tax obligations, and every form they file shapes how their NIL journey is managed. That's why you—the parent—are a critical player in this process.

1099 vs. W-2 Income: Understanding the Difference

Most NIL payments fall into one category: **1099 income**, also known as self-employment income. However, there are rare cases where a student-athlete might receive **W-2 income**, typically from part-time employment or university-based jobs unrelated to NIL.

1099 Income

- Comes from brand partnerships, collectives, content creation, camps, or merchandise sales
- No taxes are withheld from these payments
- The student-athlete is responsible for tracking income and paying taxes
- If more than $600 is earned from a single source, they will receive a **1099-NEC form**
- All income must still be reported, even if no 1099 is issued

W-2 Income

- Comes from employment where the school or employer withholds taxes
- A W-2 form is issued at the end of the year showing income and tax withholdings
- Common for work-study, internships, or summer jobs but rare in NIL

Understanding the difference is critical because most student-athletes will be functioning as **independent contractors**, not employees. That means they are running a small business—and all tax responsibilities fall on their shoulders.

Filing Quarterly Taxes

The IRS expects individuals who owe $1,000 or more in taxes for the year to pay in **quarterly estimated payments**. This is common for self-employed people who don't have taxes withheld from their income—exactly the case for most student-athletes with NIL deals.

Quarterly payments are due:

- April 15
- June 15
- September 15
- January 15 (of the following year)

Missing these deadlines or underpaying can result in penalties and interest charges. Even if your child receives a refund at year-end, they can still face late payment fees if they didn't submit enough throughout the year.

Tips for Filing Quarterly:

- Use IRS Form 1040-ES to calculate estimated tax payments
- Deposit payments online using the IRS Direct Pay portal
- Keep a spreadsheet of income and track how much is set aside monthly
- Automate the process if possible with bookkeeping apps or a financial advisor

What Happens if They Don't File or Pay? Failure to make estimated payments can lead to IRS penalties that grow over time. In addition, it can trigger audits or lead to challenges with FAFSA eligibility, financial aid, and scholarship reporting.

Deductions and Write-Offs

One of the biggest advantages of self-employment status is the ability to deduct business expenses, which reduces taxable income.

Examples of NIL-related deductions:

- Training and performance tools (resistance bands, weights, apps)
- Gym memberships used for brand partnerships or training
- Travel expenses (flights, mileage, hotels for appearances)
- Equipment and uniforms
- Content creation expenses (camera gear, editing software, lighting)
- Web design and hosting
- Business meals
- Cell phone and internet use (percentage for NIL purposes)
- Accountant or legal fees related to NIL

How to Track Deductions:

- Save all receipts and invoices (use Google Drive or Dropbox)
- Maintain a mileage log for business-related travel
- Separate business and personal bank accounts for easier tracking

Be aware: Personal items that double as NIL tools (e.g., phones) must be properly allocated. Only the business use portion can be deducted.

Hiring a CPA: When and Why

Taxes for independent contractors are complicated enough—but for student-athletes, they also come with variables like financial aid impact, school compliance reporting, and potential multi-state filings. That's where a CPA becomes a valuable asset.

Hire a CPA if your child:

- Earns over $5,000 in NIL income
- Works with brands in more than one state
- Has already formed an LLC or is considering it
- Is juggling multiple income sources (1099, part-time job, side hustle)
- Has questions about tax-deductible expenses or quarterly filing

A qualified CPA can:

- Prepare and file federal and state returns
- Advise on write-offs and income strategies
- File quarterly estimated taxes accurately
- Help with LLC or S-corp tax filings
- Reduce audit risk and help keep detailed records

What to Look for in a CPA:

- Experience with self-employed clients or small businesses
- Familiarity with NIL or athletic clients (if possible)

- Transparent about billing (hourly or flat fee)

In most cases, the value a CPA provides in tax savings, accuracy, and peace of mind far outweighs the cost.

State Taxes and Local Considerations

Not all NIL money is taxed the same way in every state. Some states:

- Have **no income tax** (e.g., Florida, Texas, Nevada)
- Tax **NIL differently** based on residency or business structure
- Require **non-resident filings** if your child earns money during travel (e.g., out-of-state appearances or deals)

If your child lives in one state and goes to school in another, they may owe taxes in both states. This dual residency scenario can get complicated quickly.

Example: A student-athlete from Texas (no state income tax) attends school in California (high tax state) and earns NIL income in both states. They may:

- Need to file a nonresident return in California
- Report income to Texas (even if no tax is owed)
- Pay differing rates or fees for their business income depending on where the LLC is registered

This is another area where having a tax professional on board is critical.

The Importance of Good Recordkeeping

One of the most common tax mistakes student-athletes make is poor documentation. Without clean records, it's hard to file accurately, justify deductions, or defend against an audit.

Encourage your child to:

- Save copies of all 1099s, W-9s, and contracts
- Use a dedicated email account for all NIL and financial matters
- Track income in real time with apps like QuickBooks, Wave, or Excel
- Reconcile bank statements monthly
- Save all receipts for expenses (digital copies are fine)

A simple Google Sheet with columns for "Date," "Income Source," "Amount," "Category," and "Notes" is a great starting point.

NIL and FAFSA: How Taxes Affect Financial Aid

NIL income must be reported on the FAFSA under "student income," and it can reduce need-based aid.

Important reminders:

- Income from NIL is considered **untaxed income**, similar to self-employment
- Reporting requirements apply even if your child didn't receive a 1099
- Over-reporting or under-reporting income can lead to aid recalculations

If your family depends on need-based financial aid, talk to the school's financial aid office and a CPA about:

- Timing income across tax years
- Filing as an independent vs. dependent student
- Structuring NIL deals to minimize aid disruption

Should You Incorporate for Tax Benefits?

For high earners, forming an LLC or electing S-Corp status may offer significant tax savings. With an LLC:

- Business deductions become easier to track and apply
- Your child may pay themselves a salary and classify other income as distributions (which can lower self-employment tax)
- Retirement plans (like SEP IRAs) become accessible

However, incorporating comes with fees, paperwork, and more complex filing. It's best to make this decision with guidance from a CPA and possibly an attorney.

Final Thoughts for Parents

NIL can be a powerful financial opportunity, but only if it's managed with the right mindset, tools, and support. Taxes aren't a one-time issue—they're an ongoing part of your child's financial life.

As a parent, your role is not to do the work for them, but to ensure they:

- Understand their obligations
- Ask the right questions
- Know where to get help
- Stay organized and proactive

By doing this, you help your student-athlete build not only a brand but also a responsible, informed foundation for their future. The money they earn from NIL can open doors, but only if they know how to keep it, protect it, and grow it.

Remember: The IRS treats NIL athletes like business owners. It's time we help our children see themselves that way, too.

Chapter 24: The IRS Doesn't Care About the Highlights

Your child just went viral. Their NIL brand is building momentum. Companies are sending direct messages, fans are buying merch, and there's a logo on their cleats that wasn't there last season.

But while everyone's watching the highlight reel, there's one very real player watching in silence:

The IRS.

And the IRS doesn't care about likes, retweets, or whether your child was "just learning the ropes."

They care about **paper trails**.

About **documentation**.

About **compliance**.

And here's the truth: in the world of NIL, the financial wins don't matter if the tax side is messy. This chapter is for the parent who's ready to help their student-athlete treat NIL like the business it is—*before* tax season becomes a season of regret.

The "Business Owner" Mindset Shift

Let's get one thing clear right now:

> ***If your student-athlete earns NIL money, they're running a business.***

Not *might be*. Not *sort of*. They *are*.

It doesn't matter if the income comes from promoting a protein shake on Instagram or running their own branded football camp. Once money changes hands for a service or promotion, the IRS considers it a business transaction.

That means this is no longer about allowance, lunch money, or casual summer jobs. This is about **building systems**. And you—the parent—are often the one with enough life experience to see the bigger picture.

You're not their accountant.

You're not their boss.

But you are their advisor-in-chief.

Their calm in the chaos.

Their financial translator.

So here's how you lead without lecturing.

The Five-Layer NIL Tax Readiness Strategy (For Parents)

Instead of diving into jargon, help your student-athlete get **tax ready** using these five layers:

1. **Visibility: Know Where the Money's Coming From**

Before anything else, make sure your child can answer this:

> *"Where did your NIL money come from this year—and how much?"*

Create a simple spreadsheet or use free tools like Google Sheets. Teach them to track who paid them, how much, and for what. This habit alone prevents chaos during tax prep and protects against **unreported income** issues.

If they're overwhelmed? Have them text you each time they get paid. You can help them log it—no judgment, just teamwork.

2. **Organization: Save Everything**

Build a digital folder (Dropbox, Google Drive, etc.) with subfolders labeled:

- Contracts
- Screenshots of payments (Venmo, Cash App, Zelle, etc.)
- Emails with deliverables
- Receipts for expenses
- Communications with brands

Explain this like keeping "receipts" in a social media argument—just in case someone tries to twist the story. You're simply keeping proof of what really happened.

3. **Protection: Avoid Audit Traps**

One of the easiest ways to get audited? Sloppy records.

Another? Claiming deductions without proof.

Even if your student-athlete doesn't owe much, their NIL activity could flag them for review if the IRS sees large income spikes with no context or "creative" expenses.

Help them avoid traps like:

- Mixing NIL money with personal Venmo spending
- Paying friends for "business services" without contracts
- Guessing on income totals instead of tracking them

If you're unsure? Google won't cut it. That's when you **call a pro** (more on that in a minute).

4. **Education: Have the Tax Talk Early**

Don't wait until April to talk taxes. The earlier the better. Here's a conversation starter:

> *"Hey, let's plan for the taxes now so you're not blindsided later. NIL is new, but the IRS isn't."*

Teach them the basics—not the forms, but the concepts:

- The more you make, the more you owe
- You can owe taxes *even if you spent the money*
- Deductions are real, but only when documented
- Refunds aren't automatic—especially with NIL

Let them ask questions. Keep it casual, but consistent.

5. **Delegation: Build a Team Sooner Than Later**

If your student-athlete is consistently earning money from multiple deals, it's time to stop winging it. You need a tax professional—**not just during tax season, but before it.**

Think of it this way:

- **An agent negotiates contracts**
- **A CPA protects what they earn**

This doesn't mean you need to drop $1,000 on an accountant right now. But it *does* mean you should start interviewing professionals, asking the right questions, and building a relationship with someone who understands student-athletes and NIL.

If your child grows into a pro athlete or entrepreneur, that team will already be in place.

The Hidden Tax Risk No One Talks About

Here's something you won't hear in most NIL seminars:

> ***If your child doesn't pay taxes properly, it could hurt their eligibility for scholarships, federal aid, housing, and even future credit applications.***

Why? Because unfiled taxes or sudden IRS debt impacts:

- FAFSA applications
- College aid verification
- Background checks
- Credit scores
- Apartment leases
- Business loan applications
- Their reputation with future sponsors

In other words, poor tax planning doesn't just cost money—it creates *barriers*.

Final Word for Parents

You're not here to become a tax expert.

You're here to be your child's *anchor* in a storm of sudden financial freedom.

The truth is, NIL income has the power to be life-changing—but only when it's handled right.

That means starting early. Staying organized. Asking for help when it's needed. And reminding your student-athlete that **real success isn't just about what you earn—it's about what you keep**.

So when the headlines fade and the lights dim, your child isn't left with receipts and regrets—they're left with structure, freedom, and a solid foundation.

Taxes might not be flashy. But neither is the steering wheel.

And without it, they're just along for the ride.

Chapter 25: Choosing the Right Financial Advisor or CPA

When a student-athlete starts earning money through NIL (Name, Image, and Likeness) deals, they are not just receiving a paycheck—they're stepping into the world of financial responsibility, taxation, and potentially even entrepreneurship. This world can be intimidating, confusing, and full of pitfalls, which is why the guidance of a competent, ethical financial advisor or CPA is crucial.

This chapter is designed to help parents and student-athletes make informed, confident decisions about selecting a financial professional. From understanding credentials to identifying red flags, this comprehensive guide covers everything you need to know about choosing the right financial ally in the NIL era.

The Stakes Are Higher Than You Think

Student-athletes used to focus solely on academics and athletics. Now, thanks to NIL, they must also think like business owners. They're negotiating contracts, managing irregular income, budgeting for taxes, and considering investments. All of this can quickly become overwhelming without the proper support system.

Unfortunately, many young earners fall prey to poor advice, opportunistic advisors, or simply make avoidable mistakes due to a lack of guidance. Choosing the right financial advisor or CPA can mean the difference between thriving and floundering in the NIL space. A great advisor doesn't just help manage money—they help shape financial behavior, provide education, and protect long-term potential.

Why a Financial Advisor or CPA Matters

NIL earnings don't come with a manual. A student-athlete's financial situation can evolve quickly, and managing money isn't just about knowing numbers—it's about:

- **Understanding self-employment taxes**
- **Filing quarterly estimates to avoid IRS penalties**
- **Maximizing business deductions**
- **Setting up the right business structure (LLC, S-Corp, etc.)**
- **Avoiding scams and high-risk investments**
- **Planning for financial aid or FAFSA considerations**
- **Budgeting for short-term needs and long-term goals**
- **Building a foundation for wealth and financial freedom**

Even financially savvy parents may find NIL complexities new or difficult to manage. This is where a qualified, trustworthy advisor becomes invaluable.

What's the Difference Between a CPA and Financial Advisor?

While these terms are sometimes used interchangeably, they have distinct roles:

CPA (Certified Public Accountant):

- Specializes in taxes, accounting, and financial reporting
- Licensed by state boards and required to pass rigorous exams
- Can represent you before the IRS
- Often prepares tax returns, helps with audits, and offers business advice

Financial Advisor/Planner:

- Focuses on investment strategy, retirement planning, budgeting, and insurance
- May or may not be certified (e.g., CFP® is a top credential)
- Can be fee-only, commission-based, or a combination
- Helps build a long-term financial plan

In an ideal world, your child should have both: a CPA for taxes and compliance, and a financial advisor for wealth building and strategy. Some firms offer both services in-house, which can be convenient.

When to Start Looking for a Professional

As soon as your child:

- Begins earning regular NIL income
- Has filed (or needs to file) taxes for NIL work
- Has more than one income source (e.g., NIL, part-time job, sponsorship)
- Is asked to fill out W-9s or signs a contract
- Starts considering forming an LLC or brand

Don't wait until tax season or until a problem arises. The best time to get professional advice is **before** the money starts flowing—or immediately after.

What to Look For in a Financial Professional

Here's what your advisor or CPA should bring to the table:

1. **Relevant Credentials**

- **CPA**: Verified with your state's Board of Accountancy

- **CFP® (Certified Financial Planner)**: Indicates rigorous training in financial planning
- **EA (Enrolled Agent)**: Specializes in tax and can represent clients before the IRS
- **RIA (Registered Investment Advisor)**: Must register with the SEC or state authorities and act as fiduciaries

2. **Experience with NIL or Young Earners**

- Has worked with student-athletes, freelancers, or influencers
- Understands irregular income and self-employment taxation
- Familiar with compliance and school regulations
- Understands NCAA reporting requirements and financial aid issues

3. **Transparency**

- Clear about how they are paid (hourly, flat fee, percentage)
- No hidden fees or vague services
- Willing to put everything in writing

4. **Education-Oriented Approach**

- Not just doing the work, but teaching your child along the way
- Explains financial concepts in plain English
- Provides tools or resources for ongoing learning

5. **Availability and Communication**

- Responds to questions in a timely manner
- Meets regularly (quarterly or more) for check-ins
- Offers virtual and in-person options
- Is available during high-pressure seasons (tax time, contract signings)

6. **Fiduciary Duty**

- Legally required to act in the client's best interest (ask them to confirm this in writing)

Questions to Ask Before Hiring

Here are some questions to ask when interviewing a financial advisor or CPA:

1. **What is your experience working with clients in similar situations (e.g., student-athletes, freelancers, young entrepreneurs)?**
2. **What licenses or certifications do you hold? Are you registered with any regulatory boards?**
3. **How do you charge for your services? Can you provide a breakdown of all fees?**
4. **Do you sell financial products or receive commissions?**
5. **What services do you offer—tax filing, budgeting, investment planning, business setup, etc.?**
6. **Can you help us structure and file for an LLC if needed?**
7. **What platforms or tools do you use for tracking, budgeting, and communication?**
8. **How do you stay updated on NIL-specific issues or changes in tax law?**
9. **Can you provide references or testimonials from similar clients?**
10. **What happens if my child moves to another state or earns income across multiple states?**

Interview at least 2–3 professionals before making a decision.

Red Flags to Watch For

- **Lack of credentials** or unwillingness to verify them
- **Pushy sales tactics**, especially around insurance or investment products
- **Promise of guaranteed returns** or "insider" investment opportunities
- **Refusal to answer questions clearly** or provide written agreements
- **Limited knowledge of NIL rules or student-athlete financial issues**
- **Negative online reviews** or complaints with regulatory agencies

Always do your due diligence. A simple online search, call to a state licensing board, or conversation with a past client can help you avoid major issues.

Where to Find Qualified Professionals

- **Referrals from your school or university**: Compliance officers, athletic departments, or career centers often have lists
- **Professional associations**:
- www.letsmakeaplan.org for CFPs
- www.natptax.com for tax pros
- www.irs.gov for Enrolled Agents
- **Online directories and reviews**:
- Google Reviews
- Yelp
- Better Business Bureau (BBB)

Also, ask other athlete families who they work with. Personal recommendations are often the most reliable.

The Importance of Compatibility

You're not just hiring someone to handle transactions—you're building a long-term relationship. It's important that your child feels comfortable asking questions, admitting what they don't know, and receiving honest feedback.

If your student-athlete feels judged, ignored, or rushed in early meetings, it's a sign the advisor may not be a good fit.

Look for someone who:

- Listens more than they speak
- Doesn't overcomplicate things
- Treats your child with respect and patience
- Supports—not controls—decision-making

What to Do After You Hire an Advisor or CPA

Once you choose a professional, set the relationship up for success:

1. **Create a document vault** with copies of:

- Tax returns
- Contracts
- Bank statements
- NIL payment records
- Receipts for business expenses

1. **Schedule regular check-ins** (monthly or quarterly)
2. **Set expectations** for communication, deadlines, and service scope
3. **Review financial goals** together and revisit them as NIL income evolves
4. **Encourage your student-athlete to take ownership**—they should be on every call, ask questions, and understand every decision

Building a Financial Team

As your child's income grows, you may need a team of professionals:

- **CPA or EA** for taxes
- **CFP®** for long-term financial planning
- **Attorney** for contracts and business formation
- **Insurance agent** for coverage advice

Many firms offer bundled services or have professionals on retainer for consulting. Don't be afraid to start small and build as needed.

Final Thoughts

Choosing the right financial advisor or CPA is one of the most important decisions a student-athlete can make in the NIL era. It's not just about compliance or getting a tax refund—it's about building a financial future with structure, clarity, and confidence.

As a parent, your job is to help your child:

- Ask smart questions
- Set clear expectations
- Vet professionals thoroughly
- Step into financial adulthood with the right support

The right advisor won't just manage money. They'll build trust, provide education, and help your student-athlete maximize every opportunity—not just in college, but in life.

Because NIL is just the beginning. Financial literacy, guided by the right professionals, is the legacy that lasts long after the deals are done.

Chapter 26: How to Vet NIL Agents and Managers

In the new world of Name, Image, and Likeness (NIL), agents and managers have become more prominent in the lives of student-athletes. These professionals can play an important role: negotiating deals, managing brand relationships, organizing appearances, and even helping build long-term career opportunities. But not all agents are trustworthy, and not every manager has your child's best interests in mind.

As a parent, understanding how to properly evaluate an agent or manager is crucial to protecting your student-athlete's financial, academic, and personal future. This chapter provides a detailed roadmap to help families navigate this often unregulated and evolving space, with more than just intuition and trust—but with facts, contracts, and clarity.

The Role of Agents and Managers in NIL

NIL agents and managers differ from traditional sports agents in that they often focus solely on branding, sponsorships, and influencer deals. They typically do not negotiate professional athletic contracts with teams or leagues. That means they may not be governed by professional associations like the NFLPA or NBAPA, and therefore can operate with fewer restrictions.

Key roles may include:

- Negotiating brand partnerships
- Securing deals with collectives or school-sponsored sponsors
- Managing social media brand outreach
- Setting up appearances or signings
- Reviewing contracts and handling communication with businesses

In short, these individuals are often acting as both marketer and business representative. In some cases, they may also function as publicists or financial consultants (though they shouldn't unless licensed).

When Should You Consider Hiring an Agent or Manager?

Not every student-athlete needs an agent. Some can manage their own opportunities using school NIL platforms, local partnerships, or digital marketplaces like Opendorse or MarketPryce.

Consider hiring an agent if:

- Your child is receiving frequent or large NIL offers
- You lack the time or expertise to vet each deal
- Your child is being contacted by major brands or media platforms
- You want help building a long-term brand or business strategy

However, more important than the "when" is the "who." The right agent can add value. The wrong one can destroy opportunities, reputation, and eligibility.

First Step: Do Your Homework

Before engaging in any discussions or signing anything, do background research:

- Google the agent or manager's name
- Search for news articles, press releases, or athlete testimonials

- Look for reviews or disciplinary actions
- Search their social media presence—does it match their promises?

Ask for:

- A resume or list of past and current clients
- Referrals from other athletes and families
- Examples of NIL deals they have negotiated

Then, verify credentials:

- Are they registered in your state (if required)?
- Are they affiliated with any sports agent associations?
- Are they certified by a school or compliance department?

What Are They Promising?

Good agents set clear expectations. Bad agents make big promises.

Watch for:

- "I can get your kid $100,000 in six months."
- "I have secret deals lined up."
- "Other parents already signed with me. Don't let your kid miss out."
- "We don't need to run this by the school."

Instead, look for:

- A realistic assessment of your child's brand and potential
- Specific strategies for growth
- Transparency about outreach, partnerships, and timelines
- Willingness to collaborate with the school's compliance office

Avoid anyone who promises earnings without showing you:

- A marketing plan
- A network of actual brand partners
- References from clients with similar profiles

Understanding Fee Structure

How and what your child will pay should be crystal clear—up front.

Common NIL fee structures include:

- **Commission-based (10–20%)**: The agent takes a percentage of each deal they bring in. This is standard for endorsement deals.
- **Flat fee**: A monthly or annual fee regardless of the number or size of deals. Good for high-volume athletes but risky for beginners.
- **Hourly consulting**: Less common, but useful for one-time strategy sessions
- **Retainer + commission**: A flat fee to retain services plus a percentage of earned deals

Questions to ask:

- What services are included in your fee?
- Are there additional costs (e.g., media kits, travel, content creation)?
- Do you take a cut of deals we bring to you, or only ones you source?
- Are you open to negotiating your percentage if we grow?

Avoid agents who:

- Are vague about pricing
- Want equity in your child's brand or LLC
- Ask for full control over decision-making

Review the Contract Carefully

Never sign anything without reading and reviewing every clause. Contracts should include:

- Duration of agreement
- Scope of work and responsibilities
- Commission structure
- Cancellation and termination policy
- Confidentiality clauses
- Non-compete or exclusivity provisions

Key clauses to understand:

- **Exclusivity**: Does this agent have exclusive rights to negotiate all deals? Can your child work with others for small or local deals?
- **Length**: Are you locked in for 12 months or longer? Is there an opt-out clause?
- **Termination**: What happens if you want to leave the relationship? Is there a fee?

Consider having the contract reviewed by an attorney or the school's compliance officer.

Are They Willing to Work With Your Team?

A red flag is any agent who wants to operate in isolation. The right manager will be open to collaboration with:

- You (the parent)
- A CPA or financial advisor
- School compliance officers
- Coaches and athletic department staff

Ask:

- Will you attend meetings with our CPA or financial advisor?
- Do you share contracts with the school's NIL team?
- Are you comfortable working within NCAA/state guidelines?

Transparency and teamwork should be non-negotiable.

Red Flags to Watch For

Keep your guard up if you notice any of the following:

- No written agreement offered
- Pressure to sign quickly without time for review
- No references or verifiable client list
- Avoids sharing deal specifics or "keeps things vague"
- Pushes products or investments as part of the deal
- Involvement with companies unrelated to sports or branding
- Prior legal trouble or licensing issues

Trust your instincts. If something feels off, it probably is.

Credential and Background Checks

Use public databases and search tools to verify an agent's legitimacy:

- State business registries
- Better Business Bureau
- LinkedIn profiles and company websites
- School NIL directories (if applicable)
- NCAA compliance tools

Case Study: Good Agent vs. Bad Agent

Athlete A signs with an agent who:

- Has a strong client list
- Sends weekly updates
- Is transparent about commissions and offers
- Includes the athlete in all decision-making
- Works with the athlete's parents and CPA

Result: Athlete A earns over $40,000 in NIL income over two years, stays eligible, and uses deals to build a strong personal brand.

Athlete B signs with an agent who:

- Promises six figures without a plan
- Takes 30% commission on all deals
- Delays payments and hides contract terms
- Discourages athlete from talking to school compliance

Result: Athlete B loses eligibility, earns less than $5,000, and struggles to exit the agreement.

The lesson: It's not just about signing with an agent. It's about signing with the *right* agent.

Final Thoughts for Parents

Hiring an NIL agent or manager is not a quick decision. It requires due diligence, open conversations, and a clear contract. As a parent, your role is to:

- Vet potential candidates thoroughly
- Empower your child to ask smart questions
- Build a support team of legal, financial, and compliance professionals

- Never rush into a relationship based on promises or hype

NIL is an amazing opportunity—but it must be managed wisely. A good agent can help your child grow their brand, build wealth, and stay focused on their goals. A bad one can derail everything.

So take your time. Protect your child. And remember: every deal, every dollar, and every decision begins with the team you build around them.

Chapter 27: Working with Brands – What to Ask

In the NIL era, one of the most exciting developments for student-athletes is the opportunity to work directly with brands. These partnerships can be empowering, lucrative, and even career-launching. But they also come with responsibilities, risks, and a lot of fine print. Whether it's a social media post, product sponsorship, or full-scale campaign, every brand deal must be evaluated with a business mindset.

This chapter will help parents and student-athletes know what to ask, what to avoid, and how to negotiate brand partnerships smartly and safely. We'll walk through timelines, content rights, exclusivity, deliverables, and more—so you don't just get paid, you get protected.

What Makes a Brand Deal Successful?

A good NIL brand partnership should meet three criteria:

1. **Aligned with the athlete's values and goals**
2. **Clear about expectations and deliverables**
3. **Legally and financially transparent**

When any of these elements are missing, the risk of misunderstanding, underpayment, or exploitation increases. Before your child signs a deal—or even agrees to a conversation—you should know the right questions to ask.

The Initial Conversation: Brand Fit and Alignment

Start with assessing the brand's values. Not every opportunity is the right opportunity.

Questions to ask:

- What does this brand stand for?
- Have they worked with other college athletes?
- Do they support causes that match my child's values?
- Is the brand appropriate for my child's age, image, and audience?

Examples of potential concerns:

- Alcohol, vaping, or gambling brands
- Political or controversial endorsements
- Conflicts with your child's school or team sponsors

Working with the right brands enhances credibility. Working with the wrong ones can damage reputation, eligibility, and relationships.

Understanding the Offer: Scope and Expectations

Before signing any deal, ask these core questions:

1. What is the brand asking your child to do?

- Instagram posts? TikTok videos? Live appearances? Merchandise modeling?
- Are the deliverables one-time or ongoing?
- How much creative control will your child have?

2. When are deliverables due?

- Specific posting dates?
- Seasonal schedules?
- Realistic time expectations alongside school and sport commitments?

3. What is the compensation structure?

- Is payment a flat rate or commission-based?
- Is product included? (And does it count as taxable income?)
- Are bonuses offered for engagement or performance?

Get every detail in writing. Even a short email or agreement template is better than verbal promises.

Payment Timelines: Don't Assume "Now"

Many brands use net payment systems (e.g., Net 30, Net 60), meaning payment is due 30 or 60 days after content is posted or the agreement is completed.

Questions to ask:

- When is payment issued?
- Is there a written agreement outlining timelines?
- What happens if a post underperforms or is delayed?
- Who handles late or missed payments?

Tips:

- Ask for part of the payment up front (especially for large deals)
- Keep records of deliverables (screenshots, analytics)
- Track invoices and due dates in a shared calendar or tool

Make sure your child isn't waiting months for money they already earned.

Usage Rights: Who Owns the Content?

Many student-athletes don't realize that once they post branded content, the brand may legally reuse it—forever. Usage rights determine who owns the photo, video, or likeness used in the campaign.

Key questions to ask:

- Will this content be reused in ads, websites, or commercials?
- For how long can the brand use your child's image?
- Can your child request removal of content later?
- Is compensation adjusted based on reuse?

Terms to watch for:

- **Perpetual rights**: Brand can use the content forever (often undesirable)
- **Exclusivity**: Your child can't work with similar brands
- **Territorial rights**: Where can content be used (U.S. only? Global?)
- **Platform rights**: Can they use content across social, print, and TV?

Protecting image rights is key to maintaining brand control and future value.

Exclusivity and Non-Compete Clauses

Many contracts include exclusivity or non-compete clauses, preventing your child from working with competitor brands during or after the partnership.

Questions to ask:

- Are there category restrictions (e.g., no other sports drinks)?
- How long does exclusivity last?
- Is it limited to specific platforms or all channels?

- Is there a buyout option if another deal comes along?

Sometimes, exclusivity can be negotiated or narrowed. If it's too broad, it may restrict more valuable future deals.

Content Control and Authenticity

A strong brand-athlete partnership should feel authentic. But brands may want input or control over what is said or posted.

Ask:

- Does your child have final approval over the caption or script?
- Can the brand request edits or removals?
- Are specific hashtags, tags, or language required?
- Can your child add their personal voice or message?

Be wary of scripted posts that don't match your child's tone. Audiences can sense inauthenticity.

FTC Disclosure: Staying Compliant

Federal Trade Commission (FTC) rules require that any paid brand partnership be disclosed publicly. Failure to do so can result in penalties for both the brand and the student-athlete.

What to ask:

- Are there clear instructions for disclosing the sponsorship?
- Does the brand require use of #ad, #sponsored, or similar hashtags?
- Will your child be coached on proper FTC guidelines?

Never agree to "quiet" partnerships without disclosure. It's not only illegal—it can damage your child's integrity and future trust with brands.

Contracts and Legal Review

Every brand deal should come with a written contract. Even for one-off or small engagements, written agreements provide clarity and protection.

What to look for in a contract:

- Scope of work
- Payment amount and timeline
- Ownership of content and likeness
- Usage rights and limitations
- Termination clauses
- Exclusivity or non-compete language

Ask a legal advisor, NIL manager, or the school's compliance office to review the agreement before signing. Contracts should never be rushed or agreed to under pressure.

Tracking and Managing Brand Relationships

As NIL grows, your child may work with multiple brands over time. Organization becomes essential.

Create a system to track:

- Brands contacted and who initiated the deal
- Terms of each contract
- Deliverables completed and posted
- Payment dates and status
- Communication history with each brand

Use a spreadsheet, CRM tool, or NIL platform to stay on top of active deals. This helps avoid missed deadlines, duplicate partnerships, and payment confusion.

Long-Term Brand Building: More Than Just a Check

Encourage your child to focus on partnerships that go beyond the one-time payout. Think about:

- How does this deal contribute to their long-term goals?
- Can this brand be part of a recurring or ambassador program?
- Are there values or causes they care about that the brand supports?
- Can this lead to internship, mentorship, or future employment opportunities?

A $250 one-off post might be fun, but a $10,000 brand partnership over six months with growth potential is better for long-term strategy.

The Parent's Role in Brand Deals

Parents should play a background role, offering oversight and support. Let your child take the lead in conversations but be available to:

- Review contracts
- Research the brand's background
- Help track payments and invoices
- Spot red flags

Model professionalism in your involvement. This is their brand, but your experience adds protection.

Common Red Flags in Brand Deals

Watch out for:

- No contract or written agreement
- Asking for personal info (SSN, bank account) too early

- Confusing or hidden compensation terms
- Promises of "exposure" instead of payment
- Vague deliverables or no clear expectations
- Requesting free product posts or trial work
- Excessive demands for posting frequency or content control

When in doubt, walk away. A bad deal isn't worth the stress, risk, or reputation hit.

Building a Media Kit

To attract better partnerships, your child can create a digital media kit that includes:

- Bio and personal story
- Athletic achievements
- Social media stats (follower count, engagement rates)
- Past brand collaborations
- Contact information and booking policies

A professional-looking media kit signals readiness and sets your child apart from competitors.

Final Thoughts: It's Business, Not Just Branding

Brand deals are business. They involve legal agreements, real money, and long-term consequences. The stakes are high, but so is the potential.

The student-athletes who succeed long-term are the ones who:

- Ask smart questions
- Vet every opportunity
- Value alignment over volume
- Track their progress

- Learn from every interaction

As a parent, your job isn't to run the business—but to help make sure it runs well.

Remember: A well-managed brand deal isn't just about income. It's about experience, integrity, and growth. Done right, it's one more way NIL can become a launchpad for a powerful future.

Chapter 28: Intellectual Property: Your Kid's Brand is a Business

In the NIL era, your student-athlete isn't just an athlete—they're also a brand. And that brand has value. It can be protected, licensed, monetized, and—if not properly safeguarded—taken advantage of. Intellectual property (IP) is the foundation of your child's NIL identity. It's what separates casual posting from real brand-building, and it's what ensures long-term control and earning power over their name, image, and likeness.

This chapter explores what intellectual property means in the NIL space, how student-athletes can protect their brand assets, and why parents should play an active role in guiding these decisions early.

What is Intellectual Property (IP)?

Intellectual property is any creative or brand asset that is legally protected by law. In the NIL context, this includes:

- **Name** (including nicknames or stage names)
- **Image** (photos, likeness)
- **Voice or catchphrases**
- **Logo or brand symbol**
- **Slogans or taglines**
- **Merchandise designs**

- **Digital content (videos, podcasts)**

Your child's Instagram handle, podcast intro, YouTube videos, and even a hashtag they created can become part of their IP portfolio.

Why It Matters Now

If your child becomes known for a specific phrase, design, or logo—and it catches on—someone else can use it if it's not protected. That's why smart brands trademark their assets, own their domains, and secure the rights to what they create.

If your child wants to:

- Sell merchandise
- Launch a podcast or brand
- License their likeness
- Use a unique stage name
- Create a digital presence outside their sport

... then intellectual property protection becomes essential.

Trademarks: Locking in the Brand

A trademark is a legal registration of a word, phrase, symbol, or design that distinguishes one brand from another. For student-athletes, this might be:

- A personal logo
- A catchphrase they use consistently
- A podcast or business name
- A stylized version of their name

Why file a trademark?

- It prevents others from using the same or similar branding
- It gives your child legal recourse if someone infringes
- It boosts brand value and investor confidence
- It can be licensed to companies for merchandise or campaigns

Steps to File a Trademark:

1. **Search**: Use USPTO.gov to make sure the name or design isn't already taken.
2. **Hire help**: A trademark attorney can assist with application strategy.
3. **File**: Submit the application through the USPTO (costs range from $250–$350 per class).
4. **Monitor**: Once registered, you must defend the mark by watching for unauthorized use.

Pro tip: Register social media handles and domain names at the same time to build consistency.

Logos and Personal Branding

Your child doesn't need to be a pro athlete to have a logo. Logos help communicate identity, values, and recognition.

A strong athlete logo is:

- Simple and scalable
- Unique to their style or initials
- Versatile across merch, video, and print

You can work with:

- A graphic designer (via Fiverr, Upwork, or a local freelancer)
- School design departments or media teams
- Branding agencies (more expensive, but professional)

Once you create a logo:

- Save the design files in multiple formats
- Trademark it if it will be used commercially
- Add it to social banners, merch, and websites

Domain Names: Owning the Online Real Estate

Securing a domain name is one of the simplest and smartest brand moves. Start by registering:

- Your child's name (e.g., JalenSmith.com)
- Their nickname or athlete name (e.g., TheRealTank.com)
- Brand or business names (e.g., WalkOnLegacy.com)

You can use platforms like:

- GoDaddy
- Google Domains
- Namecheap

Pro tips:

- Grab .com versions first, even if you're not ready to use them
- Consider registering .org or .net to protect your brand family
- Redirect domains to social pages or Linktree until you build a website

Social Media Handles: Be Consistent Across Platforms

Social handles are modern-day business cards. Make sure your child:

- Uses the same handle across platforms (if possible)
- Avoids using school names or trademarks in usernames

- Claims profiles on new platforms before someone else does
- Adds professional bios that include media contact info

You can reserve handles even if your child isn't ready to post. Protecting the brand starts with claiming the space.

Copyrights: Protecting Original Work

If your child creates original content—videos, photos, songs, training programs, or blogs—it may qualify for copyright protection.

What copyright protects:

- Music and lyrics
- Written works (books, blogs, courses)
- Photographs and videos
- Podcasts and training guides

While copyright is automatic upon creation, registering it through the U.S. Copyright Office provides additional legal protection and allows for claims if someone uses the work without permission.

Working with Designers and Creators

If someone designs a logo, video, or website for your child, make sure you have a **work-for-hire agreement** or a written release that gives full ownership to your child.

Without it, the creator may technically retain the rights to the design.

Licensing and Merchandising

Once your child has a brand, they can license it to others:

- Print-on-demand stores for merch (Shopify, Teespring)

- Local businesses or sports camps
- Partnerships for co-branded promotions

Before licensing anything, consider:

- What the brand will be used for
- How long the agreement lasts
- How revenue is split
- What quality controls are in place

Consult an attorney or brand manager before entering licensing deals. Poorly written contracts can give away too much for too little.

Parents' Role in IP Protection

Parents don't need to manage every detail but should:

- Help file trademarks and copyrights if appropriate
- Track renewal dates for domains and registrations
- Guide brand conversations with integrity
- Protect minors by overseeing public content and media use

If your child is a minor, parents may need to sign legal documents on their behalf or be listed on official registrations.

Long-Term Brand Value

An athlete's NIL career may be short, but their personal brand can last a lifetime. Many athletes go on to become:

- Coaches or trainers
- Motivational speakers
- Entrepreneurs

- Authors and content creators

Building and protecting intellectual property today gives your child leverage tomorrow. A well-managed brand creates job opportunities, credibility, and multiple income streams long after their playing days are over.

Final Thoughts

Your student-athlete's brand is more than just a social media account or jersey number. It's intellectual property. It's business. And it deserves the same level of thought, structure, and protection as any startup or influencer brand.

Help your child treat their brand like an asset:

- Own the name
- Trademark the logo
- Lock in the domain
- Protect the content
- Think long-term

Because when the games end, the brand can keep winning—as long as it's built to last.

Part VI: Life Skills Beyond the Field

NIL deals and athletic success might open the door—but life skills keep student-athletes in the game long after the spotlight fades. This section helps parents guide their children through the practical, emotional, and interpersonal skills they'll need to navigate college, career, and adulthood with confidence and purpose.

It explores the habits and character traits that define success off the field: time management, communication, leadership, mental health awareness, and decision-making. These foundational life skills are often overlooked in the rush to monetize NIL opportunities but are essential for long-term growth.

The section includes advice on how to handle peer pressure, manage stress, and balance academics, sports, and business. It also dives into the importance of networking, building a strong personal support team, and protecting one's mental health in the face of public scrutiny, digital attention, and financial pressure.

Part VI doesn't just focus on what athletes can do for their brands—it emphasizes who they're becoming as people. It equips parents with conversation starters, strategies, and resources to help their kids grow in character, self-awareness, and independence. Because no matter how far an athlete goes in sports, life will demand much more than physical ability. This section ensures they're ready.

Chapter 29: Budgeting for College Athletes

In the NIL era, college athletes are in a unique financial position: they may be receiving income through brand partnerships, collectives, and endorsements while still juggling the realities of college life. But earning money doesn't automatically lead to financial security. Without a solid plan, NIL income can disappear as quickly as it arrives. That's where budgeting becomes essential.

As a parent, one of the most valuable life lessons you can pass on to your student-athlete is how to create and stick to a realistic budget. This chapter covers how to guide your child through budgeting basics, how to distinguish between wants and needs, and how to set financial boundaries that align with long-term goals.

Why Budgeting Matters for College Athletes

Unlike a 9-to-5 job with predictable paychecks, NIL income is often irregular. One month might bring in a four-figure deal, while the next month could bring nothing. Pair that with the responsibilities of school, practice, travel, and competition, and it's easy to see how budgeting can fall by the wayside.

A budget provides structure. It turns short-term money into long-term opportunity. It also:

- Reduces financial stress
- Prevents overspending
- Encourages savings and investing
- Creates clarity around goals
- Builds financial discipline

Start with a Budgeting Conversation

You don't need to be a financial expert to start budgeting with your child. Begin with a simple, open conversation. Ask:

- What are your current monthly expenses?
- What are your biggest money challenges?
- What do you want your money to help you do this year?

This sets the tone that budgeting is a tool for freedom, not restriction.

Step-by-Step: Building a Budget

Step 1: Track All Income

Have your student-athlete write down every source of income:

- NIL deals (monthly or one-time payments)
- Stipends from collectives or boosters
- Part-time jobs or tutoring
- Parental support (if any)
- Scholarships or refunds

Remind them to account for taxes if they're receiving 1099 income.

Step 2: Identify Fixed Expenses

These are monthly costs that don't change much:

- Rent or housing

- Utilities and Wi-Fi
- Phone bill
- Transportation (car, gas, ride shares)
- Insurance (auto, health, renters)

Step 3: Identify Variable Expenses

These change month to month and often cause overspending:

- Food and groceries
- Dining out
- Clothing
- Entertainment
- Travel (personal or team-related not covered by the school)
- Subscriptions (Netflix, Spotify, etc.)

Step 4: Set Savings Goals

Encourage your child to allocate money to savings every month:

- Emergency fund (goal: 3-6 months of expenses)
- Travel savings
- Tax savings (20-30% of NIL income)
- Long-term investments (Roth IRA or brokerage)

Step 5: Use a Budgeting Tool

Help them pick a system:

- Apps like Mint, YNAB (You Need A Budget), or EveryDollar
- Google Sheets or Excel templates
- Envelopes or physical tracking (for the old-school approach)

Wants vs. Needs: The Hard Conversations

A key part of budgeting is learning the difference between wants and needs. As a parent, you can help by guiding this process without shaming them.

Needs:

- Food
- Housing
- Transportation
- Tuition and books
- Health insurance

Wants:

- Designer clothes
- Streaming subscriptions
- Impulse Amazon purchases
- Fancy takeout
- New tech or gaming systems

Questions to help them evaluate:

- Will this purchase help me meet my goals?
- Is this something I need right now or something I want?
- How will I feel about this purchase next month?

Encourage the 24-hour rule: if it's a big non-essential purchase, wait a day before buying.

Creating a "Zero-Based Budget"

This budgeting method ensures every dollar has a job. Income – Expenses = $0.

Here's how it works:

- Track all expected income for the month
- Assign every dollar to a category: housing, food, savings, fun, giving, etc.
- Adjust each month based on changes in income or priorities

This keeps students intentional about spending and makes it easier to course-correct.

Dealing with Peer Pressure and Lifestyle Creep

Many student-athletes feel pressure to "keep up" with teammates or influencers. Budgeting helps build self-control and resist comparison traps.

Tips:

- Talk about social media filters and the illusion of wealth
- Share stories of pro athletes who went broke after college
- Reinforce that being financially healthy is better than looking rich

Emergency Fund Basics

Encourage your child to build a small emergency fund, even if it's $500 to start. This money is for true emergencies:

- Car repairs
- Medical expenses
- Unplanned travel

Keep it in a separate account that's easy to access but not linked to their daily debit card.

Weekly Check-Ins

Suggest a quick weekly budget review:

- What did I spend this week?
- What do I have left?
- What's coming up next week?

Parents can check in monthly to offer support and celebrate consistency.

Final Thoughts

Budgeting is a muscle that gets stronger with use. Your student-athlete may not get it perfect at first, but that's okay. The goal is progress, not perfection.

Helping your child build a realistic, values-based budget is one of the best forms of financial mentorship you can offer. It gives them the confidence to say no, the clarity to say yes, and the discipline to prepare for life beyond sports.

In a world where NIL can bring quick money, budgeting gives them something even more valuable: long-term control.

Chapter 30: Lifestyle Inflation: When the Checks Start Coming In

For many college athletes, receiving their first NIL check is a moment of pride. It feels like recognition, a reward, and in some cases, life-changing money. But that sense of newfound freedom can also trigger a dangerous cycle: **lifestyle inflation**—the gradual increase in spending as income goes up. If left unchecked, lifestyle inflation can sabotage long-term goals and lead to financial instability.

This chapter helps parents understand how to guide their student-athletes through the emotional and behavioral shifts that come with earning money. It explores how to maintain financial discipline, spot red flags, and avoid the common trap of trying to "keep up."

What is Lifestyle Inflation?

Lifestyle inflation happens when a person increases their spending in proportion to an increase in income. Instead of saving more or investing, they upgrade their wardrobe, buy more expensive meals, or start paying for extras they didn't need before. Over time, it becomes difficult to scale back, even if the income slows down.

For student-athletes, lifestyle inflation might look like:

- Buying designer clothes after landing a deal
- Ordering takeout every day instead of meal prepping

- Upgrading to premium subscriptions
- Flying home more often or choosing luxury hotels for trips
- Gifting friends or family large items without a plan

These habits can add up quickly, especially when NIL income is irregular or short-term.

Why It's So Easy to Fall Into

1. Visibility and Peer Pressure

Athletes are often in the spotlight. When fans, teammates, and social media followers are watching, there's pressure to look successful.

2. Emotional Spending

After years of financial stress or sacrifice, that first check can feel like a reason to celebrate. Some student-athletes feel compelled to treat themselves or their families, often without a plan.

3. Lack of Experience

For most young earners, NIL is their first real experience managing income. Without budgeting tools or mentorship, money slips away unnoticed.

4. Social Media Influence

Instagram and TikTok often glorify luxury and consumption. It can be hard to distinguish someone's highlight reel from their reality.

How to Maintain Financial Discipline

1. Celebrate Without Overspending

Encourage your child to celebrate their NIL wins in meaningful but modest ways. A dinner out or small gift to themselves is fine—but not at the expense of their goals.

2. Set a Savings Ratio

Use a simple system:

- 50% for essentials (housing, food, insurance)
- 30% for savings (emergency fund, taxes, future goals)
- 20% for wants or lifestyle spending

Or try 70/20/10: 70% live on, 20% save, 10% give.

3. Create a "Fun Money" Account

Set aside a monthly amount for non-essential purchases. This gives them freedom to enjoy their money without breaking their budget.

4. Make Financial Goals Visible

Help your student-athlete write down goals: saving for a car, paying taxes, investing, or launching a business. Put the list somewhere they can see it—it helps fight impulse spending.

5. Delay Major Purchases

Use the 24- or 48-hour rule. If they want to make a big purchase, have them wait before buying. Chances are, the urge will pass.

6. Talk About the Long-Term

Ask: "What do you want your money to do for you six months from now?" Frame spending in the context of their future.

Helping Them Resist the Urge to "Keep Up"

Comparison is one of the biggest traps for student-athletes.

1. Focus on Values Over Appearances

Talk with your child about what they value most—freedom, generosity, opportunity, security. Spending should reflect those values, not just image.

2. Expose the Real Costs

Discuss the hidden side of luxury: taxes, debt, obligations. Many student-athletes don't realize that the people they're trying to keep up with may be deeply in debt or leveraged.

3. Reinforce That Money is a Tool

Money isn't about status. It's a tool to create freedom, impact, and stability. Keep that mindset front and center.

4. Encourage Authenticity

They don't need to fake a lifestyle to earn respect. In fact, staying grounded makes them more relatable to brands and fans.

5. Talk About Role Models

Point to athletes who handled wealth well (LeBron James, Kawhi Leonard) vs. those who struggled due to mismanagement. Stories stick.

Signs Lifestyle Inflation is Happening

Be on the lookout for:

- A sudden shift in spending habits
- Frequent online orders or luxury purchases
- Little to no money left at the end of the month
- Missed payments or surprise overdrafts
- Defensiveness when asked about money

These signs don't always mean a crisis, but they do mean it's time for a conversation.

How to Talk to Your Child About It

Keep the tone positive, not critical. Use open-ended questions:

- "What are you most excited to use your NIL money for?"
- "How are you tracking your spending lately?"
- "Do you want help setting up a system to organize things?"
- "What do you think your future self will thank you for financially?"

Avoid guilt or shame. Reinforce that learning to manage money is a skill—not something they should already know.

Final Thoughts

Earning NIL income is a privilege and a responsibility. It gives student-athletes financial options their peers may not have—but only if they use it wisely.

Lifestyle inflation is a quiet threat. It doesn't show up all at once. It creeps in and builds habits that are hard to break. But with the right guidance, your child can develop financial discipline early and carry it for life.

The goal isn't to deprive them. It's to empower them to make choices today that their future selves will be proud of.

Because at the end of the day, the most impressive flex isn't what you buy—it's what you build. And the strongest athletes don't just win on the field. They win with their money, too.

Chapter 31: Protecting Mental Health in the NIL Era

The introduction of NIL (Name, Image, and Likeness) into college athletics has brought tremendous opportunities—but also added layers of pressure and expectation. For student-athletes already balancing academics, performance, and social lives, the sudden role of "influencer" and "entrepreneur" can create new mental and emotional challenges. The pressure to monetize, maintain appearances, and perform both on and off the field is real. And it can take a toll.

As a parent, your role isn't just about financial guidance. It's also about emotional protection and psychological support. This chapter will help you recognize how NIL can impact your child's mental health, and when it's time to step in, step back, or seek help.

The New Pressure Points

NIL can impact mental health in several unique ways:

1. Performance Pressure

Athletes may feel like they have to perform at peak level constantly, not just for their team, but for the brands that have invested in them. They may tie their self-worth to deals, likes, and engagement.

2. Public Scrutiny

Every post, game, or misstep can be broadcast online. The fear of "cancel culture," online hate, or disappointing fans and sponsors is exhausting.

3. Comparison and Identity Crisis

Social media makes it easy to compare NIL earnings, deals, and popularity with teammates or athletes across the country. This can lead to self-doubt, imposter syndrome, and identity confusion.

4. Time Burnout

Between classes, practice, and content creation, there's little time to rest. The pressure to keep up can rob student-athletes of sleep, downtime, and balance.

5. Financial Stress

Paradoxically, making money creates new fears: taxes, budgeting, contracts, and the pressure to provide for family. For some, it shifts their role in the family from dependent to provider.

What Mental Health Struggles Might Look Like

Keep an eye out for changes in behavior or mood:

- Withdrawal from social interactions
- Increased irritability or mood swings
- Trouble sleeping or oversleeping
- Loss of interest in sport, school, or hobbies
- Anxiety around games, social media, or meetings
- Obsessive focus on money or brand image
- Self-comparison or frequent negative self-talk
- Avoiding conversations about NIL responsibilities

Even if they appear high-functioning, many student-athletes are silently struggling. Pay attention to shifts in personality and energy.

What Conversations to Have

Open, non-judgmental communication is key. Instead of assuming they're okay or pushing them to be grateful, ask intentional, supportive questions:

- "How are you feeling about everything on your plate right now?"
- "What part of NIL has been the most exciting? The most stressful?"
- "Are you sleeping well and finding time for yourself?"
- "Is there anything you're feeling overwhelmed by?"
- "Would it help to talk to someone outside the family?"

Avoid:

- "You're lucky to be making money. Why are you stressed?"
- "Back in my day, we didn't have these opportunities."
- "Just focus harder. You'll be fine."

Validation is key. Their stress is real, even if their life looks great from the outside.

When to Step In

You know your child better than anyone. If their mental, emotional, or academic health seems compromised, it's okay to intervene.

Step in when you notice:

- Academic performance dropping significantly
- Isolation or avoidance of communication
- Persistent anxiety or mood swings
- Panic attacks or visible emotional breakdowns
- Risky behaviors (substance use, self-harm, financial irresponsibility)
- Extreme fixation on their online persona or NIL status

Stepping in doesn't always mean taking control. It could mean:

- Offering to connect them with a campus counselor
- Helping them find a mental health app or support group
- Encouraging time off from social media or branding tasks
- Suggesting they speak to their coach or academic advisor

Supporting Without Smothering

Your student-athlete may not want to open up. That's okay. You can still support them by creating an emotionally safe environment:

- Be available without being intrusive
- Celebrate them for who they are, not just their performance
- Normalize therapy and emotional check-ins
- Share your own stress or mental health journey if relevant
- Encourage hobbies and friendships outside of sports/NIL

Help Them Create Mental Health Boundaries

Work together to:

- Schedule weekly breaks from content creation
- Create time blocks for NIL tasks vs. school and recovery
- Turn off phones after a certain hour
- Limit who has access to their schedule and availability
- Say "no" to deals that don't align with their values or capacity

Balance is the antidote to burnout. Teach them that mental wellness is part of their performance strategy.

Campus Resources That Can Help

Most schools have:

- On-campus counseling centers
- Performance psychologists
- Mental health peer groups
- Student-athlete support services

Encourage them to connect early, not just in crisis. These resources are confidential, judgment-free, and often free of charge.

Final Thoughts

NIL is a powerful opportunity—but it brings responsibility. And with responsibility often comes pressure.

As a parent, your presence, perspective, and unconditional support are more valuable than any NIL check. Your student-athlete may be building a brand, but they are still growing into adulthood. They need safety, not just strategy.

Mental health isn't a side conversation. It's central to everything else. Protect it fiercely. Prioritize it openly. And remind your child: they are not their earnings, followers, or statistics.

They are loved. They are enough. And they don't have to carry it all alone.

Chapter 32: Credit Cards and Building Credit Responsibly

For many student-athletes, college is the first time they'll be introduced to the world of credit. Whether it's through a flyer on campus, a social media ad, or a suggestion from a bank, the idea of getting a credit card becomes very real. And with NIL income now part of the picture, some student-athletes may be seen as more "creditworthy" than their peers.

Used wisely, a credit card can be a great tool for building financial credibility and long-term success. But without proper guidance, it can quickly become a gateway to debt, fees, and credit score damage. This chapter explores how parents can help student-athletes understand credit cards, manage them responsibly, and build strong credit habits early.

Why Credit Matters

A credit score isn't just about borrowing money. It affects:

- Renting an apartment
- Buying a car
- Getting a mortgage
- Qualifying for insurance
- Job background checks

Establishing good credit in college gives your child a major head start. But only if they learn to manage it correctly.

Credit Score Basics

Credit scores generally range from 300 to 850 and are based on:

- **Payment history (35%)**: Do they pay on time?
- **Credit utilization (30%)**: How much of their available credit are they using?
- **Length of credit history (15%)**: How long have they had accounts?
- **Credit mix (10%)**: Do they have both revolving (credit card) and installment (loan) accounts?
- **New credit inquiries (10%)**: Are they applying for multiple new accounts?

Encourage them to check their score regularly using tools like:

- Credit Karma
- Credit Sesame
- Free reports at AnnualCreditReport.com

The Right Way to Get Started with Credit

1. Become an Authorized User

Parents can add their student-athlete to an existing credit card. The account holder is responsible, but the child benefits from the credit history.

Pros:

- No risk of denial
- Builds credit without requiring income
- Good for monitoring early habits

Cons:

- If the parent mismanages the account, it can hurt the child's score

2. Apply for a Student Credit Card

Many banks offer student cards with low credit limits and manageable terms.

Requirements:

- Proof of income or a cosigner
- Limited (or no) credit history
- Must be 18+

Encourage cards with:

- No annual fee
- Simple reward structure
- No foreign transaction fees

3. Start with a Secured Credit Card

Secured cards require a deposit (usually $200-$500) that acts as the credit limit.

Pros:

- Easier to qualify for
- Helps establish payment history

Cons:

- Ties up cash temporarily
- Doesn't offer large rewards or benefits

Cosigning: The Risks and Realities

Some student-athletes may not qualify for credit alone and ask a parent to cosign.

Before agreeing, know this:

- You're equally responsible for repayment
- Missed payments affect your credit score too
- You may be legally liable for the entire balance

Only cosign if:

- You trust your child to use the card responsibly
- You can afford to cover the balance in an emergency
- You agree on clear rules for usage and repayment

Put expectations in writing, and set up alerts so you're notified of charges and due dates.

How to Use a Credit Card Responsibly

Teach your student-athlete these habits:

- Pay the balance in full each month
- Never spend more than 30% of their limit (ideally 10%)
- Use autopay to avoid missed payments
- Only charge what they can afford to pay with cash
- Avoid cash advances and late payments

Example: If they have a $500 credit limit, try to keep usage under $150 at any time.

Setting Credit Boundaries

Talk through:

- What expenses are allowed on the card (e.g., gas, groceries)
- How to handle an emergency expense
- What to do if they lose the card or suspect fraud

Encourage:

- Monthly check-ins to review statements
- Linking the card to budgeting apps like Mint or YNAB

Common Mistakes to Avoid

- Opening too many cards to chase rewards
- Using credit to finance a lifestyle
- Ignoring statements or minimum due dates
- Letting friends borrow the card or card info
- Missing a payment due to forgetfulness or oversight

Mistakes now can impact them for years. One late payment stays on a report for up to 7 years.

When to Step In as a Parent

Step in if:

- They miss payments or get hit with late fees
- They use the card for impulse shopping or gifts
- They exceed their credit limit regularly
- They ignore statements or don't know how much they owe

Intervention doesn't mean taking the card away—it means teaching and guiding. If needed, freeze the card temporarily or limit usage while reviewing credit fundamentals together.

Teaching the Bigger Picture

Remind them:

- Credit is not free money
- Credit is a tool for building their financial future
- A strong credit score opens doors, but only with discipline

Help them visualize long-term wins:

- Qualifying for their first car loan
- Renting an apartment without a cosigner
- Lower interest rates over time

Final Thoughts

Credit can be empowering or destructive. With the right education, boundaries, and habits, your student-athlete can use it to build a financial foundation that lasts beyond college.

As a parent, your job is to demystify the system and give them tools to navigate it confidently. Whether you cosign, advise, or just support from the sidelines, you're helping them build something more valuable than points or perks: **a life of financial trust and independence.**

Chapter 33: Insurance Needs for Student Athletes

Health, renter's, disability, auto, and liability insurance

One of the most overlooked but critical parts of financial literacy for student-athletes is understanding the role of insurance. When a young athlete starts earning NIL income, moves off campus, begins traveling independently, or assumes public visibility, they also assume risk. Parents often focus on income, deals, and taxes, but fail to recognize how one accident, lawsuit, or uncovered event can derail a student-athlete's academic, athletic, or financial future.

This chapter is designed to help parents understand the major types of insurance every student-athlete should consider: health, renter's, disability, auto, and personal liability. Each plays a unique role in protecting the person behind the brand.

Health Insurance

Health insurance is essential for every student, but for student-athletes—especially those whose physical performance is tied to their education and income—it's non-negotiable. Most college students are covered under their parents' plan until age 26, but that doesn't mean coverage is simple or complete.

Pros of health insurance coverage through a parent or school:

- Continued access to a familiar network of doctors, therapists, and specialists

- Full or partial coverage of doctor visits, surgeries, hospitalizations, and mental health services
- Access to telehealth and urgent care when away at school
- Athletic departments may cover treatment for sports-related injuries

However, there are significant limitations:

- If your plan is regional, your child may be out-of-network when attending school in another state, resulting in high out-of-pocket costs
- School-provided athletic insurance often covers injuries during official practices and games only—not during personal workouts or unsanctioned events
- NIL income could affect Medicaid eligibility or other need-based health programs

Parents should review their policy with their insurance provider, ask about network limitations in the college's area, and explore supplemental plans if necessary. If your child is no longer eligible under your plan, they may need to enroll in a university-sponsored plan or individual marketplace plan. Don't wait for a medical emergency to find out what is and isn't covered.

Renter's Insurance

Once your child moves out of the dorms and into an apartment or house, they need renter's insurance. Many students assume that if their belongings are stolen or damaged, their landlord or the school will cover the loss. That's rarely the case.

Renter's insurance protects personal property against damage from fire, theft, vandalism, and other risks. It also provides liability protection if someone is injured on the property.

Advantages:

- It's affordable—typically $10 to $25 per month
- It can be bundled with other insurance (like auto) for a discount
- It gives peace of mind if laptops, phones, clothes, or NIL-related gear

are stolen or damaged
- It often includes "loss of use" coverage, paying for a hotel if your child's apartment becomes temporarily uninhabitable

Potential drawbacks:

- Some policies have high deductibles that may exceed the value of lost property
- Not all renter's insurance includes flood or earthquake protection (this must be added separately depending on location)
- If your child has expensive athletic equipment or tech, coverage limits may need to be increased

Parents should check if their own homeowner's policy extends any coverage to dependents living away at school. If not, help your child shop for their own policy and educate them about what's included and excluded.

Disability Insurance

Disability insurance is a more specialized but critically important area of protection for athletes—especially those with professional aspirations or substantial NIL income. It provides income replacement if your child is unable to continue participating in sports due to injury or illness.

There are two main types:

1. Short-term disability: Covers temporary injuries or conditions that prevent participation for weeks or months
2. Permanent total disability (PTD): Pays a benefit if your child suffers a career-ending injury

Pros of disability insurance:

- It protects future earnings tied to athletic performance, including professional contracts or future NIL potential
- It may be available through athletic departments for elite prospects

- In some cases, premiums can be paid using NIL income, allowing your child to protect their own future

Cons:

- It can be expensive, with annual premiums ranging from hundreds to thousands of dollars
- The underwriting process can be rigorous and invasive
- Claims can be denied if injuries fall outside covered parameters or are considered pre-existing

This insurance isn't necessary for every athlete, but for those being recruited at the Division I level or showing pro potential, it's worth investigating. Parents should consult a sports insurance specialist or financial advisor familiar with this niche market.

Auto Insurance

If your student-athlete owns a car or regularly drives at school, having the right auto insurance is both legally required and financially critical. Beyond standard coverage, athletes who use their vehicle for NIL-related activity—such as traveling to appearances, delivering merchandise, or creating content—may need special coverage.

Benefits of proper auto insurance:

- Liability coverage protects against lawsuits from accidents your child causes
- Comprehensive and collision coverage pays for repairs or replacements
- Uninsured motorist coverage protects against accidents caused by others with no or minimal insurance

Concerns to address:

- Moving out-of-state may affect rates or require a new policy depending on residency rules

- NIL income may affect classification (e.g., business use)
- Some policies may not cover ride-share activities or commercial usage

Parents should talk with their insurance provider to ensure that the coverage reflects their child's current status. In many cases, keeping a child on the family policy is cheaper and more comprehensive, but if they're earning their own money and acting independently, an individual policy may be more appropriate.

Personal Liability Insurance

In the NIL era, student-athletes aren't just playing sports—they're operating personal brands. That makes them public figures, which increases their legal risk. A single mistake, misstatement, or misstep could result in legal action. Liability insurance protects against lawsuits stemming from personal injury, property damage, or reputation damage linked to business activity.

Advantages:

- Umbrella policies provide high-dollar protection above existing auto or renter's policies
- Helps protect against lawsuits stemming from NIL business activities
- Offers peace of mind for high-profile athletes engaging with the public, brands, or media

Challenges:

- Requires coordination with other insurance policies to avoid coverage gaps
- Can be expensive if the athlete is considered "high risk" due to public visibility
- May not cover intentional misconduct, copyright infringement, or business disputes

Liability insurance is especially important for student-athletes who travel frequently, host events, or have large social media followings. Parents should consider helping their child purchase a personal umbrella policy or assess the liability coverage included in other policies.

Additional Considerations

As student-athletes accumulate gear, income, and exposure, they are increasingly vulnerable to theft, lawsuits, accidents, or sudden loss. Insurance might feel like an "extra" expense when money starts rolling in, but the consequences of being uninsured—or underinsured—can far outweigh the monthly premium.

Athletes who run NIL businesses, sign merchandise deals, or operate online stores should also consider:

- Business liability coverage
- Errors and omissions insurance
- Content liability coverage if they operate as influencers

Not all insurance agents or companies understand the unique needs of NIL athletes, so it's important to find providers familiar with young entrepreneurs and student-athletes. Parents can play a major role in helping their child make smart decisions, shop for competitive rates, and truly understand what they're protected from—and what they're not.

Conclusion

For student-athletes navigating college and NIL, insurance is not just protection—it's preparation. Helping your child secure the right policies is an act of financial mentorship. It reinforces that their brand, body, belongings, and business are valuable—and worth protecting.

Don't wait for an accident, injury, or lawsuit to start asking questions. Be proactive. Review policies together. Compare providers. Ask what-if scenarios. Insurance won't make NIL headlines—but it will protect everything your child is working so hard to build.

Chapter 34: Social Media Mistakes That Cost Big

In the NIL era, social media isn't just a place to connect—it's a platform to profit, a portfolio to present, and for many student-athletes, a pressure cooker to navigate.

Platforms like Instagram, TikTok, YouTube, and X (formerly Twitter) have turned everyday users into entrepreneurs, influencers, and public figures. For student-athletes, who are often already in the spotlight, these platforms carry both immense opportunity and risk. With a single post, an athlete can attract a new sponsor—or lose a scholarship.

This chapter explores the most common social media mistakes student-athletes make, the real-world consequences of those errors, and how parents can help their children manage their digital footprint with confidence and care.

The NIL Shift: Why Social Media Matters Now More Than Ever

Before NIL, social media was a tool for entertainment and connection. Now, it's a business platform. Companies looking to partner with athletes for endorsements or promotional campaigns evaluate not just performance on the field, but personality and presence online.

A clean, consistent, and engaging social profile can lead to:

- Brand partnerships

- Speaking engagements
- Clothing lines
- Podcast deals
- Media appearances

But that same profile, if mismanaged, can also lead to:

- Canceled NIL contracts
- Lost recruiting opportunities
- Damaged public image
- Long-term brand distrust

Social media is now part of an athlete's resume. Coaches check it. Brands evaluate it. Fans follow it. The risks of misuse are higher, and the room for error is smaller.

Common Mistakes That Cost Student-Athletes

1. Inappropriate or Offensive Content

Offensive posts—including racist, sexist, homophobic, or vulgar language—can immediately disqualify an athlete from NIL consideration. These mistakes are often found in old tweets, Instagram captions, or even "liked" posts.

Even if the post is from middle school or early high school, the consequences can be career-altering. There have been numerous high-profile examples of athletes losing scholarships or endorsements due to resurfaced offensive content—even content they didn't write but reshared or commented on.

2. Public Partying and Substance Use

A photo holding a red cup. A snap from a party. A caption joking about being "lit." Even when harmless or legal, the perception of partying or drug use can conflict with a sponsor's image. Alcohol and cannabis brands may approach athletes in states where products are legal, but most mainstream brands will avoid athletes who appear reckless or out of control online.

Many NIL agreements include morality clauses, which can be triggered by inappropriate social media activity—costing the athlete the deal and sometimes their eligibility.

3. Retweeting, Reposting, or Liking Problematic Content

This mistake is subtle but dangerous. A student-athlete might not create controversial content themselves, but by liking or sharing it, they give the appearance of endorsement. This includes:

- Retweeting crude jokes
- Sharing conspiracy theories
- Liking posts with explicit images
- Amplifying offensive or divisive content

Brands monitor this behavior. Some use software to analyze digital footprints and flag accounts with high-risk engagement—even if the athlete never posted anything directly.

4. Arguing or Fighting with Fans, Trolls, or Peers

Student-athletes will receive criticism. Some of it will be unfair. But engaging in arguments, name-calling, or retaliation rarely ends well. These exchanges are easy to screenshot and share, even if deleted.

Sponsors want ambassadors who show professionalism under pressure. If an athlete's online persona is combative or volatile, brands may walk away—even if the athlete has a strong following.

5. Posting Too Much or Oversharing

Not every moment needs to be documented. Athletes who post excessively—especially about their income, material purchases, or personal relationships—can come off as immature or self-centered. Oversharing can also make the athlete vulnerable to identity theft, scams, or privacy breaches.

The Real Cost of a Digital Slip-Up

For student-athletes in the NIL era, the consequences of a single post can be swift and severe. Unlike private mistakes, which may stay in the locker room or classroom, social media errors are public and permanent.

Financial Consequences

When an athlete makes a social media mistake—whether it's a crude joke or an angry exchange—the impact often hits their bank account first.

How?

- **Canceled NIL contracts**: Brands can terminate deals if they feel the athlete no longer represents their values.
- **Missed opportunities**: Other companies may quietly pass over the athlete when vetting brand partners.
- **Declining value**: If followers stop engaging or negative press builds, the athlete's online influence drops—and so does their market rate.

An athlete could go from having a $10,000 deal on the table to nothing in less than 24 hours—all because of a tweet.

Reputational Consequences

Perception is reality. And in the world of social media, perception is shaped by likes, comments, and retweets. An athlete might argue, "That's not what I meant," but by then, the damage is done.

What happens when reputation takes a hit:

- **Recruiting interest cools down**
- **Coaches and teammates lose trust**
- **Media scrutiny increases**
- **Peers and fans begin to distance themselves**
- **Schools implement disciplinary action**

Even if the athlete apologizes or deletes the content, screenshots live forever. A single lapse in judgment can become the first thing that appears when someone Googles their name.

Case Studies: When Social Media Goes Wrong

Here are just a few real-world examples (names removed for privacy):

Case 1: The Scholarship Revoked

A high school football player committed to a Power Five school was found to have tweeted multiple racial slurs when he was 14. Though the tweets were years old, they resurfaced the week before Signing Day. The school pulled the scholarship, and the player issued a public apology. He eventually landed at a smaller school but lost his national platform—and likely thousands in future NIL earnings.

Case 2: The Deal That Disappeared

A women's basketball player signed a major NIL agreement with a fitness brand. Days later, she posted a TikTok poking fun at her coaching staff's appearance. The video went viral for the wrong reasons. The brand, worried about backlash, terminated the contract immediately.

Case 3: The Feud That Went Public

Two teammates began trading jabs on Instagram Stories, airing private locker room drama. What started as jokes turned into insults. A media outlet picked up the story, leading to team meetings, suspensions, and an avalanche of negative attention. Both athletes saw their NIL activity drop off as brands distanced themselves.

These aren't outliers—they are becoming increasingly common.

The Viral Effect: Fast and Unforgiving

What makes social media so dangerous is how quickly things can spread. A private joke can become public. A video meant for 10 friends can be reshared by 10,000 strangers. Once it's out, it's out—and usually taken out of context.

Here's how it happens:

1. **Athlete posts or engages with questionable content**
2. **Follower screenshots it**
3. **Post goes viral—shared in group chats, fan forums, media threads**
4. **Brands, school officials, and recruiters are tagged**
5. **Reputation suffers—even if the athlete deletes the post**

All of this can happen in less than an hour.

What's even more dangerous is that once the story is written, it's hard to rewrite. Athletes often find themselves apologizing for years—sometimes for something they barely remember doing.

How Parents Can Help: Proactive Digital Mentorship

While your student-athlete's online presence is ultimately their responsibility, parents play an essential role in shaping how they approach social media. You don't have to be a tech expert or follow every trend on TikTok—but you do need to be involved, informed, and intentional.

Here are tangible steps parents can take to help protect their child's brand, image, and future earning potential.

Step 1: Conduct a Social Media Audit

Start with a full review of your child's digital presence. Sit down together and look at all of their accounts—Instagram, TikTok, X, YouTube, Facebook, LinkedIn, Snapchat, BeReal, and any others.

What to look for:

- Posts with offensive or insensitive language
- Comments that reflect poorly on character or judgment
- Liked or reshared content that might be seen as problematic
- Party photos, underage drinking, or drug references
- Public fights, trolling, or passive-aggressive subtweets
- Cringe-worthy or overly personal oversharing

Next, Google your child's full name and social handles. Check image search results, forum mentions, and cached posts. Even if content was deleted, old posts can still appear in search engines.

Make it a routine—review accounts every few months, and definitely before:

- Recruiting visits
- NIL deals
- Public appearances
- Media interviews

This helps them stay clean and confident, knowing nothing lurking online can surprise them or derail a deal.

Step 2: Create a Family Posting Policy

You don't need to monitor every post. Instead, work with your child to develop basic guidelines. This can include:

- A rule that no post should be sent while angry or emotional
- Waiting 24 hours before posting a rant, clap-back, or meme
- Avoiding posts that include profanity, illegal activity, or private team matters
- No posting late at night when judgment may be impaired
- No engaging in fights or feeding the trolls
- Thinking long-term: "Would I want a coach or brand to see this?"

You can even print these guidelines and keep them visible near their workspace or bedroom. When student-athletes know the expectations, they're more likely to pause before posting impulsively.

Step 3: Professional vs. Personal Profiles

While nothing online is ever truly private, it can be helpful to separate public-facing content from more casual or personal posts.

- A **public professional account** should be brand-ready: clean, inspiring, athletic-focused, and well-curated.

- A **personal account** can be locked, monitored, and limited to trusted friends and family.

This separation allows your child to grow their public platform strategically while maintaining some space for expression and connection that doesn't affect their career.

Tip: Encourage consistency across platforms. Handle names, profile photos, and bios should align with their personal brand.

Step 4: Teach the 24-Hour Rule

This simple rule can prevent a majority of digital disasters: *Don't post when emotional. Write it down, think about it, and revisit it in 24 hours.*

Often, the urge to vent or react fades. What felt like a must-post moment will seem insignificant a day later.

If they're still unsure—advise them to run it by someone they trust (including you). You can be their filter, mentor, and backup until they've developed the internal discipline to do it themselves.

Step 5: Make Social Media a Branding Tool

Parents can also help their student-athlete use social media as a tool for growth, leadership, and NIL readiness.

Encourage content that shows:

- Workout routines and behind-the-scenes training
- Academic milestones or honor roll achievements
- Volunteer work or community outreach
- Family values and team camaraderie
- Goals, affirmations, or athlete motivation
- Game-day highlights and media features

This type of content tells a brand or college: "This athlete is serious, mature, and ready to represent our organization."

It also makes them more relatable and likable, which grows their following organically.

What to Do When a Mistake Happens

Even with the best preparation, young athletes are human. They'll mess up. They may post something thoughtless, share an off-color joke, or comment on something they didn't fully understand. The key isn't to prevent every mistake—it's to know how to respond when one happens.

Step 1: Don't Panic

If a post goes viral for the wrong reason, remain calm. Avoid knee-jerk reactions like instantly deleting everything or firing back defensively. Most mistakes get worse when handled impulsively.

Take screenshots of the original post and the reactions (for reference or legal use if needed), and pause. Then move to step two.

Step 2: Assess the Situation Honestly

Talk with your student-athlete and ask:

- What exactly was posted or said?
- Is it truly offensive, or just being taken out of context?
- Who is upset—and why?
- Is this an opportunity for growth and learning?

You don't have to defend the behavior to support your child. Help them see the impact without shaming them. Let them reflect and take ownership.

Step 3: Own the Mistake (If It's a Mistake)

If something inappropriate was said, reposted, or supported—acknowledge it. Brands, fans, and schools value maturity and accountability.

A simple, authentic statement like:

> *"I made a mistake. I posted something that doesn't reflect who I am or who I want to be. I'm learning from it and taking steps to do better."*

...can often stop a backlash from turning into a lasting stain.

Avoid excuses. Don't blame the media, followers, or "cancel culture." Real accountability builds trust.

Step 4: Learn from the Moment

Every misstep is a teaching opportunity. Help your child explore:

- Why did they post or engage with that content?
- What do they want their personal brand to reflect?
- How can they grow from this?

If necessary, reach out to a trusted coach, mentor, or media professional to guide the conversation or help with public relations. A private conversation with the team or school may be required.

In some cases, student-athletes have turned mistakes into turning points—apologizing publicly, taking social media breaks, or launching campaigns focused on the values they want to stand for moving forward.

Turning Social Media into Long-Term Opportunity

Once your student-athlete develops discipline, strategy, and awareness, they can transform their platform into something powerful.

That means:

- Posting consistently, but thoughtfully
- Treating NIL deals like business partnerships
- Promoting causes that reflect their personal values
- Staying out of drama and online beefs
- Building a network of followers who respect—not just admire—them

Some student-athletes have parlayed their NIL success into full-time careers in:

- Influencer marketing

- Fitness coaching
- Speaking and broadcasting
- Sports entrepreneurship
- Brand consulting

It all starts with smart, strategic, consistent social media behavior.

Final Thoughts for Parents

You don't need to understand every platform to help your child succeed online. You just need to be involved, informed, and engaged. Here's how you can support them:

- Talk regularly about what they're posting and why
- Share real-life examples of both good and bad social media behavior
- Encourage them to think long-term with every post
- Help them clean up old content and maintain a public presence they're proud of
- Remind them that attention fades, but reputation lasts

Most of all, help your child understand this truth:

In today's world, your brand is your name—and your name is your currency.

Social media is the stage where that name is shaped, tested, and promoted. It can open doors or shut them. With the right approach, your student-athlete's online presence can become one of their greatest assets, both in college and far beyond.

Part VII: Planning for Life After College

The journey of a student-athlete doesn't end on Senior Night or graduation day. For most, life after college athletics arrives quickly—and it rarely looks like what they imagined. Whether they turn pro, pursue graduate school, enter the workforce, or pivot into a completely new career, planning for what comes next is one of the most important responsibilities a parent and mentor can help guide.

This section helps families begin that transition early by discussing the financial, professional, and emotional preparation every student-athlete needs to consider well before the final season ends.

It begins by addressing the reality that very few student-athletes make it to the professional level—and even those who do will eventually face retirement. It explores how NIL can be a launchpad to build a sustainable brand or career beyond the game, but only if there's a long-term vision and financial plan in place.

This part of the book covers how to:

- Budget and save for the transition from student life to independence
- Build a resume that includes NIL experience, leadership roles, and entrepreneurship
- Network with intention—through LinkedIn, alumni groups, conferences, and brand relationships
- Explore business ventures, graduate school, or service careers
- Protect and grow what was built during the NIL years
- Prepare for the emotional shift of losing the structure, attention, and

identity tied to being a college athlete

It also offers guidance for parents on how to shift their own support style—from being active guides during college to being thoughtful advisors as their child enters adulthood.

Part VII is about preparing student-athletes to leave college confident, clear-headed, and ready—not just to find their next opportunity, but to build it.

Chapter 35: The Emotional Exit: What No One Talks About

Athletic retirement, even at the college level, can feel like a kind of grief. Your student has spent years competing, sacrificing, and building their identity around performance. When the uniform is gone, they may feel lost.

Common emotions include:

- **Loss of identity**: "If I'm not an athlete, who am I?"
- **Anxiety** about the future: "What comes next?"
- **Depression or lack of motivation** without the structure sports provided
- **Envy or comparison** when watching teammates go pro or start their own careers
- **Relief and guilt**: Some are glad it's over—but feel guilty for feeling that way

As a parent, be prepared for these emotions. Don't rush them to "move on" or focus only on the job search. Allow space for reflection and emotion, but be ready to help guide them forward.

What helps:

- Talking openly about their feelings
- Connecting them with other former athletes

- Celebrating what they accomplished—both emotionally and practically
- Reassuring them that it's normal to feel unsure and unmotivated at first
- Helping them set new goals—not just professional ones, but personal too

Reframing NIL: From Endorsement to Experience

If your student-athlete participated in NIL during college, they've already gained experience in:

- Brand management
- Public speaking
- Time management
- Contract negotiation
- Content creation
- Entrepreneurial thinking

That's a résumé—even if it doesn't come with a traditional title.

Help your child understand how to frame their NIL activity in ways that appeal to future employers:

- "Managed partnerships with national and local brands"
- "Produced social media campaigns with 50k+ views"
- "Negotiated contracts and managed income as a student-entrepreneur"
- "Balanced academics, athletics, and brand responsibilities"

NIL isn't just about income. It's real-world experience, and it can help bridge the gap from athlete to professional.

Is the Degree Enough?

A college degree is still valuable—but in today's job market, it's only the foundation. Employers want:

- Soft skills (communication, leadership, teamwork)
- Evidence of work experience (internships, part-time jobs, side projects)
- Tech literacy and adaptability
- A clear sense of purpose or passion

If your student-athlete majored in general studies, communications, or sport management, that's fine—but now is the time to focus on how they'll apply what they learned.

Questions to ask:

- Do they have work samples, a digital portfolio, or writing examples?
- Have they built a professional LinkedIn profile?
- Have they explored graduate programs or certifications?
- Have they made connections beyond the athletic department?

Many student-athletes graduate without having completed internships due to athletic time demands. Now is the time to catch up, even if it means doing free work, shadowing professionals, or taking an online course to build new skills.

Exploring Career Paths After Sports

Not every student-athlete knows what they want to do next—and that's okay. What matters now is exposure and exploration.

Encourage your child to:

- Attend alumni networking events or virtual job fairs
- Join LinkedIn and reach out to former student-athletes in various

industries
- Set up informational interviews with professionals in fields of interest
- Create a "career board" with potential paths to explore

Common industries where former athletes thrive:

- Sales and marketing
- Coaching and athletic administration
- Fitness and wellness
- Broadcasting and content creation
- Education and youth development
- Real estate, entrepreneurship, and financial services
- Military or public service roles

Their competitive edge, resilience, and time management skills give them a strong foundation. The challenge is turning that foundation into a focused pursuit.

Financial Transition: From NIL Income to Entry-Level Reality

This may be the first time your child sees their income go down instead of up. NIL may have provided a few thousand—or tens of thousands—during college. Now, they're entering the workforce, often with entry-level pay, limited benefits, and rising living costs.

Tips for parents and athletes to prepare for the financial shift:

- Adjust lifestyle expectations early
- Build a monthly budget that reflects post-college income
- Reevaluate recurring expenses (car notes, apartment leases, phone plans)
- Continue saving (especially if they saved NIL income)
- Avoid taking on new unnecessary debt during the transition

Encourage them to maintain the smart habits they developed during NIL:

- Track spending
- Set short-term and long-term goals
- Use credit responsibly
- Consult with a financial advisor if needed

The goal is not just to maintain their financial standing—but to continue building it.

The Parent's Role After the Game

Now that the cheering stops, your role begins to shift again. You're no longer just the support system behind an athlete—you're the advisor, the coach, and the motivator for an adult navigating new terrain.

What your child needs from you:

- A sounding board, not a boss
- Encouragement without pressure
- Accountability with grace
- Space to grow and even fail

Continue having conversations about budgeting, work ethic, emotional wellness, and setting new goals. Let them lead more, but be ready to offer resources, reminders, and real-world perspective.

Final Thoughts

Every athlete's career ends—but the life they build afterward can be even more rewarding, stable, and fulfilling. The key is helping them understand that their value was never limited to their performance on the field.

With emotional support, financial planning, and a proactive mindset, student-athletes can thrive beyond sports. And with your guidance, they won't just move on—they'll move forward.

Let me know if you'd like to turn this chapter into a downloadable transition worksheet or add sample action plans for job searching and budgeting after graduation.

Chapter 36: Using NIL to Fund Grad School or Business Ventures

Investing NIL income wisely

Structuring income to reduce tax liability

As student-athletes build their brands and earn money through NIL deals, many are discovering something most college students never experience: extra income in their early twenties. Whether it's a few thousand dollars a year or tens of thousands through brand deals, collectives, and appearances, NIL income opens doors—and not just for short-term spending.

With guidance and intentionality, NIL income can be a launchpad to fund bigger dreams: graduate school, business ownership, real estate, or other long-term investments. But to turn today's income into tomorrow's security, athletes (and their parents) need to think strategically.

This chapter explores how to help your student-athlete use their NIL earnings to build—not just spend. It focuses on financial literacy, investing wisely, and making decisions that position them for independence, security, and long-term success.

Turning NIL Into a Long-Term Asset

For most college students, the idea of having capital to invest in their future sounds like a fantasy. But your student-athlete is in a rare position: they may have more financial flexibility than their peers, thanks to NIL. That flexibility can—and should—be used to fund future goals.

Common long-term uses for NIL income:

- Paying for graduate school or professional programs (law, med, MBA, etc.)
- Launching a business or side venture
- Investing in real estate or stocks
- Saving for a post-college transition fund
- Building a personal brand or digital product line
- Reducing or avoiding student loan debt

Help your student shift their mindset from "I earned this, I can spend it" to "I earned this, now how do I multiply it?"

Should They Go to Grad School?

Graduate education is still a powerful way to increase lifetime earning potential and specialize in high-demand fields. But it's expensive. NIL income can give your student the freedom to choose grad school without taking on massive debt.

Before using NIL to fund further education, help your child consider:

- Is grad school required for their career goals?
- What's the return on investment (ROI) for the degree?
- Will they pursue grad school full-time or part-time while working?
- Are there assistantships, scholarships, or employer reimbursement programs available?

Using NIL to self-fund some or all of tuition can prevent them from relying on high-interest graduate PLUS loans or private loans, which are difficult to pay off with entry-level salaries.

Starting a Business with NIL Income

Some student-athletes are natural entrepreneurs. Others develop business ideas while growing their personal brand. Whether it's starting a clothing line, coaching service, podcast, or online fitness program, NIL income can serve as seed capital.

Here's how to approach it wisely:

Step 1: Validate the idea.

Is there a real market for the product or service? What problem is it solving? Is it scalable?

Step 2: Start small.

Use NIL income to test the market—build a prototype, start a website, invest in branding. There's no need to drop $10,000 upfront.

Step 3: Create a business structure.

If they haven't already, consider forming an LLC. This protects their personal assets, helps manage taxes, and signals professionalism.

Step 4: Separate personal and business finances.

Create a dedicated business checking account. Use bookkeeping software to track expenses and income.

Step 5: Work with professionals.

A CPA can help structure income to reduce tax burden. A legal advisor can help write contracts and protect intellectual property.

Encourage your student-athlete to treat any business like a business—not just a hobby. If done right, their NIL experience can become the foundation for a lifelong entrepreneurial journey.

Investing NIL Income Wisely

NIL income shouldn't just be spent—or even saved—it should be invested. Even small amounts invested early can grow significantly thanks to compound interest.

Here are smart investment strategies for young athletes:

1. Roth IRA

This tax-advantaged retirement account is ideal for young earners with relatively low taxable income. Contributions are made with after-tax dollars, and all growth and withdrawals in retirement are tax-free. As long as the athlete has earned income, they can contribute up to the annual limit.

2. Brokerage Account

If they want more flexibility, a taxable brokerage account allows them to invest in ETFs, mutual funds, or individual stocks. Unlike retirement accounts, these funds can be withdrawn at any time (with tax considerations).

3. 529 Education Plans

If grad school is on the horizon, a 529 plan can be a smart way to save tax-free for future education expenses. In some states, contributions are deductible for state tax purposes.

4. Real Estate Fund or REITs

Not ready to buy a house? Real Estate Investment Trusts (REITs) allow athletes to invest in real estate without owning property directly.

5. High-Yield Savings Account or CD Laddering

For short-term goals, placing funds in a high-yield savings account or short-term certificate of deposit (CD) helps protect capital while still earning interest.

Structuring Income to Reduce Tax Liability

NIL income is typically treated as self-employment income. That means it's subject to both income tax and self-employment tax (Social Security + Medicare). Without smart planning, taxes can eat up 30–40% of earnings.

Steps to reduce tax liability:

Track all income and expenses.

Use tools like QuickBooks, Keeper, or Wave to document income from each brand or appearance. Save receipts and records of business expenses (travel, software, phone use, training gear, branding, etc.).

Consider forming an LLC.

With an LLC, they may be able to deduct a wider range of expenses. It also allows for cleaner separation of business income.

Contribute to a SEP IRA or Solo 401(k).

These are retirement accounts specifically for self-employed individuals. They reduce taxable income and encourage long-term savings.

Hire a qualified CPA.

As income increases, so do the complexities. A CPA familiar with NIL can help file quarterly estimates, leverage deductions, and avoid underpayment penalties.

Avoid co-mingling funds.

Mixing NIL income with personal bank accounts can make tax season confusing and risk losing deductible expenses. Keeping accounts separate simplifies everything.

Helping Your Student Think Like a Long-Term Earner

Athletes are trained to think day-to-day, week-to-week, season-to-season. But NIL success requires long-term thinking. As a parent, you can help shift their mindset.

Talk about:

- Income vs. wealth: Money earned vs. money grown
- Taxes: The cost of not planning ahead
- Opportunity cost: What buying that new watch means for funding grad school
- Ownership: Why they should own assets, not just consume

Help them set goals like:

- "I want to save $10,000 toward grad school."
- "I want to launch my own training brand after graduation."
- "I want to have a 6-month emergency fund before I leave college."
- "I want to invest 20% of my NIL income each year."

The earlier they start setting goals with their money, the more control they'll have over their future.

Final Thoughts

NIL is more than a moment—it's a movement. But its real power is in what comes next. When managed wisely, even modest NIL earnings can give your student-athlete the ability to fund an advanced degree, start a business, or create a foundation of financial freedom before they ever leave college.

As a parent, your role is not to control every dollar, but to create conversations and systems that allow your child to think strategically. The same discipline and focus they've applied to sports can serve them well in money management.

The game might end. The NIL deals might dry up. But the financial mindset they build now will outlast all of it—and power the next chapter of their life with clarity and confidence.

Let me know if you'd like to turn this into a downloadable action plan for NIL investing or post-graduation financial prep.

Chapter 37: Building Generational Wealth

Teaching Long-Term Investing

Roth IRAs, Brokerage Accounts, and Compound Interest

One of the most powerful outcomes of the Name, Image, and Likeness (NIL) era is the opportunity it gives young athletes to begin thinking like wealth builders—not just short-term earners. While many student-athletes see NIL income as a way to buy what they've always wanted, the real win is using that income to build a financial foundation that can benefit not just themselves, but their future family for decades to come.

This chapter explores how parents can help student-athletes move from the mindset of income consumption to long-term investing. It outlines the tools, principles, and strategies that lead to true generational wealth—and how to start building it in college.

Why Generational Wealth Matters

Generational wealth means passing on assets—money, property, investments, businesses—that continue to benefit future generations. It's not about handing children a fortune. It's about equipping them with resources and financial literacy that can change their trajectory.

For many families, especially those who didn't come from money, the idea of building wealth that lasts more than one lifetime is new. But it starts with a single decision: choosing to save and invest money now rather than spend it all.

Student-athletes with NIL income have a unique opportunity to begin this legacy early. With guidance, they can graduate not just debt-free—but with real assets and long-term wealth potential.

The Time Advantage: Why Now Is Everything

Young adults have one key advantage that no one else can buy: time.

The earlier someone invests, the more they benefit from **compound interest**—the process by which money earns interest, and that interest earns more interest over time.

Consider this example:

- If your child invests $6,000 per year in a Roth IRA from age 19 to 25 (just 7 years), and never adds another penny…
- That investment could grow to **over $1 million** by retirement age, assuming an average 8% annual return.

The message is clear: **Start early. Even small amounts invested now have the power to grow into generational assets.**

Investing Basics for Student-Athletes

Before diving into specific accounts, it's important to teach your student-athlete these basic principles of investing:

1. **Investing is not gambling.**
2. It's not about guessing or chasing trends. It's about long-term strategy.
3. **Consistency matters more than perfection.**
4. Regular contributions, even small ones, beat one-time lump sums.
5. **Diversification protects against risk.**
6. Don't put all the money in one stock or crypto coin. Spread it across

assets.

7. **Investing is for the long term.**
8. Expect volatility. Don't panic. Don't pull out when the market dips.
9. **Inflation eats savings.**
10. Keeping money in a regular savings account over 30 years can actually reduce its value. Investing allows the money to outpace inflation.

Roth IRA: The Perfect Starter Investment Vehicle

For young earners, few tools are as powerful as a **Roth IRA**.

A Roth IRA (Individual Retirement Account) allows individuals to contribute **after-tax income**—and then grow it **tax-free**. That means no taxes on interest, dividends, or withdrawals in retirement.

Key points:

- Annual contribution limit: $6,500 (as of 2024)
- Contributions can be withdrawn at any time (no penalty)
- Earnings can be withdrawn tax-free after age 59½ (if the account is 5+ years old)

Why it's perfect for student-athletes:

- They're likely in a low tax bracket now, so paying taxes up front is painless.
- They can take advantage of decades of compounding.
- It encourages long-term thinking and financial discipline.

To contribute, the athlete must have **earned income** (from NIL, jobs, etc.). NIL income qualifies.

Parents can help:

- Set up the account through a reputable brokerage (Fidelity, Vanguard, Schwab, etc.)

- Match their contributions (e.g., for every $1 they contribute, you add $1)
- Explain the long-term impact using growth calculators and visuals

Brokerage Accounts: Flexibility and Opportunity

While Roth IRAs are for retirement, **brokerage accounts** provide flexibility. They allow for investing in stocks, ETFs, and mutual funds with **no restrictions on when money can be withdrawn**.

Why it matters:

- Athletes may want to invest toward short- and mid-term goals (buying a car, launching a business, putting a down payment on a home).
- Brokerage accounts can be managed with mobile apps, making investing feel accessible.

Important lessons to teach:

- **Use low-cost index funds** (like S&P 500 ETFs) to reduce fees and simplify investing
- **Avoid day trading**—teach the difference between investing and speculation
- **Track performance monthly** but don't obsess over daily changes
- **Set up automatic contributions** from their NIL income each month

What to Avoid

As your student-athlete begins investing, steer them away from common traps:

- **High-fee advisors or platforms** that charge 1–2% annually
- **Overhyped meme stocks** or "get rich quick" pitches
- **Unregulated crypto platforms** with no investor protections

- **Borrowing to invest (margin accounts)** without deep understanding

Teach them to vet opportunities, seek professional advice, and stay grounded in their goals.

Building a Wealth Plan During College

Here's a sample monthly plan for using NIL income wisely:

- 50% — Save or invest (Roth IRA, brokerage, 529)
- 30% — Spend on essentials (food, rent, travel)
- 10% — Donate or give (charity, church, causes)
- 10% — Fun money (clothes, shoes, outings)

You can adjust the percentages, but the goal is to **build structure and discipline**. Every dollar earned through NIL should have a purpose.

Teaching Legacy: Beyond Their Own Lifetime

Help your child see how wealth building is not just about them.
It's about:

- Creating stability for future children
- Paying for future education without debt
- Giving generously to causes they care about
- Building a platform of independence that allows them to choose meaningful work

That's what generational wealth really means. And it starts now—with a clear plan, strong habits, and the right support.

Final Thoughts

Most student-athletes won't play professionally. Even fewer will earn millions through NIL. But any athlete—at any level—can build wealth if they start early and manage wisely.

You don't need millions to build a legacy. You need a plan, consistency, and vision.

Help your student-athlete see beyond today's income and into the power of long-term investing. Because what they do now with $1,000 matters far more than what they might do later with $100,000.

When they understand compound interest, Roth IRAs, smart investing, and the value of time, they begin to shift from just making money—to building a life their future family will benefit from for generations.

Let me know if you'd like to include a printable "Wealth Plan Starter Guide" or a visual chart on compound interest in this chapter.

Chapter 38: Real Estate, Cars, and Big Purchases

Helping Your Child Make Wise Choices

Avoiding Predatory Lenders

Big purchases like cars, apartments, and even homes are exciting milestones for any young adult. For student-athletes earning NIL income, these moments often come sooner—and with more temptation—than for their peers. The sudden availability of money combined with pressure from social media, peers, and even family can lead to impulsive decisions and long-term financial mistakes.

This chapter will help you guide your student-athlete through the big-spending years. It covers how to think about real estate and vehicle purchases, how to evaluate whether a major buy makes sense, and—critically—how to identify and avoid predatory lenders and scams that often target young earners.

The Psychology of "Having Money for the First Time"

Let's acknowledge something that often goes unsaid: when a young person comes into money—especially if they grew up without it—there's emotional weight behind every dollar. Buying a car or a flashy outfit isn't just about style or transportation. It's about validation. Confidence. A declaration that "I made it."

That mindset is understandable, but unchecked, it can lead to:

- Overspending on luxury items that lose value
- Buying liabilities instead of assets
- Signing contracts without understanding the terms
- Becoming a target for manipulation or exploitation

Helping your student-athlete shift from *spending to prove* toward *spending with purpose* is one of the most powerful gifts you can give them.

Buying a Car: What They Need to Know

Cars are often the first big-ticket purchase a student-athlete considers. The right vehicle can improve mobility, safety, and independence. But too often, athletes overextend financially or get taken advantage of at the dealership.

Help them consider:

1. New vs. Used

- New cars depreciate up to 20–30% in the first year.
- Used cars (2–4 years old) offer better value.
- Athletes should avoid financing flashy vehicles that stretch their monthly income.

2. Cash vs. Financing

- If they have the cash, buying outright saves on interest.
- If financing, compare interest rates from banks, credit unions, and the dealer.
- Never accept a loan without understanding the full APR, loan term, and total cost over time.

3. Insurance Costs

- NIL income may affect how insurers classify them (especially if tied to business use).

- Sports cars or luxury models bring much higher premiums.

4. Additional Costs

- Registration, maintenance, gas, and unexpected repairs should be part of the decision.

Red Flag: Predatory Auto Lenders

- These companies offer "easy approvals" but hide massive fees, inflated interest rates, or balloon payments.
- If the rate is higher than 8–10% or the loan term exceeds 5 years, it's a warning sign.
- Always review contracts carefully and encourage your child to walk away from high-pressure sales tactics.

Real Estate: When (and If) to Buy

Some student-athletes consider buying a home or investment property during or right after college. On the surface, this sounds like a mature move—but it must be carefully evaluated.

Buying During College:

- Generally not advisable unless they're working with a financial advisor or parent with experience.
- Complicates taxes, financial aid, and lifestyle flexibility.
- Better to rent or sublet unless there's a long-term plan in place.

Post-Graduation:

- Buying a home or condo might make sense if your child has stable income and plans to stay in one place for 3–5 years.
- NIL income typically won't count as "stable income" in the eyes of

mortgage lenders unless it's structured properly (through LLCs or with documented contracts).

Investment Properties:

- Owning rental properties can be an excellent path to wealth—but it requires education, patience, and management skills.
- Encourage your student to start by learning: read books, follow real estate investors, and understand the numbers (cap rate, cash flow, maintenance costs).

Things to Consider Before Buying:

- Will this asset grow in value over time?
- Can they afford it without sacrificing savings or emergency funds?
- Do they understand all the responsibilities and risks?
- Are there better uses for this money right now?

Big Purchases Beyond Homes and Cars

NIL income brings opportunities to buy other high-ticket items:

- Watches and jewelry
- Travel and vacations
- Private trainers or chefs
- Studio equipment or production gear
- Business tools or technology

Each of these could be a meaningful investment—or an expensive distraction.

Help your child evaluate:

- **Utility**: Does this add long-term value to their brand, business, or

career?
- **Appreciation vs. depreciation**: Is it likely to gain value or lose it?
- **Cash vs. credit**: Can they afford it without debt?
- **Delayed gratification**: Would waiting 6 months change the decision?

Encourage them to make one or two meaningful purchases they'll value—and to delay others until their financial house is in order.

Predatory Lending: Spotting the Traps

Predatory lenders thrive on young people with cash and limited financial education. They're often found in:

- Auto dealerships
- Payday loan shops
- Online "instant approval" sites
- Lease-to-own stores
- Social media promotions disguised as luxury credit

Tactics include:

- Hiding fees in complex contracts
- Charging sky-high interest rates
- Preying on the desire for status or speed
- Encouraging cosigners (often parents or friends) without transparency

Signs of a predatory loan:

- Vague or rushed explanations
- Penalties for early repayment
- "No credit check required" for large loans
- Rates above 15% (sometimes 100%+)
- Payments that keep the borrower locked in without reducing principal

Teach your child to read every contract. If they don't understand it, they shouldn't sign it.

Smart Habits Around Big Purchases

To help your student-athlete build good decision-making muscles, instill these habits:

- **The 30-Day Rule**: Wait 30 days before making any purchase over $1,000.
- **The Rule of 3**: Compare three vendors, products, or price options before buying.
- **The Research Rule**: Spend at least 2 hours researching any purchase over $2,500.
- **The "Would You Still Buy It Without Social Media?" Test**: Would they still want it if no one could see it?

Encourage them to celebrate their success with meaningful purchases—but always within the context of a long-term wealth plan.

Final Thoughts

Big purchases aren't the problem—impulsive ones are. Helping your student-athlete slow down, ask the right questions, and think long-term will protect them not only from financial harm, but from regret.

Remind them:

- A car doesn't define their worth.
- A house doesn't guarantee stability.
- A luxury item doesn't equal long-term success.

True freedom comes from control—not consumption. NIL income gives them a head start. Help them use it to build a life, not just a lifestyle.

Part VIII: Scams, Frauds, and Red Flags

With new income, exposure, and opportunity comes new risk—especially for young athletes who are new to managing money and building their brand. In the NIL era, student-athletes are prime targets for scammers, shady agents, fake endorsement offers, identity theft, and financial manipulation. This section prepares parents to serve as the first line of defense.

Part VIII explores the most common scams that student-athletes face and gives parents the tools to spot red flags early. It includes fake NIL deals, phony financial advisors, predatory loan offers, exploitative contracts, and social media phishing tactics. It also explains how bad actors use flattery, urgency, or complexity to confuse and pressure young athletes into bad decisions.

This section helps parents teach their student-athletes how to:

- Recognize too-good-to-be-true offers
- Verify the credentials of agents, advisors, and brands
- Read contracts carefully and insist on transparency
- Understand the risks of sharing personal data or signing without legal guidance
- Set up systems of accountability and "pause rules" before any deal is accepted

Most importantly, this part reinforces the idea that your child doesn't have to figure it out alone. You, along with a vetted team of professionals, can help them filter out noise, stay grounded, and focus on legitimate, long-term growth.

Because in the world of NIL, the opportunities are real—but so are the risks. And staying protected is just as important as staying promoted.

Chapter 39: NIL Scams to Watch Out For

As Name, Image, and Likeness (NIL) opportunities grow, so does the risk of exploitation. While NIL has created life-changing financial possibilities for student-athletes, it has also opened the door to unethical individuals and organizations looking to take advantage of their inexperience. Many of these athletes are teenagers or young adults, often new to contract negotiations, legal documents, and business partnerships. This makes them prime targets for scams, misinformation, and manipulation.

This chapter explores the most common NIL scams, how to spot them, and how parents can help their student-athletes avoid costly mistakes before signing any deal, sharing personal information, or working with anyone claiming to "help them monetize their brand."

Why Student-Athletes Are Targets

Student-athletes are new to the business world. Most are focused on performance, school, and social life—not business operations, tax codes, or contract law. Their visibility makes them attractive targets, especially when they gain followers on social media or get mentioned by local or national outlets. The NIL era introduces an entirely new level of risk, especially when the athlete's brand becomes tied to money.

Scammers and shady operators rely on two things: excitement and inexperience. Offers that seem exciting often come with strings attached, and scammers know that most families won't catch the fine print until it's too late. Your child might be contacted by someone with a great pitch, slick presentation, or the right connections—but that doesn't make the deal legitimate or safe.

Let's explore the most common types of NIL scams today and how to protect against them.

1. Fake Endorsement Deals

This is one of the most common NIL scams. A student-athlete receives a DM or email from a "brand" offering to pay them to promote a product—usually clothing, supplements, gear, or accessories. In some cases, the athlete is promised a flat rate; in others, they're offered free products or commissions for sales.

The catch? The brand doesn't really exist. Or worse—they're using the athlete to get free advertising, financial info, or content.

How It Works:

- A fake company offers a "sponsorship opportunity."
- The student is told to buy a product up front with a promise of reimbursement.
- They're asked to post about the product and tag the brand.
- No payment ever arrives. The product may never ship.
- In some cases, the goal is to steal financial or personal information.

What to Watch For:

- Unverified or newly created social media pages
- Poor grammar or overly generic pitches
- Urgency ("We only have one spot left!")
- Requests for banking info or upfront payment
- No formal contract or vague terms

How to Respond:

- Never agree to promote a brand without a signed contract.
- Research the company—Google their name, look them up on LinkedIn or BBB.
- Don't provide banking details or make purchases as a "requirement."
- Show every deal to a parent, coach, or trusted advisor before responding.

2. Shady Agents and Talent Managers

As the NIL space matures, more agents and managers are entering the market—but not all of them are legitimate. Some are opportunists looking to charge student-athletes for access to deals or promise things they can't deliver.

A reputable agent should work on commission and have a track record of managing clients. They should never ask for large upfront fees or pressure your child into exclusive, long-term contracts.

How It Works:

- An "agent" contacts your child and promises exposure to brands.
- They claim they have worked with pro athletes or major companies.
- They ask for a fee to begin or ask for 25-50% of deals they bring in.
- They may disappear once they're paid or introduce harmful contracts.

What to Watch For:

- No verifiable client history or business license
- Asking for immediate decisions or upfront money
- Pressuring the athlete to sign a long-term deal
- No involvement of legal counsel in the agreement

How to Respond:

- Ask for references and past clients. Contact those athletes directly.
- Request all terms in writing. Don't sign anything without review.
- Verify that the agent is registered with your state (some states require this).
- Avoid anyone who isn't transparent about how they are paid.

3. Identity Theft and Personal Data Harvesting

Some scammers don't want money upfront—they want information. By pretending to be recruiters, sponsors, or NIL platforms, they trick athletes into sharing sensitive personal details.

Once they have your child's Social Security number, birth date, address, or banking info, they can commit fraud, file fake tax returns, or open credit cards in your child's name.

How It Works:

- The student receives a form requesting "basic info" to "set up payment."
- They're told to complete a W-9 or upload documents.
- These forms may be routed to a fake platform.

What to Watch For:

- Early requests for Social Security numbers or personal data
- Links that lead to suspicious websites
- Pressure to "sign up quickly to get paid"
- Misspellings in emails or URLs

How to Respond:

- Don't share sensitive information unless the company is verified.
- Use a professional email and keep NIL dealings separate from personal accounts.
- Use secure platforms like DocuSign or encrypted uploads when sharing

official forms.

4. MLMs Disguised as NIL Opportunities

Multi-level marketing companies often approach athletes as "brand ambassadors." These offers can seem harmless but quickly become exploitative.

The athlete may be asked to sell products, recruit others, or maintain quotas in exchange for commissions. In many cases, income is tied to recruiting—not actual NIL value.

How It Works:

- The athlete is offered a percentage of sales using a personal code or link.
- They are encouraged to post often and buy inventory.
- They're asked to recruit teammates or followers into the "program."

What to Watch For:

- Commission-based models that focus on recruitment over sales
- Pressure to buy inventory or meet monthly minimums
- Lack of real NIL connection—just sales jobs in disguise

How to Respond:

- Say no to any "deal" requiring payment or recruitment.
- Ask: "Is this about me as an athlete, or just me as a sales rep?"
- Avoid companies that can't show results for other college athletes.

5. Bad Contracts and Long-Term Lock-Ins

Even legitimate companies can offer contracts that are harmful. Some lock athletes into multi-year agreements, take too high of a percentage, or require exclusivity.

Your student may sign a deal thinking it's for one post—but discover they've given away rights to their image for years.

How It Works:

- A student signs a vague agreement quickly.
- The contract includes terms about exclusivity, automatic renewals, or ownership of content.
- The athlete later finds out they can't work with other brands—or can't leave.

What to Watch For:

- No legal review offered or allowed
- Lengthy contracts for low compensation
- Transfer of image rights without clear usage terms
- Unclear payment timelines or vague deliverables

How to Respond:

- Always read the fine print with a legal or compliance advisor.
- Avoid contracts longer than a year unless the income justifies it.
- Maintain ownership of personal brand, image, and content.
- Insist on fair exit clauses or termination language.

Teaching Your Athlete to Spot the Red Flags

The best defense is education. Parents can't monitor every DM or email, but you can train your student-athlete to think critically.

Teach them to ask:

- Who is this person, and can I verify their background?
- What exactly am I being asked to do?
- Is any money or personal info being requested upfront?

- What's the urgency—and why?
- Have I shown this to someone I trust?

Remind them that in NIL, **real opportunities don't require you to act immediately, pay first, or give away rights** without understanding the full scope of the deal.

What To Do If Your Student Falls for a Scam

If your child has already engaged with a bad actor or scam:

- Immediately stop communication and block the contact.
- Alert your child's school compliance officer or coach.
- Contact your bank if financial data was shared.
- Freeze credit if identity info was shared.
- Report the scam to the Federal Trade Commission or your state attorney general.
- Consult a lawyer to determine if the contract can be voided.

Do not shame your student—use the moment as a learning experience. Many professionals have made worse mistakes with more at stake. What matters is what happens next.

Final Thoughts

As long as NIL exists, scams will too. But your student-athlete doesn't need to live in fear—they need to be informed.

Teach your child to slow down, research, ask questions, and never feel rushed to sign or commit. NIL should be empowering, not risky. With your support and guidance, they can navigate this new world with wisdom and confidence.

A deal isn't an opportunity if it costs them their peace, their reputation, or their name. Help them protect all three.

Chapter 40: Internet Fame and the Dangers of Viral Exposure

The rise of NIL has thrust many young athletes into the spotlight in ways that go far beyond the field. Social media platforms like TikTok, Instagram, YouTube, and X (formerly Twitter) allow athletes to build massive audiences in short periods of time. While viral fame can lead to NIL success, brand deals, and media attention, it also comes with very real risks: doxxing, identity theft, and impersonation.

This chapter explores the darker side of viral visibility and helps parents understand how to protect their student-athletes in a digital landscape where being well-known also means being vulnerable.

What Happens When Athletes Go Viral

Going viral feels like winning the lottery. A post gets shared thousands—or millions—of times, followers pour in, and suddenly, your child is a public figure. This kind of attention can lead to real NIL money, media features, interviews, and even national recognition. But it also draws the attention of strangers, trolls, scammers, impersonators, and even hackers.

The moment your child gains visibility, their image becomes a commodity. And in that moment, they may face challenges like:

- Fake accounts pretending to be them
- Unwanted public scrutiny

- Unsolicited DMs and sponsorships
- Targeted harassment
- Data exposure from too much sharing

Fame can be rewarding, but without preparation, it can also be disorienting and dangerous.

Doxxing: When Privacy Disappears

Doxxing is the act of publishing someone's private or identifying information online without their consent. It's a tactic often used by trolls and online harassers to intimidate or threaten individuals. For student-athletes who go viral, doxxing can include:

- Posting their home address or school name
- Sharing their class schedule or dorm location
- Publishing their cell phone number or private email
- Circulating personal or family information

The consequences of doxxing can be severe. It can lead to safety risks, psychological trauma, and a need to change phone numbers, housing arrangements, or even routines.

How to Protect Against Doxxing

- Turn off location tagging on social media apps.
- Avoid posting photos with school IDs, addresses, or easily identifiable locations.
- Do not share personal schedules, routines, or locations in real time.
- Encourage the use of a P.O. box for any business or NIL correspondence.
- Consider using privacy settings to control who can comment, tag, or view posts.
- Google your child's name regularly to see what information is publicly

visible.

Impersonation and Fake Profiles

The more followers and recognition your child gains, the more likely someone will try to impersonate them. Fake profiles can look legitimate and often scam followers by pretending to represent the real athlete. This can include:

- Asking fans for money through Cash App or PayPal
- Promoting fake giveaways
- Messaging brands with false NIL proposals
- Posting offensive or misleading content under your child's name

These accounts not only damage your child's reputation but also create confusion that is hard to clear up—especially if the impersonator has already interacted with brands, teammates, or the media.

How to Prevent and Respond to Impersonation

- Secure social media handles across all major platforms, even ones your child isn't active on yet.
- Use a consistent profile image and bio to build legitimacy.
- Set up two-factor authentication on all social and email accounts.
- Report impersonators immediately using platform tools (Facebook, Instagram, TikTok, etc.).
- Keep a record of usernames and account links for documentation.
- If NIL income is significant, consider trademarking your child's name or brand.

Identity Theft and Account Hacking

Viral fame can make your child a target for cybercriminals looking to steal personal data, banking info, or control of high-traffic accounts.

If a student-athlete's account is hacked, it can cause serious damage:

- Loss of access to their social media platforms
- Distribution of spam, scams, or inappropriate content under their name
- Blackmail or ransom attempts to regain account control
- Unauthorized brand deals or fake business pitches

Preventative Tips

- Use complex, unique passwords for each platform.
- Never share login credentials—even with friends or teammates.
- Activate two-factor authentication for all major accounts.
- Regularly review app permissions and connected devices.
- Store sensitive documents and files in secure cloud services, not phones or desktops.
- Avoid logging into accounts on public or shared computers.

The Mental Health Toll of Viral Attention

The pressure that comes with being suddenly visible can take a serious toll on a young athlete's mental health. What starts as excitement may quickly turn into anxiety, paranoia, or burnout. The constant expectation to post, reply, promote, and perform can feel exhausting and intrusive.

Your child may experience:

- Difficulty sleeping
- Fear of judgment from peers or strangers
- Stress about saying or doing the wrong thing online

- Depression or mood swings tied to negative comments or cyberbullying
- A distorted self-image based on likes, views, and engagement metrics

As a parent, it's critical to stay tuned in to your child's emotional state and provide a safe space for them to express when the online attention becomes overwhelming.

Creating a Plan for Managing Exposure

Having a plan in place for managing social media and public attention helps your student-athlete stay in control of their narrative. Here are some practical steps:

Establish posting boundaries.

Decide in advance what types of content are on and off-limits. Personal life, family, politics, real-time locations, and injury updates should be discussed carefully.

Build a professional bio and visual identity.

This makes it easier to differentiate the real account from fakes. It also strengthens their brand presentation for NIL opportunities.

Keep a trusted adult or advisor in the loop.

Make sure your child has someone they can run things by—a parent, coach, mentor, or media-savvy friend who can help vet ideas before they go public.

Separate personal and professional accounts when appropriate.

Some athletes benefit from having a professional-facing profile and a private, friends-only account to decompress.

Plan downtime and digital detoxes.

Encourage your athlete to set screen-time limits, take breaks from posting, and focus on real-world relationships and recovery.

How Parents Can Help

You don't need to manage your child's accounts to protect them. You just need to stay informed, involved, and approachable. Here's how you can help without micromanaging:

- Talk regularly about what they're seeing, feeling, and dealing with online.
- Offer to help report impersonation or harassment cases.
- Help them establish a strategy for engagement and growth.
- Praise how they handle challenges or show restraint—not just the wins.
- Stay connected with their coach or school's compliance officer about digital conduct policies.

The goal isn't to scare your child away from the spotlight—but to help them navigate it wisely.

Final Thoughts

In the NIL era, fame can be fast, exciting, and financially rewarding—but it also comes with real vulnerabilities. Your student-athlete deserves to be celebrated and supported—but they also need to be protected.

Teach them that it's not just about going viral—it's about building something real, sustainable, and secure. Help them understand that a powerful public image starts with strong private habits. And most importantly, remind them that their worth isn't defined by likes, followers, or view counts. It's defined by who they are, not just how many people are watching.

Chapter 41: Peer Pressure, Influencer Culture, and Overspending

Why Your Child Needs a Financial Accountability Partner

In today's NIL-driven world, student-athletes are not only navigating the demands of their sport and academics—they're also managing money and image in a world shaped by influencer culture and constant comparison. Social media showcases highlight reels of brand deals, new cars, designer clothes, and luxury travel. It's easy for a student-athlete to feel like they're behind or not doing enough, even if they're doing just fine.

This chapter explores how peer pressure and online influence can lead to poor financial decisions, and why every student-athlete needs a financial accountability partner—a trusted person who helps them stay grounded, manage money wisely, and make decisions with long-term goals in mind.

The Pressure to "Keep Up"

Student-athletes used to compare stats, playing time, and school rankings. Now, they're comparing follower counts, NIL payouts, and sponsorships. NIL has introduced a financial scoreboard into the locker room, and not every athlete is equipped to handle it.

Some of the common pressures include:

- Teammates or peers flexing new clothes, jewelry, or cars

- Social media posts that showcase extravagant purchases or luxury trips
- Influencers promoting a lifestyle that's more about appearance than financial sense
- The belief that "if I don't spend, I won't look successful"
- Fear of missing out on the image of success, not just the reality of it

This culture creates an environment where spending is expected—even when it's unwise. And because many student-athletes are experiencing their first significant income, they often have no baseline for comparison or guidance.

Influencer Culture Is Not Real Life

Social media is a curated reality. Influencers, including other athletes, post highlights, not budgets. That "gifted" car might be a lease. That paid trip might be part of a one-time promotion. That new wardrobe might come with an unpaid invoice or sponsorship strings attached.

But from the outside looking in, it appears that everyone else is living better, spending more, and getting further ahead. This illusion can cause your child to:

- Overspend to match a false standard
- Use their NIL income for show rather than for savings or investments
- Feel pressure to accept every deal, even if it doesn't align with their values or brand
- Feel inadequate, anxious, or depressed when they can't "keep up"

Parents can help by reminding their child that most people—even successful influencers—don't show their full financial reality. Debt, taxes, obligations, and burnout rarely make the highlight reel.

The True Cost of Overspending

For student-athletes with NIL income, the issue isn't just spending—it's overspending without a plan. Many young athletes:

- Don't set aside money for taxes
- Spend before saving or investing
- Fail to budget for school, rent, travel, or emergencies
- Don't track where their money is going

Overspending in college isn't just a financial issue—it's a habit-forming one. Left unchecked, it sets the tone for how they'll manage money well into adulthood.

Consequences of NIL overspending include:

- Unexpected tax bills
- Inability to cover medical or travel expenses
- Missed opportunities to grow savings or invest
- Long-term financial insecurity even after major earnings

It's not about saying no to fun or lifestyle—it's about building financial habits that support independence, responsibility, and freedom.

Why Your Child Needs a Financial Accountability Partner

An accountability partner isn't someone who manages your child's money for them. It's someone who asks the right questions, provides a sounding board, and helps them slow down before making impulsive decisions.

This person can be:

- A parent or guardian
- A coach or mentor
- A financial advisor

- A trusted older teammate with strong money habits

Their role is to check in, offer perspective, and reinforce long-term thinking. Not to control—just to support.

An accountability partner helps student-athletes:

- Review spending decisions before they're made
- Talk through peer pressure moments or "should I buy this?" decisions
- Set realistic short- and long-term goals
- Celebrate smart choices and model consistency
- Build confidence in managing money intentionally

This partnership doesn't have to be formal. It starts with a conversation. But the impact can be enormous.

How to Talk to Your Child About Accountability

If you're a parent, this conversation may feel delicate. You want to support independence, not control. Here's how to approach it with empathy and respect.

Lead with your own experiences.

Talk about your own money mistakes and how having someone to talk to might have helped.

Focus on goals, not control.

Frame the conversation around what they want for their future—freedom, ownership, security—and how financial habits support those goals.

Ask, don't dictate.

"Would it help to have someone you check in with about money stuff?" is different from "You need to let me see your spending."

Offer support without judgment.

Create a space where they can share without fear of being shamed or lectured.

Encourage outside accountability if it's a better fit.
Sometimes a financial coach or advisor feels less personal and more objective—especially for older college students.

Building the Habit of Financial Check-Ins

Encourage your student-athlete to build a monthly or bi-weekly financial check-in with their accountability partner. These meetings can include:

- Reviewing income (from NIL, part-time work, etc.)
- Tracking spending and identifying trends
- Checking in on goals (saving for a car, travel, business)
- Looking ahead to future expenses or tax payments
- Talking through any big decisions (large purchases, new deals)

The idea is not to make it feel like homework—but like health for their wallet. Just as they track reps, practice hours, and meals, they should learn to track their money.

Final Thoughts

In an NIL world shaped by visibility, deals, and comparisons, your student-athlete needs more than just financial knowledge—they need financial support. Influencer culture, peer pressure, and the illusion of constant success can push even the most grounded athlete into reckless spending.

But with the right accountability, guidance, and habits, they can build a financial foundation that will serve them for decades.

Because long after the spotlight dims, it's not about what they spent—it's about what they built.

Let me know if you'd like this paired with a budgeting template, goal tracker, or accountability journal.

Chapter 42: When to Intervene – The Parent's Safety Net

Warning Signs That Your Child Needs Help and How to Build an Emergency Plan

In the NIL era, student-athletes are balancing more than just practice and classes. They're running small businesses, building brands, managing public images, and for many, handling money for the first time. That's a heavy load. While independence and responsibility are crucial parts of this journey, so is support. And sometimes, your student-athlete may not ask for help—even when they need it most.

This chapter is for parents who are trying to respect their child's autonomy but also recognize when it's time to step in. Whether the issue is emotional, financial, academic, or safety-related, you are the net beneath the tightrope. This chapter outlines warning signs to watch for, what types of intervention are appropriate, and how to build an emergency plan that everyone agrees on.

Understanding Your Role as the Safety Net

Your child may be technically an adult. They may be earning money, managing followers, and making big decisions. But they're also still learning. NIL has created a fast-moving environment where mistakes can have public and financial consequences. Even the most mature student-athlete needs guidance.

You don't need to be a watchdog or a warden. But you do need to be present, involved, and ready to act if things veer off course. You're not just their parent—you're part of their foundation.

Warning Signs That Your Child May Be Struggling

Here are common signals that your student-athlete may be overwhelmed, off-track, or in trouble—and may need a safety net:

Emotional or Behavioral Changes

- Mood swings, irritability, or shutting down emotionally
- Withdrawal from teammates, friends, or family
- Loss of interest in their sport or NIL activities
- Increase in anxiety or visible stress

Financial Red Flags

- Constantly running out of money despite earning from NIL
- Avoiding conversations about spending or taxes
- Large, impulsive purchases without a plan
- Asking for loans or advances

Academic or Athletic Warning Signs

- Missing classes, workouts, or study halls
- Declining grades or feedback from coaches
- Apathy toward school or practice commitments

Online Presence Shifts

- Deleting social media accounts suddenly
- Posting emotional, erratic, or uncharacteristic content
- Engaging in arguments or controversy online

- Sharing too much personal information

Health and Lifestyle Concerns

- Erratic sleep patterns
- Weight gain or loss, fatigue, or signs of burnout
- Frequent injuries or chronic stress without addressing them

If one or two of these things show up briefly, it may be situational. But if you start to see multiple signs persistently, it's time to ask questions and offer help.

How to Intervene Without Pushing Them Away

Knowing your child needs help is one thing. Getting them to accept that help is another. Here's how to approach intervention with care, respect, and effectiveness.

Start With Curiosity, Not Judgment

Use open-ended questions like:

"I've noticed you seem a little off lately. What's been on your mind?"

"Want to talk through what's been stressing you out?"

These are invitations, not accusations.

Normalize Struggle

Remind them that everyone needs help sometimes—especially when juggling as much as they are. Normalize therapy, tutoring, financial coaching, or mentorship.

Offer Options, Not Ultimatums

Give your student choices when possible.

"Would you prefer to talk to me, or should we find someone else to go over this with you?"

"Do you want help building a budget or would it be easier if I connected you with someone else?"

Respect Their Voice

Let them express how they feel, even if it's hard to hear. Listening is the foundation of trust—and trust makes intervention work.

Stay Consistent and Calm

If you're worried, keep checking in. Don't get discouraged if they brush you off the first time. They'll remember your presence when they're ready to talk.

Building an Emergency Plan in Advance

The best time to prepare for crisis is before it happens. Work with your student-athlete to build a mutual plan for how you'll both respond if things go sideways. This isn't just for big emergencies—it's for anything that feels overwhelming.

What to Include in an Emergency Plan:

1. **Who They Can Call (Besides You)**
2. Encourage them to list 2–3 trusted adults: a coach, mentor, mental health provider, older teammate, or family member.
3. **Signs It's Time to Ask for Help**
4. Agree on key indicators that mean they need to speak up—trouble sleeping, panicking about money, feeling depressed or stuck.
5. **What You Will and Won't Do**
6. Clarify boundaries:

- "I'm here to talk, not take over."
- "I'll only call your coach if it's a safety concern."
- "We'll handle problems together, not with blame."

1. **Mental Health Resources**
2. Save the numbers for on-campus mental health services, national hotlines, or a therapist they feel comfortable with.
3. **Financial Backup**
4. Set guidelines for when you'll help with money—e.g., emergency travel,

tax errors, or medical expenses—and when they're expected to manage things on their own.

5. **Digital Safety**
6. Talk about what to do if they're hacked, impersonated, or harassed online.

Scenarios Where Immediate Intervention Is Needed

Some situations call for stepping in, even if your child resists:

- **Serious mental health crisis** (suicidal thoughts, panic attacks, self-harm)
- **Physical injury that affects academics or athletics**
- **Signs of substance abuse or addiction**
- **Legal trouble or involvement with law enforcement**
- **NIL-related fraud, scams, or identity theft**
- **Ongoing isolation and withdrawal from all support systems**

In these cases, your responsibility as a parent overrides the desire to "let them figure it out." Just like you'd protect them from harm on the field, you're protecting them off of it.

Final Thoughts

Parenting a student-athlete in the NIL era requires a delicate balance—supporting their independence while remaining a consistent safety net. You may not be able to stop every mistake or prevent every moment of overwhelm, but you can show up, stay engaged, and create a system where they know they're never alone.

Your job isn't to catch them every time they fall. It's to be the steady hand that helps them back up—and the guide who helps them prepare before the fall ever happens.

Let me know if you'd like to turn this into a downloadable emergency plan worksheet for parents and student-athletes to fill out together.

Chapter 43: Culture and Cash: How Your Background Shapes Your Money Mindset

As a parent raising a student-athlete in the NIL era, you are more than just a cheerleader. You are their first coach in life, especially when it comes to money. Long before your child signs endorsement deals or opens a business account, they've already been learning how to think about money—by watching you.

Whether consciously or unconsciously, you've been teaching them through your words, your choices, and your reactions. And more often than not, your own financial habits were shaped by your upbringing, your culture, your community, and the world you were raised in.

This chapter is about owning that truth—not with guilt, but with clarity. Because how we think about money is deeply cultural, and if you want your child to have financial success, you first have to understand your own money story.

Your Money Lens: What Did You Learn Growing Up?

Every person carries a "money lens." This lens is shaped by what you saw, heard, and experienced during your childhood and teenage years. Maybe you grew up in a household where money was tight. Maybe it was taboo to talk about money at all. Maybe your parents did well financially, but never explained how.

Your money lens might be rooted in:

- Survival mode ("We can't afford that")
- Shame ("Money causes problems")
- Entitlement ("Money will always be there")
- Avoidance ("I just don't think about finances")
- Security ("We always had just enough")
- Scarcity ("We never had enough")

These lenses impact how you save, spend, invest, and even talk to your child about their NIL income. If you've never examined your lens, it's easy to pass down the same mindset—whether it's helpful or not.

Ask yourself:

- Did your family talk about bills and budgeting?
- Was there open conversation about saving or investing?
- How did your family view wealth? Was it admired, envied, resented, or ignored?
- How were financial mistakes handled—were they learning moments, or hidden secrets?

Culture, Community, and the Money Mindset

Now let's zoom out. Beyond your household, your culture and community also shaped your view of money. Race, ethnicity, class, religion, gender—all of these layers affect what financial behaviors are encouraged, discouraged, or stigmatized.

Below are common cultural influences—not to stereotype, but to help you recognize inherited narratives that may need updating.

1. The Black American Experience

Generational wealth in Black communities has historically been obstructed by systemic barriers: redlining, segregation, employment discrimination, and lack of access to capital. As a result, many Black families emphasized financial survival over wealth-building.

Cultural themes may include:

- Giving back to extended family, church, or community
- Prioritizing image (designer clothes, nice cars) as a form of status and pride
- Distrust of banks, investing, or "the system"
- Viewing financial conversations as private or uncomfortable

What to model now:

- Teach that ownership—of land, businesses, and investments—is real power
- Encourage open conversations about money, credit, and generational planning
- Shift the mindset from "get money" to "grow money"

2. The Immigrant or First-Generation Experience

Immigrant families often pass down discipline, sacrifice, and hard work. But financial education isn't always included. Money may be viewed as something to protect—not something to grow.

Cultural themes may include:

- Avoiding debt at all costs
- Sending money back home
- Fear of government systems (taxes, banks)
- Saving cash but avoiding investments

What to model now:

- Introduce responsible credit and its role in financial life
- Teach that investing is not a gamble, but a strategy for growth
- Show that it's possible to support family *and* build wealth

3. White Middle-Class or Affluent Upbringings

In many white or suburban households, money was available but rarely discussed. Wealth was assumed, but financial planning wasn't always modeled.

Cultural themes may include:

- College and home ownership seen as a "given"
- Little discussion about budgeting, debt, or long-term goals
- Financial struggles hidden or considered shameful

What to model now:

- Teach your student-athlete that income requires stewardship
- Don't assume they "get it"—talk openly about taxes, saving, and risk
- Prepare them to handle real-world money decisions, not just inherit habits

4. Rural, Working-Class, or Underserved Communities

Many rural or working-class families rely on cash income, side hustles, or local opportunities. Exposure to financial literacy may be limited by geography or school funding.

Cultural themes may include:

- "We get by with what we have"
- Hard work praised over financial strategy
- Banks or online tools underused
- Investing seen as risky or unnecessary

What to model now:

- Emphasize the difference between income and wealth
- Use technology to bridge gaps (apps, online learning, podcasts)
- Introduce the idea that money can work for you—not just the other

way around

Breaking Generational Cycles

If you didn't learn about budgeting, saving, or investing as a child, you're not alone. Most parents didn't. But you're here now, trying to do better. That's powerful.

Here's how to begin breaking unhelpful financial cycles:

1. **Acknowledge your own gaps.**
2. Say it out loud: "I didn't learn this as a kid, but I want us to learn together now."
3. **Speak the language.**
4. Normalize words like "budget," "interest," "compound growth," "taxes," and "credit score."
5. **Model curiosity.**
6. Let your student-athlete see you asking questions, reading, or working with professionals.
7. **Avoid shame.**
8. Don't project guilt about past mistakes. Focus on the future.
9. **Keep it simple.**
10. You don't need to teach estate planning in high school. Start with budgeting, saving, and taxes.

Avoiding Cultural Stereotypes in NIL

The NIL world comes with attention, assumptions, and sometimes unfair narratives. Your child might face subtle or direct messages like:

- "You're just an athlete, not a businessperson."
- "You don't need to worry about taxes—you're young."
- "Black athletes just spend all their money."
- "First-gen kids don't know how to manage income."

- "Girls in sports don't earn as much—it's not worth worrying about."

Shut that down. These stereotypes are dangerous, limiting, and flat-out false. As a parent, you are your child's defense against these narratives. Help them see that:

- Financial literacy is for everyone
- They have the right to ask questions, get professional help, and protect their brand
- Money isn't about where you come from—it's about what you do with it

Your Child is Watching

Your student-athlete will earn money. That's a blessing—but also a responsibility. They will look to you to interpret what that money means. You don't need to be perfect. But you do need to be intentional.

They are watching you when:

- You make a budget—or avoid one
- You explain a tax form—or ignore it
- You say, "We'll save up for that"—or "We deserve this today"

You are their first financial role model. Whether you realize it or not.

Chapter 44: Navigating NIL as Divorced Parents: A Unified Approach to Financial Literacy

Being a parent to a student-athlete already comes with high stakes. But when you're a divorced parent navigating the evolving NIL (Name, Image, and Likeness) landscape, the challenges multiply. Different households. Different philosophies. Different financial priorities. And one student-athlete caught in the middle.

This chapter is dedicated to parents who may no longer be together as a couple but are united by one critical mission: preparing your child for life, leadership, and financial literacy in the NIL era.

Divorce doesn't disqualify you from being an excellent financial role model. In fact, it gives you an even more important role: to model how collaboration, communication, and consistency can thrive—even in complexity.

A New Financial Chapter, Together

Whether your divorce was amicable, turbulent, or somewhere in between, the truth is that your student-athlete is now entering a new life phase that will require structure, support, and guidance from both parents.

They need more than sideline cheers. They need help managing money, taxes, contracts, business decisions, and brand development. They need financial wisdom—not family conflict.

Let's walk through how to handle NIL in a co-parenting situation, while also modeling responsibility, trust, and teamwork for your child.

The Emotional Layer: Divorce, Identity, and Influence

Divorce changes more than living arrangements. It reshapes communication patterns, decision-making power, and emotional dynamics. Many student-athletes with divorced parents feel torn:

- Who do I listen to when advice conflicts?
- What if one parent pushes for deals while the other says to wait?
- Who handles taxes if I live with one but earn money in both households?

Parents, your job isn't to "win" influence—it's to create clarity.

Your student-athlete must know that both parents are rooting for them—and that NIL is about their future, not about revisiting the past.

Step 1: Have an NIL-Co-Parenting Conversation (Even If It's Hard)

Schedule time to meet, call, or video chat specifically about NIL. This isn't a conversation about child support or parenting time. It's about your child's income, responsibility, and brand.

Topics to align on:

- How will you communicate about NIL matters? (Group text? Email? Shared folder?)
- Who will track deals, payments, and documentation?
- Will both parents be listed as emergency contacts for contracts, banking, or legal needs?
- What's the tone you want to model—respectful, collaborative, united?

You don't need to agree on everything. But you must agree on this: the student-athlete comes first.

Step 2: Establish a Unified NIL Financial System

Your student-athlete will likely be receiving payments, merchandise, or sponsorships. That means you need a central way to track what's happening—even if the athlete lives primarily with one parent.

Tips for organizing finances across two households:

- Use a shared spreadsheet or money app (like Mint or Monarch) with limited view-only access
- Set up a joint email account for NIL communication
- Agree on who oversees tax filing, banking, and professional services
- Keep all contracts, 1099s, and receipts in a shared Google Drive or Dropbox

This isn't about control. It's about visibility, consistency, and adulting—together.

Step 3: Avoid Competing Financial Philosophies

One of the biggest risks in a divorced household is contradictory money advice. One parent may say "Save everything." The other might say "Enjoy the moment."

These mixed messages confuse your student-athlete and create tension. It turns smart financial decisions into loyalty tests.

What to do:

- Schedule a parent-only check-in once a quarter to revisit goals
- Agree on foundational principles: budgeting, saving, taxes, no spending sprees
- Use a financial advisor or CPA as a neutral third-party to help guide decisions

- Keep arguments about money philosophies away from the athlete

You're not just teaching your child how to earn. You're teaching them how to listen, discern, and lead.

Step 4: Clarify Tax Filing and Custody Considerations

If your student-athlete is earning NIL income and is still listed as a dependent, tax time can get complicated.

Questions to address early:

- Which parent claims the student on taxes?
- If the child is filing a return for NIL income, who is responsible for helping them prepare it?
- Will earnings affect FAFSA or other financial aid applications?

Tip: Consult a tax professional familiar with divorced-family dynamics and student-athlete income. Don't assume. Don't guess. Do it right.

Step 5: Present a Unified Front to Brands and Professionals

When brands approach your child—or when your child begins working with agents, managers, or collectives—it's important they see professionalism, not division.

If brands feel like they're caught in the middle of parental disagreements, they may walk away. Or worse, they may try to manipulate the situation.

What professionals need to see:

- Clear communication channels
- Parental involvement that supports—not dictates—decisions
- A student-athlete who knows who to go to with questions
- A consistent message about values, expectations, and long-term goals

Let your family structure be a strength, not a liability.

Step 6: Talk About Financial Literacy Together

This book is about helping your student-athlete become financially wise—not just rich. One of the best things you can do as co-parents is to be equally involved in your child's financial education.

How to do that in a split household:

- Pick a monthly topic and share notes or resources (e.g., "Let's both talk to them about taxes this month.")
- Attend webinars, NIL workshops, or school events together when possible
- Read the same book or listen to the same podcast, then discuss it as a family
- Praise your child when they make a smart money move—whether they did it with your help or the other parent's

When both parents are financially literate, the child feels supported—not split.

Step 7: Set Boundaries Around NIL Money

Sometimes, NIL income creates new tension: one parent feels entitled to a say in how money is spent, even if the student lives with the other. Or one parent begins expecting financial support from the athlete.

Here's the truth: NIL money belongs to the athlete.

Unless you are managing it legally or contractually (through a trust or business structure), you should not control or depend on your child's income.

Set clear boundaries:

- NIL money is not child support

- NIL money is not a bargaining chip
- NIL money is not family income

Instead, help your child learn to:

- Save 20–30% of every deal
- Spend intentionally
- Ask for help before signing
- Plan for taxes and future goals

If you need financial support, be transparent. But don't pressure. Your student-athlete is still learning.

Step 8: Celebrate Milestones—Together

Don't let NIL become just another thing that highlights what's different between your households. Let it become a bridge.

When your child:

- Lands a deal
- Files taxes for the first time
- Buys their first car with cash
- Creates a budget
- Makes their first investment

Celebrate that. Together if possible.

Say: "We're proud of you."

Say: "You handled that like a professional."

Say: "Keep going. We've got your back."

Because that's the real win.

Final Thoughts: Divorce Doesn't Mean Disconnected

This chapter wasn't about being perfect. It's about being present.

You don't need to be in the same house, same city, or even the same chapter of life as your former partner to show up for your student-athlete. You just need a shared vision:

> *That your child deserves to build a life of financial freedom, confidence, and clarity.*

NIL has introduced brand-new dynamics—but it also introduces brand-new chances to lead, guide, and grow.

You may no longer be spouses—but you are forever partners in raising someone exceptional.

Lead with respect. Parent with purpose. Learn together.

Because in the NIL era, legacy isn't about wealth—it's about wisdom.

You've still got time to give them both.

Chapter 45: Impact on Financial Aid and Scholarships: What Every Parent Needs to Know

As exciting as NIL earnings can be, they introduce a new layer of complexity when it comes to how your student-athlete qualifies for financial aid, scholarships, and other forms of support. The truth is: **NIL income isn't "free money" in the eyes of financial aid offices, the federal government, or your child's school**.

This section will walk you through how NIL earnings can affect:

- Pell Grants and other federal aid
- Institutional aid or need-based scholarships
- FAFSA filing
- State and local assistance programs

1. FAFSA: Where NIL Income Gets Reported

FAFSA (Free Application for Federal Student Aid) uses **income from two years prior** (the "prior-prior year" rule) to determine your child's financial aid eligibility. That means NIL income earned today may not affect aid *immediately*—but it will in future years.

For example:

- If your child earns NIL income in 2025, it could reduce their eligibility for aid in the **2027–2028** school year.

Where it shows up:

- If your child files their own taxes and reports NIL earnings, that income is factored into their Student Contribution on the FAFSA.
- If you, as a parent, manage NIL earnings through a family business, or deposit income into a joint account, it could potentially be counted as parental income.

Important: NIL income is considered **untaxed income**, **taxable income**, or **business income**, depending on how it's earned and reported. Consult a tax professional to report it accurately.

2. Pell Grant Eligibility Could Be Affected

Pell Grants are awarded based on financial need, determined by your Expected Family Contribution (EFC), now called the **Student Aid Index (SAI)**.

If NIL income increases your child's income significantly:

- Their SAI goes up
- Their Pell eligibility may go down—or be eliminated entirely

For families who depend on federal grants and aid to make college affordable, this could be a painful surprise. That's why early planning matters.

3. State Grants and Need-Based Scholarships

Many states offer their own grant or tuition-assistance programs, often based on FAFSA data or household income.

In addition, colleges may offer:

- **Need-based institutional scholarships**
- **Athletic scholarships with need-based supplements**
- **Emergency financial aid or housing assistance**

NIL earnings, especially if not documented clearly, may disqualify your student from these programs.

Questions to ask your school's financial aid office:

- "Does NIL income affect my child's aid package?"
- "Will my child's athletic scholarship be reduced if they earn more money?"
- "If they file a tax return as an independent contractor, how will that impact future aid?"
- "Does the school count NIL earnings as income in internal aid formulas?"

4. Impact on Work-Study Eligibility

Federal work-study is also awarded based on financial need. If your student-athlete earns substantial NIL income, they may:

- Lose eligibility for work-study
- Be expected to self-fund more of their college expenses

For many families, this trade-off is worth it—but it should still be understood up front.

5. Housing, Food, and Public Assistance Programs

If your family or your student-athlete qualifies for programs such as:

- SNAP (food stamps)
- Section 8 housing

- State-based healthcare subsidies
- Local assistance for low-income students

... then NIL income could put those benefits at risk. Many programs have income thresholds, and NIL earnings—even if inconsistent—may push your child above those limits.

Tip: Encourage your child to meet with a financial aid counselor and social services case manager *before* signing NIL deals that could affect aid.

6. Athletic Scholarships & School-Based Aid

NIL income does **not** reduce or "count against" a student-athlete's athletic scholarship from an NCAA compliance perspective. However, some schools may adjust institutional aid packages based on total income—especially private colleges.

Ask directly:

- "Will NIL earnings reduce my child's institutional need-based scholarship?"
- "Is there a cap on outside income that affects university support?"
- "How does your school interpret income for aid purposes?"

7. Tax Filing and Aid Timing

Sometimes families delay tax filing or make errors on FAFSA that delay aid processing. NIL income complicates this even more.

Avoid delays by:

- Filing taxes early and accurately with a CPA familiar with NIL and self-employment
- Making sure your child uses the correct FAFSA year (check the income look-back period)
- Keeping accurate records of all NIL deals, invoices, and 1099 forms

8. Long-Term Financial Tradeoffs

Here's the hard truth: NIL income may reduce aid—but that doesn't automatically mean it's a bad thing.

Would you rather:

- Qualify for a $5,000 Pell Grant, or
- Help your child manage $30,000 in NIL earnings with a strong financial plan?

The key is **understanding the impact, running the numbers, and planning ahead.**

Summary: What Parents Should Do Right Now

Meet with a financial aid officer

Have a frank conversation about how your child's NIL income might affect aid, both now and in future years.

Talk to a CPA or tax preparer who understands FAFSA

Filing taxes correctly can avoid overreporting or underreporting income.

Keep meticulous records

Have your child track NIL income, expenses, and contracts. This helps during audits, tax prep, and appeals.

Ask about "professional judgment" or "special circumstances"

Financial aid offices have discretion to make exceptions. If your financial situation changes or if NIL income is irregular, appeal processes may be available.

Plan for the long-term

Don't avoid NIL just to preserve aid. Instead, plan around the income—so it serves your child, not surprises them.

Bottom Line:

NIL income can be a blessing—but it's not a blank check. As a parent, your job is to help your student-athlete make informed decisions, stay compliant, and maximize both their financial aid *and* their NIL opportunity.

Chapter 46: NIL Income and Financial Aid: What Every Parent Needs to Know

When student-athletes began signing NIL deals, it unlocked more than financial opportunity. It also introduced financial complexity—especially for families relying on financial aid, scholarships, and public support systems to make college possible.

As a parent, your job isn't just to celebrate the money coming in. It's to understand how that money might affect your child's ability to receive Pell Grants, school-based need aid, work-study eligibility, or other state and federal programs.

This chapter takes a deep dive into one of the most misunderstood aspects of NIL: the impact it can have on financial aid.

Even a $5,000 NIL deal can change a student's financial aid picture—either this year or in years to come. That's why this issue can't be ignored, and why you need to be proactive, informed, and strategic.

Understanding the Financial Aid Landscape

Before we break down how NIL affects financial aid, let's define the major forms of aid student-athletes might receive:

1. **Federal Aid** – Based on the FAFSA (Free Application for Federal Student Aid), includes:

- Pell Grants (need-based)
- Federal Supplemental Educational Opportunity Grants (FSEOG)
- Federal Work-Study
- Federal student loans (subsidized and unsubsidized)

1. **State Aid** – Based on state rules; may include:

- Tuition assistance
- State scholarships and grants

1. **Institutional Aid** – Aid provided by the college or university, including:

- Need-based grants
- Athletic scholarships
- Merit scholarships
- Emergency aid funds

1. **Private Scholarships** – Aid from nonprofits, foundations, or private donors.

All of these categories can be impacted—directly or indirectly—by how NIL income is earned, reported, or perceived by the awarding body.

FAFSA and the "Prior-Prior Year" Rule

The FAFSA doesn't look at current income. It looks at income from **two years ago** (the "prior-prior year" rule).

Example: The FAFSA for the **2025–2026** school year looks at **2023** income.

That means NIL income your child earns now could reduce aid **two years later**.

Parents must understand that:

- NIL income earned in high school could affect freshman-year aid
- NIL income earned during freshman year might affect junior-year aid

This delayed effect catches many families by surprise.

How NIL Income Is Reported on the FAFSA

FAFSA separates income into:

- **Taxed income** (W-2, 1099, business income)
- **Untaxed income** (child support received, contributions to retirement accounts)

Most NIL income is classified as **self-employment income** and will:

- Appear on a Schedule C if your child files taxes
- Be considered **taxable income** and counted toward the Student Aid Index (SAI)

If your student files a tax return:

- The IRS Data Retrieval Tool may pull their income directly into FAFSA

Even modest NIL income—$5,000 to $10,000—can raise the student's financial responsibility in the federal formula, which lowers aid eligibility.

Parent vs. Student Income

If you're managing your child's NIL income (e.g., via joint accounts or using it to pay household bills), **some of that income may be considered parental income**.

This is especially relevant if:

- You file jointly with your child
- You claim your child as a dependent but use their income
- The NIL income is deposited into your account

You need to structure NIL finances carefully to avoid unintentionally increasing the family's reported income on the FAFSA.

Pell Grants and Federal Aid

Pell Grants are strictly need-based. If your student's income or your household income rises, they may:

- Lose eligibility for Pell
- Receive a reduced grant

Even modest NIL earnings can affect this. Other federal aid (like subsidized loans and work-study) can also be impacted.

State Aid Rules Differ

Many states use FAFSA data to determine eligibility, but others apply their own rules.

Some states:

- Set specific income thresholds
- Require separate applications
- Review aid annually rather than using FAFSA's two-year delay

Call your state's higher education office to find out how NIL earnings might affect state-based aid.

Institutional Aid and Merit Awards

Colleges and universities set their own internal policies.
Some may:

- Adjust need-based aid for students who earn outside income
- Require updated income documentation annually
- Combine NIL income with “expected family contribution”

This is especially important at private schools, where institutional grants can be substantial.

Work-Study and Campus Jobs

Work-study eligibility can decrease if a student earns significant income through NIL. Work-study is still valuable, though:

- It provides on-campus connections
- It may offer academic/career relevance
- It builds financial discipline in structured ways

A student who earns $10,000 from NIL may not qualify for work-study the next year.

Public Assistance Impacts

If your family depends on:

- SNAP (food stamps)
- Medicaid or CHIP
- Free/reduced lunch
- Section 8 or subsidized housing

... then NIL income may put those programs at risk. Some assistance programs consider household income, while others look at individual income.

This is especially critical if your child is still considered part of your household while earning NIL money.

Dependency Status and FAFSA

Even if your student files their own taxes, they may still be considered **dependent** on your FAFSA unless:

- They're 24 or older
- They're married or supporting a child
- They're an emancipated minor
- They're a veteran or ward of the court

This means **your income AND their NIL income** gets reported.

There are limited paths to declaring a student independent, but those require documentation and special review.

"Professional Judgment" and Appeals

Financial aid offices can adjust FAFSA numbers under special circumstances, such as:

- Loss of income
- One-time financial windfall
- High medical bills
- Sudden NIL opportunity that skews the formula

Ask about **Professional Judgment** or **Special Circumstances Appeal**. This may preserve need-based aid in years when NIL income temporarily rises.

Planning Tips for Parents

Here's how to avoid surprises:

1. **Track All NIL Income**

- Use apps or spreadsheets
- Keep receipts, 1099s, and contracts

1. **File Taxes with Strategy**

- Consider when to claim your child as a dependent
- Work with a CPA who understands NIL

1. **Create Separate Financial Accounts**

- NIL money should go into a student-owned checking account

1. **Communicate With Financial Aid Office**

- Ask how NIL will affect aid before the next FAFSA cycle

1. **Plan Ahead for Reductions**

- If Pell or school-based grants will be reduced, save enough now to offset

Case Example

Jaylen is a sophomore wide receiver. He earns $15,000 in NIL in 2024.

- In 2026–27, his FAFSA reflects that income.
- His Pell Grant drops by $2,500.

- His school reduces institutional need-based aid by $2,000.
- Total lost aid = $4,500

But with strong planning, Jaylen saved $6,000 and used a CPA to file properly—minimizing penalties and keeping eligibility.

Final Word for Parents

Don't fear NIL. Plan for it.

When your student-athlete begins earning, it's a proud moment. But it also comes with strings—especially when it intersects with aid.

NIL doesn't have to cancel financial support—but it does require smart timing, accurate reporting, and proactive communication.

You've made it this far. Keep showing up, keep asking questions, and keep building a path where your child can thrive—on the field, in the classroom, and in the world of finance.

Chapter 47: Breaking Down the Market for Parents

You've probably heard people say:

"The market is crashing!"

"The S&P 500 is hot right now!"

"The Fed raised interest rates again."

"Inflation is out of control!"

It's the kind of noise that makes you want to change the channel — especially when you're focused on helping your child navigate NIL, recruiting, classes, and maybe even paying bills.

But here's the thing: this financial stuff? It's not rocket science. It's a game — just like sports. And once you learn the rules, the players, and the plays, it starts to make sense.

There's momentum. There are hot streaks and cold stretches. There are coaches, teams, and strategies. It's not about being a math genius — it's about getting in the game and staying consistent.

Let's break it down — in plain language — so you can help guide your student-athlete, and maybe even build something stronger for your own financial future.

What Is the Stock Market?

The stock market is just a place where people buy and sell small pieces of companies. These pieces are called "stocks." Buying a stock means you own part of that company — whether it's Nike, Apple, or Amazon.

It's like owning a piece of a team. When that team wins, you win too. Your investment grows if the company grows.

What Makes the Market Go Up or Down?

Supply and demand. That's it.

If everyone wants to buy, the price goes up.

If everyone wants to sell, the price goes down.

What changes that demand? News, interest rates, elections, company earnings, global events — and sometimes just hype or fear.

Think of it like a player's buzz before the draft. If the media loves them, their stock rises. One bad headline? Their value drops. The market works the same way.

Stock Market vs. Economy: What's the Difference?

The stock market is like the scoreboard — it reflects what people *think* will happen in the future.

The economy is the actual game — people working, companies making money, goods being sold.

Sometimes they match up. Sometimes they don't. A team might look good on paper, but underperform on the field. Same with markets and the economy.

Is Investing Risky?

It can be. If you put all your money in one stock, and that company fails, you could lose big.

But if you spread your money across many companies using something called an "index fund" or "ETF," your risk goes way down. You've got depth on your team. One player struggles, but the rest carry the load.

What's the Smart Way to Invest?

You don't need to be flashy or complicated. The best approach for most people is:

- Invest in index funds or ETFs (which include many companies)
- Use a Roth IRA or a brokerage account
- Keep your money invested over the long term
- Be consistent — invest a little every month

It's like running a strong offense — simple plays, executed well, win games.

When's the Best Time to Start?

Now. Always now.

Just like an athlete needs time in the weight room to grow stronger, your money needs time in the market to grow. The earlier you start, the more time it has to build.

What's the S&P 500?

It's a list of the 500 biggest U.S. companies. When people say "the market is up," they often mean the S&P 500 is up.

Think of it like the AP Top 25 in college sports. If most of the teams are winning, the rankings rise. Same concept.

Bull Market vs. Bear Market

- A bull market is when prices are rising and people feel confident
- A bear market is when prices fall 20% or more and everyone starts to panic

It's the difference between a winning streak and a slump. In both cases, staying level-headed matters most.

Should You Sell When Prices Drop?

No. That's when most people lose money.

Imagine pulling your kid out of the game after one missed shot. Doesn't make sense, right? Same here. You've got to let the game play out. Stay invested.

How Much Money Do I Need to Start?

Not much. You can start with $50 or $100. You can even buy partial shares of big companies.

You don't have to be rich to begin. Just get in the game. Reps build results.

Can I Make Fast Money?

You *can* — but that's not investing, that's gambling.

Trying to make fast money in the market is like jacking up half-court shots and hoping for the best. You might hit one. But you're more likely to lose.

Real investing is about playing smart, consistent ball — high-percentage shots and good defense.

What's an ETF?

An ETF is a bundle of different stocks or bonds you buy all at once. It gives you variety without having to pick individual companies.

It's like drafting an entire all-star team with one move. Safer. Smarter.

Is Investing Just for Rich People?

No. Investing is how people *become* wealthy. You don't need a lot to get started — just commitment and consistency.

Think of it like your child's athletic journey. No one starts in the spotlight. But day by day, it builds.

Stock vs. Bond

- A stock means you *own* a part of a company.
- A bond means you *loan* money to a company or the government.

Stocks have more potential upside — and more risk. Bonds are slower, but steadier.

It's like a flashy freshman vs. a seasoned vet. You want both in your lineup.

What's Diversification?

Diversification means spreading your money out. Don't put all your money into one company, one industry, or one idea.

It's like building a balanced team. You don't want five point guards on the court. You need strength, speed, size, shooters, and defenders.

Why "Buy Low, Sell High" Is Hard

Everyone says "buy low, sell high," but emotions get in the way.

People panic when prices drop and buy when everything's hyped up. Reverse that. Stay cool. Think long-term.

You don't trade your kid after a bad game — you trust their potential. Do the same with your investments.

What Should I Invest In?

Start with:

- Total market or S&P 500 index funds
- Low-cost ETFs
- Reinvesting dividends
- Long-term goals

It's not about being flashy — it's about getting buckets with smart, simple plays.

What's a Recession?

It's when the economy slows down — job cuts, less spending, and more uncertainty.

It's not the end of the world. It's just a rebuilding season. Happens every few years. Winners are the ones who stay calm and keep working.

Do I Need a Financial Advisor?

Not to start. You can use apps like:

- Fidelity
- Vanguard

- Schwab
- M1 Finance
- Public
- Betterment

But if your child's NIL money grows, or you've got complex tax issues or multiple income streams, it's smart to work with a fiduciary — a financial coach who works in your best interest.

What's the Golden Rule of Investing?

Start early. Be consistent. Don't panic.

That's it. That's the game plan.

What's a Dividend?

Some companies pay you a little bonus — called a dividend — just for holding their stock.

It's like your kid earning extra scholarship money just for showing up and staying eligible. Bonus points for doing what you were already doing.

How Often Should I Check My Investments?

Not every day. Once a month is fine. Once a quarter is better.

Checking every five minutes is like constantly watching the scoreboard during practice. Focus on execution, not every little stat.

What's a Stock Split?

If a company's stock gets too expensive, it might split its shares.

If you had 1 share at $100, now you have 2 shares at $50. Same value — just easier to buy.

It's like changing your jersey number — you're still on the team.

What's a Market Correction?

If the market drops 10%, that's called a correction. It's normal and even healthy.

It's like halftime after a rough stretch. You regroup, adjust, and come back stronger.

Should I Invest During a Down Market?

Yes. That's when everything's on sale.

Same product. Better deal.

You wouldn't pass up the best cleats on discount — same with great companies at lower prices.

Can I Lose Everything?

If you bet it all on one company, yes.

But if you spread it out across funds and stay diversified, the risk drops a lot. The market has *always* bounced back — even after crashes.

A deep bench keeps you in the game.

Mutual Funds vs. ETFs

Both are bundles of investments.

- Mutual funds: slower, may have higher fees
- ETFs: faster, cheaper, more flexible

ETFs are the modern play. Easier to manage and better for beginners.

Why Do Interest Rates Matter?

Interest rates are the cost of borrowing. When they go up, loans (car, home, business) get more expensive. That slows spending and cools the economy.

It's like when your coach turns up the conditioning. It hurts now, but builds discipline for later.

What's Dollar-Cost Averaging?

It means putting in the same amount of money on a regular schedule — no matter what the market is doing.

$100/month. Rain or shine.

It's like showing up to practice, even on the days you're tired. Reps compound.

Final Thoughts: Play the Long Game

The financial world isn't reserved for the wealthy or the Ivy League. It's for all of us — especially parents who want to help their student-athletes win on and off the field.

Build your plan like you build a team:

- Diversify
- Stay consistent
- Think long-term
- Tune out the noise

Your child is building a brand, a career, a legacy. Help them build a financial future to match.

And as you guide them, don't forget — you're allowed to build, too. Your future matters just as much as theirs.

Chapter 48: Wrong Examples for your Student Athlete

Real Talk: Learn from the Legends... and Their Mistakes

Let's take a moment and be honest.

As a parent, it's natural to want your child to enjoy their success — especially after all the early mornings, long road trips, and sacrifices that went into getting that scholarship or NIL deal. But the last thing you want is for their money to disappear faster than it came in.

Here's the truth: just because a young athlete earns money doesn't mean they know how to manage it. And sadly, history has shown us what happens when there's no plan, no boundaries, and no trusted financial guidance.

The following stories are not meant to shame. They're meant to teach. These are real athletes — some household names — who made millions and still ended up broke, struggling, or starting over. Help your child understand that money without a strategy is a short-term victory. But money with a purpose? That's legacy.

1. Allen Iverson (NBA)

Career Earnings: $200+ million

What Happened: Lavish spending, flying friends on private jets, gifting jewelry, and spending thousands in a single trip to the mall. His generosity had no limits — but neither did his expenses. Divorce and lack of financial planning made things worse.

How He Survived: Reebok had the foresight to set up a $32 million trust for him — which he can't touch until age 55. That move likely saved his future.

Lesson: Just because you're earning doesn't mean you're building wealth. Have something set aside that you can't touch until later in life.

2. Antoine Walker (NBA)

Career Earnings: $108 million

What Happened: Bad real estate deals, supporting 70+ friends and family members, and a high-roller lifestyle led to bankruptcy two years after retirement.

Lesson: Saying "no" doesn't make you selfish. It makes you smart. You can't carry everyone, or you'll sink with them.

3. Vince Young (NFL)

Career Earnings: $35 million

What Happened: $5,000 a week at The Cheesecake Factory. Buying out all the seats on Southwest flights. Zero financial discipline. Trusted the wrong people. Filed for bankruptcy in 2014.

Lesson: Even moderate wealth can disappear if you don't know how to manage it. NIL money feels big now — but it's small if you burn through it without a plan.

4. Delonte West (NBA)

Career Earnings: $16 million

What Happened: Poor money decisions, personal struggles, and a lack of mental health support. Years after playing in the NBA, he was seen panhandling on the street.

How He's Rebuilding: With help from Mark Cuban, he entered rehab and is working toward recovery.

Lesson: Mental health and financial health are connected. Don't ignore either.

5. Bernie Kosar (NFL)

Career Earnings: $20+ million

What Happened: Opened dozens of checking accounts and business partnerships — most of which failed. Tried to be everyone's financial savior. Filed for bankruptcy.

Lesson: You are not a bank. Not every friend or relative needs access to your income. Boundaries are financial protection.

6. Lenny Dykstra (MLB)

Career Earnings: $36 million

What Happened: Lived large, borrowed heavily, and invested in risky business ventures. Declared bankruptcy in 2009 and later went to prison for fraud.

Lesson: Being bold with your money without a plan doesn't make you a boss — it makes you a liability to yourself.

7. Mike Tyson (Boxing)

Career Earnings: Over $400 million

What Happened: Mansions, exotic animals, fleets of luxury cars, and a million-dollar-a-month lifestyle. Filed for bankruptcy in 2003.

Where He Is Now: He's rebuilt his career with a podcast, entertainment, and cannabis ventures — but it took decades.

Lesson: It's not about how much you make — it's about how much you keep.

8. JaMarcus Russell (NFL)

Career Earnings: $40 million

What Happened: One of the biggest rookie contracts in NFL history, but little structure or accountability. Spent on jewelry, cars, and hype — and never became a consistent starter.

Lesson: Earning power means nothing if you're not ready to handle the responsibility that comes with it.

9. Sheryl Swoopes (WNBA)

Career Earnings: Millions from salary and endorsements

What Happened: A trailblazer in women's sports who filed for bankruptcy after poor investments and mismanagement by advisors.

Lesson: Even pioneers need a plan. Representation and inspiration don't guarantee financial literacy — guidance does.

10. Evander Holyfield (Boxing)

Career Earnings: $200+ million

What Happened: Bought a 109-room mansion, had 11 kids with multiple partners, and maintained an unsustainable lifestyle. Lost his home and faced financial disaster.

Lesson: No matter how iconic your status, money that isn't managed eventually runs out. Lifestyle inflation is real.

Final Word to Parents: Be the Reminder They Need

These stories aren't just headlines. They're lived realities.

So what can you do as a parent?

- **Bring these stories up in conversation.** Not to scare — but to teach.
- **Remind your student-athlete:** You don't need tiger cubs and private

jets to be successful.

- **Help them set limits.** Saying "no" today helps them say "yes" to freedom tomorrow.
- **Encourage them to have a plan.** Budget. Save. Invest.
- **Normalize advisors, not enablers.** They need someone who knows money — not just someone who nods yes.

Because whether your child makes $10K or $10 million through NIL, what matters most is what they *do* with it.

Let's help them make sure their name, image, and likeness become more than just a temporary paycheck.

Let's help them build something that lasts.

Chapter 49: Every Athlete Needs a Game Plan (So Does Every Parent)

Think of your child's financial future like a championship season. You wouldn't send them into a game without a coach, a playbook, or a clear role. Same goes for money.

NIL may feel like a quick payday, but without a financial game plan — a strategy for how to grow and protect that money — even a strong season can end in regret. That's where a smart **portfolio** comes in.

A portfolio is just a fancy word for a lineup — a team of investments. Each one has a job to do. Some are built to score, some to defend, some to step in when things go sideways.

If you're a parent trying to help your athlete think bigger than the next endorsement deal or brand collab, here's how you talk to them about building a *financial* team that wins.

What's in a Portfolio? Think Roles, Not Just Numbers

A portfolio is a mix of different types of investments — your child's personal financial starting five. And just like no winning team is made up of all point guards or all post players, a good portfolio needs variety.

Here's the breakdown:

- **Stocks** are the scorers — aggressive, high-risk, high-reward

- **Bonds** are the defense — reliable, steady, protective
- **Cash** is the bench — ready to step in for emergencies
- **ETFs, Mutual Funds, and Real Estate** are your utility players — flexible, versatile, and often low-cost

If your child throws all their NIL money into one "hot" stock, it's like betting the season on one player staying healthy and hot all year. We all know how that turns out.

The better play? Diversify. Build depth. Balance the floor.

Why Diversification Matters

Imagine your child's team loses their star player halfway through the season. If the roster is deep, the team adjusts and still competes. But if it's a one-player show, the season's over.

Same with money.

Putting all of their NIL income into one stock, one property, or one crypto coin is gambling, not investing. When the market drops (and it will), they need other investments to hold them up — not drag them down.

Help them build a **team** — not a highlight reel.

Three Portfolio "Teams" to Choose From

Every athlete has a style. Some play fast. Some play smart and slow. Some are all-in on the long game. Same goes for investing.

Depending on your child's age, goals, and personality, they'll want a different financial lineup.

1. The Conservative Portfolio — Protect the Lead

This is the slow-it-down, manage-the-clock strategy. Heavy on bonds, light on stocks. Prioritizes stability over growth.

For athletes who:

- Need the money soon (within 5 years)

- Are cautious about risk
- Already have a solid base and want to protect it

Pros:

- Lower risk
- More predictable
- Easier to manage during downturns

Cons:

- Less growth
- May not keep up with inflation

Think of it as playing not to lose.

2. The Moderate Portfolio — Balanced and Flexible

This is your two-way team. A mix of growth (stocks) and stability (bonds). The athlete equivalent of a forward who can score *and* defend.

For athletes who:

- Have 5–10 year goals
- Want to build wealth steadily
- Don't like chaos, but still want to grow

Pros:

- Well-rounded
- Manages risk without killing potential
- Good for most college-age athletes

Cons:

- Not flashy

- Still vulnerable during market drops

Think of it as running a balanced offense — smart plays that work in different situations.

3. The Aggressive Portfolio — Go for the Win

This strategy leans heavy into stocks. It's built to grow fast over time but comes with mood swings and big risks. Not for short-term needs.

For athletes who:

- Are in their teens or twenties
- Don't need the money for 10+ years
- Are comfortable watching the market rise and fall

Pros:

- Maximum long-term growth potential
- Ideal for early wealth building
- Takes full advantage of time and compound interest

Cons:

- Big dips along the way
- Requires strong emotional discipline

Think of it like playing fast-break offense. When it works, it's beautiful — but it only works when your team is built to run.

When to Be Aggressive, and When to Chill

As a parent, you've seen seasons shift. What works in non-conference play might not work in March. Same with investing.

Encourage your athlete to **be more aggressive** when:

- They're early in their career
- They won't need the money for years
- They're okay riding the emotional rollercoaster of the market

Encourage them to **get more conservative** when:

- They need money soon (for grad school, real estate, or life after sport)
- They're nervous about losing what they've built
- They've made enough and just want to preserve it

Your Investment Strategy Grows with You

NIL income is a blessing — but without a plan, it's a missed opportunity. The same mindset your child uses to grow in their sport applies to money:

- Early years = build muscle = aggressive investing
- Mid-career = refine and balance = moderate strategy
- Later = protect the win = conservative approach

Help them understand: your portfolio should evolve like your playing style.

Final Thoughts: Don't Just Win One Game — Build a Dynasty

Your child's NIL opportunity can be the start of something much bigger. But the only way to make it last is to build like a champion: with vision, patience, and a deep team of investments.

- Don't chase every hype stock or TikTok trend
- Don't panic when the market takes a dip
- Don't sit on the sidelines with all cash either

Instead:

- Build a smart, diversified portfolio
- Adjust your game plan as your goals change
- Stay consistent

Because when the spotlight fades, the deals slow down, and the cleats are hung up… the financial team they built will still be winning games.

That's how legacies are built.

That's how parents help their athletes win long after the final whistle.

Chapter 50: Why Time Is the Most Powerful Asset Your Student-Athlete Has (Compound Interest!)

When it comes to building wealth, most people think it takes a six-figure paycheck or winning the lottery. But the truth is, wealth is built with something even more powerful — **time**.

As a parent, you already understand the long game. You've seen how consistency, repetition, and showing up every day create growth. Whether it's training, grades, or discipline — it's not about one big moment. It's about what happens over time.

The same is true with money.

The most powerful tool your student-athlete has right now is not a signing bonus or brand deal. It's **compound interest** — and the earlier they start using it, the harder it works for them.

You don't have to be a financial expert to help them. You just need to understand the basics, encourage the right habits, and remind them: "Don't waste the one thing you can't get back — time."

What Is Compound Interest?

Compound interest is when your money earns money — and then that money starts earning even more money.

It's interest earning interest.

Instead of just earning income on the original amount (that's **simple interest**), compound interest lets your investment grow faster each year, because each year, your balance gets a little bigger — and that bigger amount earns even more.

It's like a snowball rolling downhill. At first it's small. But the longer it rolls, the bigger it gets.

Example:

If your child invests $1,000 at 10%:

- Year 1: $1,100
- Year 2: $1,210
- Year 3: $1,331

By year 10, they'd have $2,593 — without ever adding another penny.

Now imagine what happens if they keep adding more.

Why Compound Interest Is a Game-Changer (Especially for Young Athletes)

Your child's biggest advantage is **not** their NIL deal or endorsement contract.

It's their age.

Starting early gives compound interest more time to work — and time multiplies money. That's why it's so important to talk to them about saving and investing now, not "once they go pro" or "after they graduate."

Let's Compare:

- **Athlete A** starts investing $200/month at age 18 and stops at age 28.
- **Athlete B** waits until age 28 and invests $200/month until age 65.

Assuming both earn 8% per year:

Athlete A, who invested less and for fewer years, ends up with **more money** by retirement.

Why? Because those early dollars had more time to grow. That's the compound interest advantage.

Timing the Market vs. Time in the Market

Many young people wait to invest because they want to "time it right."

But when it comes to investing, *time in the market beats timing the market.* Every day your child waits is a day they miss out on growth.

Encourage them to start small — but start now.

The Rule of 72 – A Quick Wealth Calculator

Want to know how fast your child's money will double?

Use the **Rule of 72**:

Just divide 72 by the interest rate.

- 72 ÷ 6% = 12 years
- 72 ÷ 9% = 8 years
- 72 ÷ 12% = 6 years

So if they invest $10,000 at 9%, it becomes:

- $20,000 in 8 years
- $40,000 in 16
- $80,000 in 24

No additional deposits needed — just time and patience.

What Waiting Really Costs

Here's how much delay can cost in real terms:

If your child starts investing $100/month at 8%:

- **Start at 18**: ~$351,000 by age 65
- **Start at 28**: ~$165,000
- **Start at 38**: ~$74,000

Ten years of delay can cut their retirement savings in half — or more. That's why now is always better than later.

Where Can Compound Interest Work For Them?

You don't need to be wealthy to start benefiting. Here are common ways your child can grow their NIL income using compound interest:

- **Roth IRA** – Tax-free growth. Perfect for students in a low tax bracket.
- **Traditional IRA or 401(k)** – Great for long-term, tax-deferred growth.
- **High-yield savings accounts** – Lower return, but great for emergency funds.
- **Brokerage account** – For investing in stocks, ETFs, and mutual funds.
- **HSA (Health Savings Account)** – If eligible, it has tax advantages too.

As a parent, you can help by encouraging them to set up these accounts — or even helping them get started.

The Flip Side: Compound Interest Can Hurt Too

While compound interest can grow wealth, it can also grow **debt**. And fast.

Credit cards, payday loans, and high-interest car loans compound *against* them. The longer the balance stays, the faster the debt snowballs.

Example:

Owing $5,000 on a credit card with 22% interest? That balance could double in a few years if they don't pay it off. That's financial quicksand.

Encourage your student-athlete to treat debt like a full-court press — get rid of it fast.

How to Keep Compound Interest on Their Side

Here's how you can help them win:

- **Pay off credit cards in full every month**
- **Avoid financing things they don't need**
- **Start investing early, even small amounts**
- **Automate savings and investments**
- **Don't pull money out early**
- **Think long-term, not short-term hype**

You don't need a financial degree to help them with this. You just need to keep them grounded.

A Mental Shift: Raise an Investor, Not Just a Spender

When your child gets NIL money, the pressure to spend is real. But every dollar spent now is a dollar that won't grow later.

Help them shift their mindset.

Ask them:

- "Is this helping you build a future?"
- "Are you putting this money to work?"
- "Could you invest this and create long-term options for yourself?"

Money is like a seed. Spend it, and it's gone. Plant it, and it can grow into something that supports them for years.

Action Steps for Parents to Encourage

- **Help your child open a Roth IRA** — $6,500/year max (2025 limit)
- **Set up auto-contributions** — even $50/month builds a habit
- **Encourage simple investments** — index funds like S&P 500 or Total

Market

- **Celebrate patience** — remind them investing isn't flashy, but it works
- **Help them avoid "get rich quick" traps** — hype fades, wealth lasts

Final Thoughts: Make Time Their Teammate

Your child is learning how to manage their name, image, and likeness. But this isn't just about branding — it's about *building*. Building financial confidence. Building independence. Building freedom.

Compound interest rewards those who start early, stay consistent, and resist the urge to cash out too soon.

Help them understand: NIL isn't just about making money. It's about **multiplying it**. About using that early check to create options later in life — whether they go pro or not.

They may not fully understand now. That's okay.

That's why they have *you*.

Because the earlier they learn this, the brighter their future becomes.

Time is undefeated. Teach them how to make it work for them.

Chapter 51: Help them say NO

The moment NIL money starts coming in, the energy changes. The excitement is real. Your child is signing endorsement deals, getting paid for social media content, selling merch, making appearances, and experiencing financial independence for the first time.

But something else shows up, too: **the pressure.**

The phone starts ringing more. Family members ask for help. Old friends show up with new business ideas. People assume that because your child got a check, they've also become everyone's solution.

This is where your role as a parent becomes powerful. It's your job to help your student-athlete protect not just their money, but their peace, their boundaries, and their future.

Saying "no" isn't selfish. It's smart. And it may be the most important financial skill your child ever learns.

Why It's So Hard to Say "No"

Let's acknowledge the emotional weight, especially for first-generation earners:

- Your child may feel like they're carrying their family and community.
- They may want to "make up for" the past by giving big now.
- They may feel guilty having money when others don't.
- They may fear backlash or losing love if they don't say yes.

You know these feelings. You may have felt them yourself. But always saying yes — especially without a plan — is the fastest way to turn a blessing into a burden.

Your child didn't work hard just to become someone else's ATM. They worked hard to build a life. Help them protect it.

What Always Saying "Yes" Really Costs

It feels good at first. You help someone pay rent. You pick up dinner. You say yes to that cousin's new "investment opportunity." But over time, here's what usually happens:

- **Savings disappear.**
- **Goals get pushed back.**
- **People stop asking and start expecting.**
- **Saying no later becomes even harder.**
- **Bitterness builds — on both sides.**

This isn't generosity. It's quiet sabotage. And it ends with your child drained — emotionally, mentally, and financially.

What Parents Can Teach Their Athletes to Say Instead

Saying "no" doesn't mean being disrespectful. It means setting boundaries with clarity and care. Here are some scripts you can help them use:

- "I've created a financial plan, and I'm sticking to it. Everything's already allocated."
- "Right now I'm focused on building something long-term, so I'm not giving out money."
- "I'm working with an advisor and I'm not making any financial commitments right now."
- "I care about you, but I'm not in a position to help financially."

- "I can't give money, but I'm happy to support you in other ways."

Remind your child: **blame the plan, not the person.** They aren't rejecting loved ones — they're prioritizing their future.

Enabling vs. Empowering

Yes, giving money can feel good. But giving without structure becomes a cycle. Today's gift turns into tomorrow's expectation.

Empowering looks different:

- Teaching someone how to build a budget.
- Connecting them with a job lead or a free financial course.
- Offering guidance and accountability instead of just a check.

One creates independence. The other creates dependence. Help your child learn the difference.

You Are Not Their Financial Plan

As parents, we know how often our kids are told, "You made it — now take care of everyone." But here's the truth you must help them hold on to:

They are not the bank. They are not the bailout.

Here are boundaries that protect them:

- No loans, period.
- No investing in businesses without full vetting.
- No co-signing for anyone.
- No recurring gifts.
- If they give, it's one-time, budgeted, and without guilt.

They can love people and still say, "I'm not your financial plan."

Legacy Over Likes

Many athletes fall into the trap of trying to impress: picking up every tab, funding projects, showing up like a hero.

But being liked isn't the same as building legacy.

Legacy looks like:

- Buying their first home
- Building generational wealth
- Investing in something real
- Helping their future family thrive
- Giving back on their own terms, at the right time

Likes fade. Legacy lasts.

When Your Child Is the First to "Make It"

Being the first to have money is powerful—and heavy.

They feel responsible. They feel watched. They feel guilt.

But remind them:

- **They can't help others until they're stable.**
- **They don't have to carry the whole village alone.**
- **Their best gift is example, not just expense.**

What people really need isn't just help — it's hope. Your child gives them that by showing what *wisdom* with money looks like.

Boundaries Are Not Betrayal

Help your child understand this: setting limits is not turning your back on loved ones.

It's turning toward a future where they can keep showing up, in ways that truly matter.

If someone walks away because they heard "no"? That tells you more about them than it does about your child.

Help Them Create a Go-To Script

Preparation beats pressure.

Here's one they can practice:

> *"I've made a decision not to give or lend money right now. I'm focused on building something that lasts, and I hope you understand."*

If needed, help them role-play different versions for different people: friends, family, teammates. Let them find their tone, but help them hold their boundary.

Ways to Help Without Giving Money

Here's what you can encourage your child to offer instead:

- A ride to a job interview
- A resource or connection
- Financial literacy tools
- Emotional support
- Career or college guidance

Support doesn't always have to be financial. And often, the non-financial kind lasts longer.

If They Do Decide to Say Yes...

Help them do it wisely:

- Be crystal clear about the amount
- Set expectations: "This is a one-time gift"
- Never loan what they can't afford to lose
- Never jeopardize their own stability
- Write down loan terms if they go that route (and be prepared that it might not come back)

And remind them: giving once doesn't mean giving always.

Watch Out for These Red Flags

Teach them how to recognize manipulation:

- "You owe me."
- "If you really loved me..."
- "You've got it, why can't you help?"
- "Just this one time..." (for the fifth time)

If someone won't respect their no, they don't respect their peace.

What Happens When You Don't Learn to Say No

Many athletes don't learn this lesson until it's too late.

They give and give. And then the money stops coming in — but the asks keep coming.

And suddenly:

- The bank account's empty.
- The pressure becomes resentment.

- The same people they gave to? Nowhere to be found.

Help your child avoid that moment by setting them up with the strength to say "no" now — and the wisdom to know when to say "yes" later.

Closing Thoughts: "No" Is a Gift

Saying no now allows your child to say yes to what matters most later:

Yes to buying a home.

Yes to investing in their dream.

Yes to retirement.

Yes to giving back when they're truly able.

Yes to peace of mind.

So help them learn that **"no" is not rejection — it's redirection.**

And it may be the most powerful word in their NIL journey.

Because in the end, the best way to help others… is to build something solid yourself first.

Chapter 47: NIL Out-of-State Tax Filing Checklist

For Parents of Student-Athletes

Use this checklist throughout the year to stay on top of your student-athlete's multi-state NIL tax responsibilities. Review quarterly and again before tax season.

1. Income Tracking

- Keep a detailed log of every NIL payment
- Include the amount, date, brand or organization, service performed, and location (state/city)
- Record the state in which each deal was performed
- Did the event take place in another state? Is the brand headquartered elsewhere?
- Save all relevant documents
- Contracts, invoices, payment receipts, 1099s, W-9s, and any correspondence confirming work done and income earned

2. Tax Preparation Calendar

Use this schedule to plan quarterly estimated tax payments:

- April 15 – For income earned from January through March

- June 15 – For income earned from April through June
- September 15 – For income earned from July through September
- January 15 (of the following year) – For income earned from October through December

Set calendar reminders to avoid missing deadlines for both federal and state estimated taxes.

3. Professional Support

- Hire a qualified CPA or tax advisor who understands:
- Self-employment income
- Independent contractor status
- Multi-state income reporting
- NIL-specific financial and tax planning for student-athletes
- Schedule a pre-tax season planning meeting to:
- Allocate income correctly by state
- Prepare quarterly estimates
- Plan for deductions and credits
- Avoid penalties for underpayment

4. Accounting and Structure

- Open a separate checking account for all NIL income
- Keep business and personal expenses separate to simplify tax reporting
- Use basic bookkeeping software or apps to track income
- Tools like QuickBooks Self-Employed, Keeper, or FreshBooks can categorize income by state and help organize documentation
- Label each transaction by state
- This makes it easier to assign income correctly when filing state tax returns

5. Filing by State

- File a resident return in your child's home or primary state
- This return covers all income and should include any tax credits for income already taxed in other states
- File non-resident returns in every state where NIL income was earned
- These returns only report income tied to work or activity in that state
- Apply for tax credits where eligible
- Many resident states offer credits for taxes paid to other states, which helps prevent double taxation
- Use apportionment when allowed
- Some states permit you to report only the portion of income earned within their borders

6. Red Flags to Watch For

- NIL earnings from California, New York, Illinois, or other aggressive tax states
- These states actively enforce non-resident income tax rules
- NIL campaigns that are digital but target specific states
- Even virtual appearances or promotions may create state nexus
- Brand contracts that lack tax documentation
- If a company doesn't provide a W-9 or 1099, that doesn't mean taxes aren't owed
- Missing 1099s for income over $600
- Even if one isn't issued, the income must still be reported
- Payments from collectives or sponsorships that come from national events or televised appearances in another state

7. Residency and Domicile

- Determine your child's legal state of residency
- Where is their driver's license issued? Where do they vote? Where do they live most of the year?
- Be clear on whether they are full-year residents, part-year residents, or non-residents for tax purposes
- If they have ties to multiple states, work with a tax advisor to correctly determine residency and filing requirements

8. Communication with Brands and Professionals

- Ask brands in advance:
- Where is the company headquartered?
- Will they issue a 1099?
- Do they expect tax withholding or reporting?
- Stay in contact with NIL agents, compliance officers, and school advisors
- They can provide early notice of NIL events that may trigger a state filing requirement
- Encourage your student-athlete to disclose all NIL deals to you or a trusted advisor, even small ones

9. Student-Athlete Financial Literacy

- Teach your child:
- The difference between resident and non-resident taxes
- Why some states require separate filings
- What it means to be self-employed
- Involve them in tracking income and organizing documents
- Help them understand how business income differs from a traditional job

10. Year-End Review

- Reconcile total NIL income for the year and break it down by state
- Match contract terms, bank deposits, and any 1099 forms
- Confirm you have all necessary tax forms
- 1099-NEC, 1099-K (for payment platforms), W-2s (if applicable)
- Meet with your tax advisor before tax deadlines
- Plan for any state-specific extensions or payment obligations
- Double check all estimated payments made throughout the year
- Ensure you're not underpaid in any state
- File all required resident and non-resident tax returns on time

This checklist can save your student-athlete from unexpected tax bills, penalties, or future audits. Consider reviewing it each quarter with your child and using it as a tool to teach real-world financial responsibility.

Chapter 48: Don't Just let your Student Athlete get paid—Build Something With It

Your child just got that first big NIL check. Maybe it's $1,000. Maybe it's $100,000. Either way, it's a moment that feels like a win — because it is.

But now comes the hard part: making sure that check isn't just a flash but a foundation.

As parents, you want the best for your child. And that includes more than making sure they train hard, stay focused, or pick the right major. It also means helping them think through what to do *after* the money hits their account.

Because the real flex? It's not a new chain or a trip to Miami.

It's building a future.

This chapter gives you the framework to help your child turn NIL income into long-term wealth — starting with a clear plan and smart investments. You don't have to be a financial expert to guide them. You just have to understand the basics, ask the right questions, and help them play the long game.

Step 1: What Is Investing, Really?

Investing simply means putting your money somewhere it can grow over time.

Instead of blowing through NIL money on Uber Eats or sneakers, investing means using that money to buy *assets* — things like stocks, ETFs (exchange-traded funds), or mutual funds — that increase in value over time and can pay them back later.

You've probably heard the phrase "make your money work for you." This is what that means. Let it earn while they sleep.

Step 2: Know the Goal and Time Horizon

Help your child ask the right questions:

- When will I need this money?
- Can I handle some short-term ups and downs?
- Am I planning for next month — or the next 10 years?

If the money is for rent, tuition, or groceries? It shouldn't be in the market.

But if they're looking to build long-term wealth — money they won't need for 5+ years — investing is the move.

Step 3: Pick the Right Type of Account

Not all investment accounts are created equal. The *type* of account determines how their money is taxed and how accessible it is. Here's the breakdown for you and your student-athlete:

Roth IRA

- Funded with after-tax money
- Grows tax-free
- Withdrawals in retirement are 100% tax-free

- 2025 contribution limit: $6,500
- Must have earned income to contribute (NIL counts!)

Why it's great: Most student-athletes are in a low tax bracket now, so paying taxes up front means they'll *never* owe taxes on that money again. That's a rare financial win.

Traditional IRA

- Contributions may be tax-deductible
- Grows tax-deferred
- Taxes paid later when the money is withdrawn
- Same $6,500 limit
- Not as good for most students unless they need the deduction now

Taxable Brokerage Account

- No contribution limits
- Fully flexible
- Taxes owed on earnings
- Great for investing beyond the IRA cap or for medium-term goals

SEP IRA

- Best for high-earning NIL athletes running a business through an LLC
- Contribute up to 25% of net earnings (up to $66,000 in 2025)
- Tax-deductible contributions
- Grows tax-deferred

SIMPLE IRA

- Best for NIL athletes who hire others (videographer, agent, marketing help) under a business
- $16,000 contribution limit plus employer match

- Grows tax-deferred
- Good for business owners with employees

Step 4: What If Your Kid Just Got a $100,000 NIL Check?

Let's walk through what that could look like. Whether it's your child or another athlete in your circle, this breakdown is about mindset.

Step 1: Save for Taxes

Unless taxes are being withheld, assume 30%. Set it aside immediately.

$100,000 × 30% = $30,000

That money goes in a separate account. Not negotiable.

Step 2: Max Out a Roth IRA

Assuming they're eligible, this is a no-brainer.

$6,500 invested in a low-cost index fund = decades of tax-free growth

Step 3: Open a Taxable Brokerage Account

They can put $30,000–$40,000 in a simple investment portfolio using ETFs or index funds. This builds wealth and gives flexibility.

Step 4: Emergency Fund

Set aside $10,000–$15,000 in a high-yield savings account. NIL isn't guaranteed to last. A financial cushion is protection.

Step 5: Spend *Some* Guilt-Free

Yes, let them enjoy a little. $5,000–$10,000 is plenty to celebrate without sabotaging the future.

Sample Breakdown:

- $30,000 for taxes
- $6,500 Roth IRA
- $35,000 brokerage account
- $15,000 savings
- $8,500 fun money

This balance sets them up to win both today and tomorrow.

Step 5: If You Don't Have $100K... Same Game Plan

The number doesn't matter. The approach does.

Even if your child only made $1,500 in NIL income this semester, you can still:

- Set aside a third for taxes
- Open a Roth IRA with what's left
- Put a small amount in savings
- Let them enjoy $100 or so without guilt

Investing isn't about the amount — it's about the habit.

Final Thoughts: Turn NIL Checks Into Long-Term Change

As a parent, you want your child to succeed — not just in sports or school, but in life.

NIL income is an incredible opportunity. But if it's not handled well, it can become a missed one.

You don't have to control their money — but you *can* help shape their mindset. Talk to them about investing. Share this chapter. Encourage them to open an account. Remind them that short-term fun doesn't have to cancel out long-term freedom.

Because at the end of the day, it's not just about getting paid.

It's about building something that lasts. Something that grows. Something that gives your student-athlete power — on and off the field — for years to come.

Chapter 48: Conclusion From Awareness to Action – Your NIL Family Game Plan

As you close this book, take a moment to reflect: you didn't just read pages about NIL—you stepped into your power as a parent, advocate, protector, and partner in your student-athlete's journey. Whether this journey started with confusion, curiosity, or concern, you now hold tools that will make a difference—not just in your child's athletic career, but in their life.

This book wasn't written to overwhelm you. It was written to **equip you**—with confidence, questions, strategies, and structure.

You've just walked through the essential areas that most families never get to learn together. And now, you're in a stronger position to help your child handle opportunity like a professional and avoid pitfalls like a pro.

What This Book Has Given You

A Cultural Lens – You've explored how your background, upbringing, and beliefs about money shape what you can teach and how your student-athlete learns. No shame. Just awareness.

Year-by-Year Guidance – From freshman year of high school to senior year of college, you now have a roadmap for every key conversation, milestone, and teachable moment.

NIL Education Basics – You've learned what NIL is, how it works, and how your student-athlete can protect themselves while participating wisely.

Business & Financial Literacy – You've been introduced to foundational principles like budgeting, saving, taxes, LLCs, contracts, and working with professionals.

Mental and Emotional Awareness – You've seen how fame, pressure, and digital visibility affect student-athletes—and what support systems they need to stay grounded.

Action Steps for Every Season – From compliance deadlines to tax forms, from brand deals to scams, you've been given checklists, questions, and timelines to stay ahead of the game.

Rules of Thumb to Carry Forward

1. **NIL income is business income.**
2. Treat it like a job—track everything, file taxes, and plan for tomorrow.
3. **Scams prey on confusion.**
4. If it sounds too good to be true, it probably is. Always review, research, and ask.
5. **Visibility is not invincibility.**
6. Just because your child is getting attention doesn't mean they're financially protected or emotionally supported.
7. **Your culture is your context—not your cage.**
8. You can honor where you came from while building new financial habits and beliefs.
9. **Money is a tool, not a trophy.**
10. Use it to build stability, freedom, and choices—not just to show off.
11. **No one succeeds alone.**
12. Financial literacy is a team sport. Don't be afraid to bring in coaches, advisors, and mentors.

10 Action Steps for Parents After Finishing This Book

1. **Schedule a financial check-in with your student-athlete.**
2. Go over what they earn, what they spend, and what they're saving.
3. **Create a basic NIL tracking system.**
4. A spreadsheet, a folder, or even a notebook—just start organizing deals, documents, and deadlines.
5. **Build your financial support team.**
6. Identify or hire a trusted CPA, financial advisor, NIL agent, or attorney when needed.
7. **Establish monthly conversations.**
8. Talk about one money topic each month—budgeting, credit, taxes, contracts, etc.
9. **Review social media accounts together.**
10. Ensure your child's digital footprint supports, not sabotages, their brand.
11. **Set savings goals.**
12. Whether it's an emergency fund or future business venture, help your child plan for it now.
13. **Prepare for tax season early.**
14. Keep track of 1099 forms, expenses, and quarterly payments.
15. **Get educated together.**
16. Watch financial videos, listen to podcasts, or attend webinars together.
17. **Help your child understand contracts.**
18. Never let them sign something they don't understand. Review everything.
19. **Celebrate progress, not perfection.**
20. Small wins matter. Keep showing up.

Your Legacy Starts Here

Every decision your child makes with money now impacts their future. Every conversation you have about NIL, taxes, values, and life skills lays a brick in the foundation they're building.

You may not have had this kind of guidance growing up—but that ends with you.

You've just become your student-athlete's greatest financial asset.

So, don't stop here.

- Keep learning.
- Keep asking questions.
- Keep setting the example.
- Keep empowering your child to think, plan, and build boldly.

Because this NIL window might close, but financial wisdom lasts forever.

You've got this. And they've got you.

Let's build legacies—not just brands.

About the Author

Pat Brown, MBA

Pat Brown, MBA, is a former collegiate athlete turned financial advisor, dedicated to enhancing financial literacy among student-athletes, coaches, and sports professionals. As a linebacker for the University of Kansas Jayhawks, Pat served as team captain his senior year, helping lead the team to a national ranking as high as 6th. He earned Big 12 Conference All-Academic Team honors and was recognized with KU's Iron Hawk Award for strength, leadership, and dedication.

After transitioning from the field to the financial world, Pat saw a critical gap: athletes were being handed life-changing opportunities through NIL (Name, Image & Likeness)—but without the tools to manage them. In response, he launched a series of financial literacy platforms and books that speak directly to the athletic community, including:

- *Financial Literacy For NIL* (for college student-athletes)
- *Financial Literacy For NIL – High School Student-Athletes Edition*
- *Financial Literacy For NIL – International Student-Athletes Edition*
- *Financial Literacy For Student Athletes*
- *Financial Literacy For College Coaches*
- *Financial Literacy For Pro Athletes*

Through these works, Pat equips athletes and those who support them with the practical skills and strategies needed to make informed financial decisions—on and off the field. He also hosts the *Financial Literacy For Student Athletes* podcast and travels the country speaking to teams, families, and athletic departments.

Pat's mission is clear: to bridge the gap between sports and financial education, and to ensure that every athlete, from high school hopeful to seasoned pro, is empowered to build lasting wealth and make wise decisions with confidence.

Glossary of 50 Financial, Investment, Banking, Credit & Tax Terms

Banking Terms

1. **Checking Account** – A bank account used for everyday spending, paying bills, and receiving deposits.
2. **Savings Account** – A bank account that earns interest and is used to store money for future needs or emergencies.
3. **Routing Number** – A nine-digit number used to identify your bank when transferring money or setting up direct deposit.
4. **Account Number** – A unique number assigned to your specific bank account.
5. **Overdraft** – When you spend more money than you have in your checking account, possibly triggering a fee.
6. **Direct Deposit** – A method of payment where money is electronically deposited into your bank account.
7. **Mobile Banking** – Using a smartphone or app to manage your bank accounts, transfer money, or pay bills.
8. **FDIC Insurance** – Protection provided by the Federal Deposit Insurance Corporation, insuring deposits up to $250,000 per account.
9. **Bank Statement** – A monthly report from your bank showing all your deposits, withdrawals, and balances.
10. **Wire Transfer** – A method of sending money electronically between banks, often for large sums or urgent payments.

Credit Terms

1. **Credit Score** – A three-digit number that represents your creditworthiness, used by lenders to assess risk.
2. **Credit Report** – A detailed history of your borrowing and repayment activity, issued by agencies like Equifax, TransUnion, or Experian.
3. **Credit Limit** – The maximum amount you are allowed to borrow on a credit card.
4. **APR (Annual Percentage Rate)** – The annual interest rate charged on borrowed money.
5. **Minimum Payment** – The smallest amount you must pay on a credit card bill to avoid a late fee.
6. **Secured Credit Card** – A credit card backed by a cash deposit, often used to build or repair credit.
7. **Co-Signer** – A person who agrees to be legally responsible for a loan or credit card if the primary borrower fails to pay.
8. **Utilization Rate** – The percentage of available credit you're using. Keeping this below 30% helps your credit score.
9. **Hard Inquiry** – A credit check that can temporarily lower your credit score, often done when applying for new credit.
10. **Delinquency** – Failing to make payments on time, which can damage your credit score.

Investment Terms

1. **Stock** – A share of ownership in a company. When you own stock, you own part of that business.
2. **Bond** – A loan made by an investor to a borrower (typically a corporation or government), with fixed interest payments.
3. **Mutual Fund** – A pooled investment managed by professionals, consisting of stocks, bonds, or other assets.
4. **ETF (Exchange-Traded Fund)** – Similar to mutual funds, but traded like stocks on exchanges.

5. **Portfolio** – A collection of investments owned by an individual or institution.
6. **Diversification** – Spreading investments across different types of assets to reduce risk.
7. **Compound Interest** – Earning interest on both your initial investment and the interest already earned.
8. **Dividend** – A portion of a company's profits paid to shareholders.
9. **Capital Gain** – Profit earned from selling an investment for more than it cost.
10. **Roth IRA** – A retirement account where contributions are made with after-tax dollars and qualified withdrawals are tax-free.

Financial Planning & Budgeting Terms

1. **Emergency Fund** – Money saved specifically to cover unexpected expenses like medical bills or car repairs.
2. **Budget** – A financial plan that outlines expected income and expenses over a specific time period.
3. **Net Worth** – The value of your assets (what you own) minus liabilities (what you owe).
4. **Cash Flow** – The movement of money into and out of your accounts; income minus expenses.
5. **Asset** – Something valuable you own, such as a car, house, stock, or savings.
6. **Liability** – A financial obligation or debt you owe.
7. **Debt-to-Income Ratio** – A percentage that shows how much of your monthly income goes toward debt payments.
8. **Financial Advisor** – A professional who helps you plan and manage your money, investments, and goals.
9. **401(k)** – A retirement savings plan offered by employers with tax advantages and sometimes matching contributions.
10. **Estate Planning** – Organizing your assets and wishes for distribution after death, often involving wills, trusts, and insurance.

Tax Terms

1. **W-2 Form** – A form employers give employees that shows total earnings and taxes withheld for the year.
2. **1099 Form** – A form used to report non-employee (contractor) income, often for NIL or freelance earnings.
3. **Adjusted Gross Income (AGI)** – Your total income minus specific deductions; used to determine tax liability.
4. **Taxable Income** – The amount of income that is subject to federal or state taxes after deductions and credits.
5. **Standard Deduction** – A fixed dollar amount that reduces your taxable income; available to most taxpayers.
6. **Itemized Deduction** – Specific expenses that can be deducted from your income, such as mortgage interest or charitable giving.
7. **Withholding** – The portion of income your employer holds back to pay your taxes throughout the year.
8. **Estimated Taxes** – Payments made quarterly by those with non-wage income (like NIL income) to cover taxes due.
9. **Filing Status** – A category that determines your tax rates and standard deduction (e.g., single, head of household).
10. **Tax Credit** – A direct reduction of your tax bill, often more valuable than deductions because it lowers what you owe dollar-for-dollar.

How to Read Investment Statements, Tax Forms, and NIL Contracts

As your student-athlete begins to earn income through Name, Image, and Likeness (NIL) deals, they're not just entering the world of athletics and branding—they're entering the world of adult financial responsibility. With that responsibility comes documentation: investment statements that track where their money is growing, tax forms that show what they owe (and what they might not know they owe), and legally binding NIL contracts that will shape their future.

This chapter is designed to help you—the parent—understand these documents, explain them to your child, and use them to protect their present and future. We'll go deep into three core areas:

1. Investment Statements
2. Tax Documents
3. NIL Contracts

Each section is packed with explanations, breakdowns, examples, questions to ask, red flags to watch out for, and strategies you can apply immediately.

Part 1: How to Read an Investment Statement

Why It Matters

Many student-athletes earn money but don't invest it. Or worse, they hand it off without understanding what's happening. Learning how to read an investment statement early helps athletes monitor performance, understand risk, control costs, and think long-term.

Breaking Down the Statement

Most investment statements come monthly or quarterly. They usually include:

Account Summary

- Beginning Balance
- Ending Balance
- Deposits & Withdrawals
- Net Investment Gain or Loss

Holdings

- Stock/fund names (e.g., Apple, Vanguard S&P 500 ETF)
- Ticker symbol
- Number of shares
- Price per share
- Market value

Performance

- Year-to-date return
- 1-year, 3-year, and 5-year performance
- Performance vs. benchmark

Asset Allocation

- How the money is spread across:
- Stocks (equities)
- Bonds (fixed income)
- Cash or cash equivalents
- Alternatives (REITs, commodities, crypto)

Fees and Expenses

- Management fees
- Expense ratios of funds
- Transaction fees

What to Look For

- **Diversification**: Is the money spread out or overly concentrated?
- **Fee drag**: Is a high fee eating away your return?
- **Risk level**: Is the account aggressive, balanced, or conservative?
- **Performance vs. goals**: Is this account growing as expected?

Key Questions to Ask

- What is our risk tolerance?
- Are we investing for 5, 10, or 30 years?
- Are these investments tax-efficient?
- Are we using the right type of account (Roth IRA, brokerage, etc.)?

Parent Action Steps

- Review the statement together quarterly.
- Ask your financial advisor to explain all fees.
- Help your student-athlete set clear investment goals.
- Talk about the difference between saving and investing.
- Show them compound interest in action.

Part 2: How to Understand Tax Documents

Why It Matters

Most NIL income is paid as 1099 income—not W-2 wages. That means your student-athlete is considered self-employed. The government sees them as a business. And that changes everything about how taxes are filed, paid, and tracked.

Key Tax Forms to Know

Form 1099-NEC

- For non-employee compensation.
- Issued by any brand or business that paid your child $600 or more.
- No taxes withheld—your child must pay them.

Form 1040

- Main federal income tax return.
- Lists total income, deductions, credits, and amount owed or refunded.

Schedule C

- Required if your student-athlete is self-employed.
- Shows income and deductible business expenses.
- Determines net profit or loss.

Schedule SE

- Calculates self-employment tax (Social Security and Medicare).
- 15.3% of net earnings.

State Tax Forms

- Required in many states where income was earned.
- Multi-state income may require filing in multiple states.

Common Deductible NIL Expenses

- Travel (to appearances or events)
- Web design or hosting
- Graphic design or branding
- Equipment used in business
- Photography or video content
- Phone/internet (if used for business)
- CPA or legal services

Quarterly Estimated Taxes

If your student-athlete is projected to owe more than $1,000 in taxes for the year, they are required to make **estimated tax payments** every quarter:

- April 15
- June 15
- September 15
- January 15 (of the next year)

Failing to pay these on time can result in penalties and interest.

Key Mistakes to Avoid

- Ignoring 1099 income just because no taxes were withheld
- Forgetting to track business expenses
- Failing to make quarterly payments
- Trying to "guess" on deductions without guidance

Parent Action Steps

- Hire a CPA familiar with NIL and self-employment tax.
- Use accounting software or spreadsheets to track income/expenses.
- Open a separate savings account just for taxes.
- Encourage your child to set aside 25–30% of every NIL check for taxes.
- Review deductions and expenses every quarter.

Part 3: How to Read and Understand NIL Contracts

Why It Matters

NIL contracts are legally binding agreements that outline your child's responsibilities and rights in exchange for compensation. If they don't understand what they're signing, they could lose money, damage their reputation, or even lose eligibility.

What Every NIL Contract Should Include

1. Parties Involved

- Full legal names of all parties
- Contact info for future correspondence

2. Scope of Work

- What exactly is your student-athlete agreeing to?
- Deliverables (number of social posts, appearances, interviews)
- Platforms (Instagram, TikTok, YouTube, etc.)

3. Compensation

- How much will they be paid?

- Is it a flat fee, per post, percentage of sales, or a hybrid?
- What's the payment schedule (upon signing, monthly, after work is completed)?

4. Usage Rights

- How will the company use your child's name, image, or likeness?
- Can they use it in perpetuity (forever)?
- Can they resell or repurpose the content?
- Are there limitations or approvals required?

5. Exclusivity

- Is your student-athlete restricted from working with other companies?
- How broad is the exclusivity clause (e.g., "all athletic apparel")?

6. Term and Termination

- How long does the agreement last?
- How can either party exit the deal?
- Are there penalties for cancellation?

7. Dispute Resolution

- What happens if there's a disagreement?
- Is the case handled in court, arbitration, or mediation?
- Which state's laws apply?

8. Indemnification

- Who's responsible if something goes wrong?
- Is your student-athlete being asked to take on unreasonable liability?

9. Compliance Clauses

- Must reference NCAA, state, and school NIL rules.
- May require school compliance officer to review the contract.

10. Confidentiality

- Prohibits either party from disclosing contract details.

Red Flags to Watch Out For

- No defined deliverables or payment schedule
- Rights granted "in perpetuity" without limits
- No ability to terminate the contract
- Excessive exclusivity that blocks future opportunities
- Clauses that hold your student-athlete responsible for the company's legal problems

Parent Action Steps

- Always get a second opinion (attorney, school compliance, or both).
- Never sign a contract on the spot or under pressure.
- Review every clause with your child before signing.
- Create a folder to keep all signed contracts organized.
- Set up a master calendar to track obligations, deadlines, and payment dates.

Final Summary: Bringing It All Together

In the NIL era, your student-athlete is no longer just an athlete—they're a business.

Investment statements show how their money grows. Tax documents reveal their financial responsibilities. Contracts define how they earn and protect their name, image, and likeness.

You, as a parent, play a key role in helping them navigate all of it. That means reading the documents, asking the hard questions, seeking professional help when needed, and creating an environment where financial literacy isn't just expected—it's a family standard.

This chapter gave you the tools to read between the lines, to understand what your child is signing or submitting, and to lead with confidence, even in unfamiliar territory.

Because NIL money isn't just about right now.

It's about what happens after the lights go off, after the season ends, and long after their final endorsement.

With your help, your student-athlete won't just be earning money.

They'll be building something that lasts.

50 Questions Parents Can Ask Coaches, Administrators & Compliance Teams

Questions to Ask High School Coaches (NIL, Recruiting & Development)

1. Does our state allow high school athletes to participate in NIL opportunities?
2. Are there specific school or district policies regarding NIL activity?
3. How do you support student-athletes who want to build a personal brand?
4. Are you comfortable if my child signs an NIL deal?
5. What's your policy on social media for student-athletes?
6. Do you communicate with college coaches on behalf of athletes?
7. How can we help support the recruiting process from home?
8. Will you assist with highlight reels, recommendations, or stats tracking?
9. How do you help athletes manage exposure from AAU/7v7/travel teams?
10. How many athletes have you helped move on to the college level?

Questions to Ask College Coaches (Recruiting, NIL, and Culture)

1. How do you support players with NIL opportunities once they arrive on campus?
2. Are athletes in your program currently earning NIL income?

3. Are there restrictions for NIL activity in your program (e.g., during season, travel)?
4. How involved are you in helping athletes evaluate NIL offers?
5. Do you offer media, branding, or social media training?
6. How do you ensure that student-athletes are not distracted by NIL?
7. Do players have access to business mentors or financial education?
8. How many of your athletes graduate with a degree?
9. What's your policy if a player gets injured and can't play?
10. What expectations do you have for parents during the season?

Questions to Ask College Administrators or Athletic Directors

1. What resources does the university provide for NIL support and education?
2. Are there partnerships with platforms or marketplaces to help students secure NIL deals?
3. Does the university help student-athletes with taxes, legal, or contract questions?
4. What percentage of athletes at your school are earning from NIL?
5. Are there specific rules around team logos, facilities, or gear being used in NIL promotions?
6. Do athletes receive financial literacy training as part of their onboarding?
7. What mental health services are available to student-athletes?
8. Are there career development or life-after-sports programs offered?
9. How are academic advisors integrated into the athletic experience?
10. What happens if a coach leaves during my child's time at the university?

Questions to Ask NCAA/NAIA/School Compliance Departments

1. What is your process for reviewing and approving NIL deals?
2. Do you provide a list of do's and don'ts when it comes to NIL activity?
3. Is my child allowed to use their school logo or uniform in sponsored

content?

4. Can my child hire a lawyer or agent to assist with NIL?
5. What must be reported, and how often, when my child signs a new deal?
6. Are there limits to how much a student-athlete can earn?
7. How do NIL deals affect scholarship eligibility or financial aid?
8. What's the policy on out-of-state NIL income and tax implications?
9. If my child forms an LLC or business, does that need to be reported?
10. What happens if my child violates NIL policy unintentionally?

General Questions for Any Coach or Administrator

1. What's the team's GPA average?
2. How is playing time determined, and what's your communication policy?
3. What academic support is offered to help with time management?
4. Do athletes have mandatory study hall or tutoring?
5. How do you manage team culture and athlete accountability?
6. What's your policy on social media behavior?
7. How do you address mental health and performance stress?
8. How does your program handle athlete discipline or legal issues?
9. Are athletes involved in community service or leadership programs?
10. Can you walk me through the onboarding process for new student-athletes?

50 Questions Parents Can Ask Professionals in the NIL Space

Questions to Ask Financial Advisors

1. Are you a fiduciary, and are you legally required to act in my child's best interest?
2. Do you have experience working with student-athletes or young clients?
3. How do you charge for your services—flat fee, hourly, or commission?
4. Can you help us create a budget for NIL income?
5. How do you assist with savings goals like emergency funds or retirement?
6. Do you help with Roth IRA or SEP IRA setup for student-athletes?
7. Can you educate my child on credit, debt, and responsible spending?
8. What is your investment philosophy, especially for someone young and new to investing?
9. Do you offer services to help manage cash flow and taxes year-round?
10. What red flags should we look for in NIL-related investments or offers?

Questions to Ask CPAs or Tax Professionals

1. Do you have experience working with 1099 income and self-employed clients?
2. Can you help us file quarterly estimated tax payments?

3. How much of my child's NIL income should be set aside for taxes?
4. Can you advise on state-specific tax obligations for NIL income?
5. What deductions or write-offs are available for a student-athlete earning NIL?
6. Can you help us file taxes for a student-athlete with an LLC or S-Corp?
7. Are there any IRS red flags we should be aware of when filing?
8. How do NIL earnings affect financial aid or FAFSA eligibility?
9. What are the tax differences between cash payments, gifts, and merchandise received?
10. What records should we keep for NIL-related tax documentation?

Questions to Ask NIL Agents and Managers

1. Are you licensed or certified to represent athletes in NIL negotiations?
2. How do you charge—percentage of deals, retainers, or other methods?
3. Can we review a sample contract or agreement you use with clients?
4. What brands or companies have you worked with in the past?
5. How do you determine which deals are right for a student-athlete?
6. Do you handle contract negotiations and brand communication?
7. Will you help ensure compliance with NCAA and university NIL policies?
8. What's your approach to protecting my child's brand and reputation?
9. Do you require exclusivity in your agreements?
10. What happens if my child wants to terminate the relationship?

Questions to Ask Brand Representatives or Companies

1. Is this NIL partnership a one-time deal or part of a longer campaign?
2. What is the scope of work required (posting, attending events, etc.)?
3. Will there be a written contract outlining deliverables and payment terms?
4. When and how will my child be compensated?
5. Will you own or reuse content created by my child for the campaign?

6. How will my child's name, image, or likeness be used?
7. Are there any exclusivity clauses or conflict-of-interest concerns?
8. How do you handle taxes and 1099 documentation?
9. Will you provide legal review or support for the agreement?
10. Can my child decline certain types of content or messaging?

General Questions Parents Should Ask Any NIL Professional

1. What's your experience in the NIL space, and how long have you been involved?
2. How do you keep up with changing NCAA, state, and federal NIL laws?
3. Do you have liability insurance or legal support if issues arise?
4. Can you help us evaluate the risks versus rewards of any NIL opportunity?
5. How do you protect my child's data, privacy, and social media accounts?
6. Do you work with attorneys to review or draft contracts?
7. Will you teach my child about long-term financial planning, not just short-term deals?
8. How do you ensure brand alignment with my child's values and goals?
9. Can we involve a parent or trusted advisor in all major communications?
10. What safeguards are in place to protect my child from scams, fraud, or exploitation?

Key Dates for Student-Athletes: Taxes, Sports Seasons, Contributions & Compliance

- JANUARY
- **Jan 1**: NCAA **official start of spring semester sport eligibility**
- **Jan 10–15**: Universities may require **compliance check-ins** (return from winter break, NIL disclosures)
- **Jan 15**: **Quarterly Estimated Tax Payment (Q4) Due** – For prior year NIL income (Form 1040-ES)
- **Jan 31**: Deadline for companies to send **1099-NEC** or **W-2 forms** to athletes
- **Mid-Jan**: NCAA winter sports in full swing (basketball, indoor track, wrestling)
- **Mid-Jan**: College Football players return for spring semester/offseason training
- FEBRUARY
- **Feb 1**: **NCAA Regular Signing Period begins** (football, basketball, all sports)
- **Feb 10–15**: Most schools require **spring NIL disclosures** and updated compliance filings
- **Feb 15**: **State sales tax filings due** for LLCs in some states (if NIL merch is sold)
- NCAA sports in season: Basketball, Wrestling, Indoor Track, Swimming & Diving, Gymnastics

- Spring seasons start: Baseball, Softball, Tennis, Golf
- MARCH
- **March 1–15**: Tax prep season begins for athletes with NIL income
- **March 15**:
- **S-Corp and Partnership (LLC) Tax Returns Due**
- **Form 2553 S-Corp Election Filing Deadline**
- NCAA Conference Basketball Tournaments
- **Spring Football Practice begins** (NCAA & high school)
- NCAA sports in full swing: Baseball, Softball, Track, Tennis, Golf, Lacrosse
- APRIL
- **April 1**: Final FAFSA corrections due for prior year
- **April 15**:
- **Federal Individual Tax Return Deadline (Form 1040)**
- **Q1 Estimated Tax Payment Due (Form 1040-ES)**
- **Last day to contribute to IRA or Roth IRA for previous year**
- **Mid-April**: Universities begin **fall eligibility audits**
- NCAA Championships: Gymnastics, Swimming, Wrestling, Bowling
- MAY
- **May 1**: National College Decision Day (for high school seniors)
- **May 10–15**: Compliance and **NIL reporting due before summer break**
- **May 31**: Deadline to enter **NCAA Transfer Portal** (spring sports)
- High School state playoffs begin: Baseball, Track, Softball, Tennis
- NCAA Postseason: Lacrosse, Golf, Tennis
- JUNE
- **June 1–30**:
- College athletes must **disclose NIL income to universities** (if required)
- New NIL collective enrollments typically begin
- **June 15**:
- **Quarterly Estimated Tax Payment (Q2) Due**
- NCAA Coaches can begin **non-football recruiting** for rising juniors

(D1 rules)

- High School summer leagues begin: AAU Basketball, 7-on-7 Football, Summer Baseball
- JULY
- **July 1**: New NCAA year begins (calendar resets)
- **July 1–15**: NCAA **compliance sessions for fall athletes**
- **July 15–31**: **Open recruiting periods** (football and basketball – varies by division)
- **Mid-July**: MLB Draft, AAU Nationals, College Summer Training
- **End of July**: Return to campus begins for fall college sports
- Financial focus: Begin organizing **Q3 expenses**, review **NIL earnings**, track savings goals
- AUGUST
- **Aug 1**:
- **NCAA D1 Fall Sports Official Practice Opens**
- **University compliance clearance deadlines** (physicals, NIL, insurance)
- **Aug 15–30**: Move-in, orientation, academic eligibility finalizations
- High School fall sports begin: Football, Volleyball, Soccer, Cross Country
- NCAA Sports Begin: Football, Women's Soccer, Volleyball, Men's & Women's Cross Country
- Athletes should review insurance policies (health, renter's, disability)
- SEPTEMBER
- **Sept 1**: NCAA **official recruiting contact begins** (for juniors in most sports)
- **Sept 15**:
- **Quarterly Estimated Tax Payment (Q3) Due**
- **Extended S-Corp and Partnership Tax Returns Due** (if filed for extension)
- High school and college football in full swing
- Fall compliance meetings and mid-semester grade tracking begin
- OCTOBER

- **Oct 1**:
- **FAFSA Opens** for upcoming academic year
- **Fall NIL disclosure deadlines** at most universities
- **Oct 15**:
- **Extended Individual Tax Return Deadline (Form 4868)**
- **SEP IRA and Solo 401(k) Employer Contributions Due** (if extended)
- Fall sports peak: Cross Country Regionals, Volleyball, Soccer Playoffs
- High School: Senior athlete recruiting visits and transcripts sent to NCAA Eligibility Center
- NOVEMBER
- **Nov 1–15**:
- NCAA Early Signing Period for many sports (Basketball, Baseball, Track, etc.)
- Coaches begin **prepping rosters and compliance rosters for spring**
- **Late November**:
- High School Football State Championships (varies by state)
- NCAA Football winding down; Bowl eligibility checks
- Encourage year-end financial prep:
- Tax projection for NIL income
- Plan Roth IRA or Solo 401(k) contributions
- Assess Q4 NIL revenue
- DECEMBER
- **Dec 1–10**:
- Final compliance updates due before winter break
- Academic progress reports due to maintain spring eligibility
- **Dec 15–20**:
- **NCAA Football Early Signing Day**
- NCAA Transfer Portal opens (fall sports)
- **Dec 31**:
- Deadline to contribute to 401(k), Roth 401(k), or employer plans for current year
- Final date to make **charitable contributions** for tax deduction

- Review or start new LLC planning for upcoming NIL year
- Begin prepping **Q4 tax filing and January quarterly payments**
- BONUS: Year-Round NIL Responsibilities
- **Monthly**: Track income, expenses, and save 20–30% of NIL earnings for taxes
- **Quarterly**:
- Reconcile NIL deals and receipts
- Submit estimated tax payments (if required)
- **Per Deal**:
- Disclose to school compliance officer
- Retain contract, invoice, and proof of payment
- Report any deal that involves merchandise sales, affiliate marketing, or team usage

Disclaimer

Important Notice to Parents and Readers

Financial Literacy For NIL for Parents of Student Athletes was written to empower, educate, and encourage parents like you to play an informed and active role in your child's financial future. NIL (Name, Image, and Likeness) has opened exciting new doors for student-athletes—but with that opportunity comes complexity, pressure, and responsibility.

This book aims to give you the tools, language, and perspective to support your child's journey with greater confidence. The guidance offered is based on the author's personal experience, professional background, and over two decades working in financial services, education, and athlete development.

That said, please understand:

This Book Is for Educational Purposes Only

This publication is designed for **general education and information**. It does not serve as legal, financial, tax, accounting, or investment advice.

While it shares strategies, ideas, and real-life examples, this book is **not a substitute for personalized professional help**. Every family's situation is different—what works for one student-athlete may not be right for yours.

Encourage your child to make financial decisions only after speaking with trusted, licensed professionals who understand their goals and unique circumstances.

This Is Not Legal Advice

NIL has created new legal territory—and while this book references legal issues such as contracts, LLC formation, and intellectual property, it does **not** offer legal counsel.

If your child is reviewing or signing NIL agreements, establishing a business, or dealing with branding or sponsorship issues, they need to work with a licensed attorney who specializes in **sports law, entertainment law, or NIL-specific matters**.

NIL laws vary by state, school, and athletic association. You and your child are responsible for staying in compliance.

This Is Not Personalized Financial or Investment Advice

This book covers topics like saving, budgeting, investing, and managing NIL money—but only from a **general educational lens**. The content is designed to raise awareness, not to give specific recommendations.

Any decisions about investing, insurance, retirement planning, or business formation should be made in partnership with a **Certified Financial Planner™, licensed advisor, or other qualified expert**.

This Is Not Tax or Accounting Advice

The author is not a CPA or tax preparer. While the book touches on important tax-related topics (like self-employment taxes, business deductions, and estimated payments), these are for informational purposes only.

If your child is earning NIL income—especially if they are self-employed or managing a business entity—consult with a **licensed tax professional** to ensure everything is structured correctly and reported properly.

No Guarantees of Financial Outcome

Nothing in this book guarantees NIL success, long-term wealth, or specific financial results. Every student-athlete's path is different. Factors like discipline, decision-making, timing, market conditions, and personal support systems all impact the outcome.

This book is designed to **spark conversations, create awareness, and guide decision-making**—not to promise results.

Limitation of Liability

By reading this book, you agree that the author—Pat Brown, MBA—and any affiliated websites or platforms (including FinancialLiteracyForNIL.com, FinancialLiteracyForStudentAthletes.com, and others) are **not liable** for any actions taken or consequences resulting from the information provided herein.

You and your student-athlete are responsible for all financial and legal decisions. This book is a tool, not a legal or financial safety net.

Build the Right Team

The author strongly encourages you to help your child build a trustworthy team that includes:

- A financial advisor
- A sports or NIL attorney
- A tax professional
- Mentors and support systems beyond sports

This book was created to **complement—not replace—that team**.

If your family doesn't have that support system in place yet, let this be your starting point. The earlier your child gets proper guidance, the more confident and protected their future will be.

Your involvement matters. Your guidance matters. And your knowledge can make all the difference.

This journey is about more than NIL—it's about setting your child up for financial success, security, and stability for years to come. Let this book be one of many tools you use to help them build something that lasts.

40

Made in the USA
Monee, IL
04 November 2026

67387585R00216